T0117039

STRATEGIC
COST MANAGEMENT

STRATEGIC COST MANAGEMENT

THE NEW TOOL FOR COMPETITIVE ADVANTAGE

John K. Shank

Vijay Govindarajan

THE FREE PRESS

The Free Press
A Division of Simon & Schuster Inc.
1230 Avenue of the Americas
New York, N. Y. 10020

Printed in the United States of America

printing number

     15 17 19 20 18 16 14

Library of Congress Cataloging-in-Publication Data

Shank, John K.
   Strategic cost management : the new tool for competitive advantage
/ John K. Shank, Vijay Govindarajan
     p.   cm.
   Includes bibliographical references.
   ISBN 978-1-4391-5036-8   ISBN 1-4391-5036-2
   1. Cost accounting.   2. Managerial accounting. I. Govindarajan,
Vijay. II. Title.
HF5686.C8S459   1993
657'.42 – dc20   93-3370
                                              CIP

CONTENTS

We dedicate this book to our wives, Diane and Kirthi, without whose unfailing encouragement and support the countless hours invested in the effort could not have come to fruition.

STRATEGIC
COST MANAGEMENT

PROLOGUE

Corporate management accounting systems are inadequate for today's environment. In this time of rapid technological change, vigorous global and domestic competition, and enormously expanding information processing capabilities, management accounting systems are not providing useful, timely information for the process control, product costing, and performance evaluation activities of managers.
—H. Thomas Johnson & Robert S. Kaplan, 1987

Most large companies seem to recognize that their cost systems are not responsive to today's competitive environment . . . the methods they use to allocate costs among their many products are hopelessly obsolete. . . . Quite simply, accurate cost information can give a company a competitive advantage.
—Ford S. Worthy, *Fortune* Magazine, 1987

Cost-accounting is wrecking American business. If we're going to remain competitive, we've got to change (our costing systems).
—Thomas E. Pryor, *Business Week*, 1988

This book responds to these harsh criticisms of the current cost accounting systems by providing a new framework, *strategic cost management,* which adapts the traditional body of knowledge called cost analysis to the rapidly developing body of knowledge on strategy formulation and implementation.

CHAPTER 1

AN INTRODUCTION TO STRATEGIC COST MANAGEMENT

New Wine, or Just New Bottles?

This book represents a new emphasis in managerial accounting. It is based on the premise that managerial accounting must explicitly consider strategic issues and concerns. We believe that the incorporation of strategic concerns into cost analysis represents a very natural, overdue extension of managerial accounting, which itself only became popular about thirty years ago.

NEW WINE?

In 1963 Sidney Davidson wrote a paper for the *Accounting Review* marking the fortieth anniversary of the publication of J. M. Clark's book, *Studies in the Economics of Overhead Costs.* Davidson titled his retrospective of Clark's book "Old Wine into New Bottles." Davidson's paper acknowledge Clark's contributions to the development of relevant cost analysis—one of the "new bottles" of managerial accounting in 1963. Though times change, this metaphor remains apt. Are the new ideas fomenting today in management accounting really new wine, or merely old wine recycled in new bottles? It is our belief that we really have new wine.

To coin a new mixed metaphor, although the winds of change are clearly blowing for management accounting, some observers believe that too many management accountants are asleep at the switch. What is

Portions of this chapter appeared in the *Journal of Management Accounting Research*, 1,1, Fall 1991, pp. 47–65. Reproduced with permission.

the evidence that the fundamental concepts of management accounting are changing or that they need to change? What is the evidence that too many management accountants are lagging behind this change rather than leading it? What is the evidence to support the assertion that the management accounting practiced for the past thirty years (since Anthony, 1956; Shillinglaw, 1961; and Horngren, 1962 popularized the term) is becoming obsolescent? These are the questions this book addresses.

It is not our intent to belittle the accomplishments of the management accounting field over the past thirty years or to belittle the leadership efforts of those who have shaped and refined the current underlying conceptual framework. Management accounting could not go forward were it not for the achievements that have brought it this far. But, it must go forward. New times often call for new thinking.

Looking back over the past thirty years, the transition from cost accounting to managerial cost analysis is one primary accomplishment. This transition has led to the prominence management accounting enjoys today in industry, commerce, and academe. The transition from managerial cost analysis to what is called here *strategic cost management* (defined below) is one primary challenge looking forward. Success in that next transition will help determine the prominence of cost management in the future.

Interest in strategic cost management derives from the rise to prominence of strategy over the past twenty years. Several influential books have contributed to the current widespread prominence of strategy.[1] In addition, since the early 1970s, the major academic journals regularly have begun to publish articles about strategy.[2] Also during this period two journals have been started that are devoted to strategic analysis, *Strategic Management Journal* and *Journal of Business Strategy.* The major management journals (*Harvard Business Review, Sloan Management Review, Business Horizons,* and *California Management Review*) now also regularly publish articles about strategy.

Finally, a billion-dollar-a-year industry in strategic analysis has arisen. Even the CPA firms are now heavily involved in this consulting segment. Clearly, strategic analysis is an important element of what is taught in business schools, what is written about in academic and management journals, and what companies are concerned about.

However, to date there has been little attention to this topic in the major research journals in accounting. Except for two papers in the *Ac-*

counting Review (Kaplan, 1984b; Patell, 1987) there are no references to strategic analysis in the *Accounting Review, Journal of Accounting Research,* or *Journal of Accounting and Economics.* One journal, *Accounting Organization and Society,* has published articles on strategy and control but not on strategic cost issues. Two new journals are emerging to fill this void: The *Journal of Cost Management* and the *Journal of Management Accounting Research.*

The dearth of attention to strategic analysis in the traditional research journals in accounting carries through to the managerial accounting textbooks as well. Only a few of the topics of strategic cost management receive some attention in only a few of the best-selling management accounting texts.[3] Further evidence of the lack of concern among management accountants with strategic topics is found in a 1988 survey by Robinson and Barrett of management accounting curricula. Their study measured the extent to which the topics prescribed by the American Assembly of Collegiate Schools of Business for managerial accounting were being covered in accredited and nonaccredited programs. Strategic topics were not mentioned anywhere in the report. The reader must look outside the major accounting journals and the accounting curricula in most AACSB schools to find the literature about strategic cost management.

In summary, two observations emerge. First, there is an extensive and rapidly growing literature on the concept of strategic cost management. Second, the ideas reflected in the concept have to date received scant attention in the leading accounting research journals, the leading textbooks, or graduate and undergraduate curricula. Which of these two observations is more reflective of the attention the concept deserves involves a value judgment that the reader is encouraged to consider very carefully. Tektronix is an example of one firm in which the new concepts have essentially replaced traditional managerial accounting, as described by Turney and Anderson (1989). Johnson & Johnson is an example of a huge, world-famous company that is in the process of totally revamping the focus of its managerial accounting efforts.

To help frame the reader's consideration of the concept, this chapter presents a definition of strategic cost management. Chapter 2 summarizes the development of the field in terms of the three principal themes deemed to underlie it. Chapters 3 through 14 explain our perspective on each of these three themes in more depth. They represent a summary of the state of the art as of 1993.

STRATEGIC COST MANAGEMENT—
DEFINITION AND OVERVIEW

Cost analysis traditionally is viewed as the process of assessing the financial impact of alternative managerial decisions. How is strategic cost management different? It is cost analysis in a broader context, where the strategic elements become more conscious, explicit, and formal. Here, cost data is used to develop superior strategies en route to gaining sustainable competitive advantage. No doubt cost accounting systems can help in other areas as well (inventory valuation, short-term operating decision, etc.). However, the use of cost data in strategic planning has not received the attention it deserved, either in cost accounting textbooks or in management practice. The billion-dollar-a-year market in strategic cost management consulting services is dominated by such firms as Bain & Company, Boston Consulting Group, Booz, Allen & Hamilton, McKinsey & Company, and Monitor, Inc. Yet, the Amos Tuck School of Business Administration at Dartmouth College is one of only a few business schools in the country that teach a course built around the specific techniques used by these firms in this business niche. A sophisticated understanding of a firm's cost structure can go a long way in the search for sustainable competitive advantage. This is what we refer to as "strategic cost management."

Consistent with this perspective, the central theme of the book is that accounting exists within a business primarily to facilitate the development and implementation of business strategy. Under this view, business management is a continuously cycling process of: (1) formulating strategies, (2) communicating those strategies throughout the organization, (3) developing and carrying out tactics to implement the strategies, and (4) developing and implementing controls to monitor the success of the implementation steps and hence the success in meeting the strategic objectives. Accounting information plays a role at each of the four stages of this cycle.

At stage one, accounting information is the basis for financial analysis, which is one aspect of the process of evaluating strategic alternatives. Strategies that are not financially feasible or that do not yield adequate financial returns cannot be appropriate strategies.

At stage two, accounting reports constitute one of the important ways that strategy gets communicated throughout an organization. The things we report are the things people pay attention to. Good accounting reports are thus reports that focus attention on those factors that are critical to the success of the strategy adopted.

At stage three, specific tactics must be developed in support of the overall strategy and then carried through to completion. Financial analysis, based on accounting information, is one of the key elements in deciding which tactical programs are most likely to be effective in helping a firm to meet its strategic objectives.

And finally, at stage four, monitoring the performance of managers or of business units usually hinges partly on accounting information. The role of standard costs, expense budgets, and annual profit plans in providing one basis for performance evaluation is well accepted in businesses around the world. These tools must be explicitly adapted to the strategic context of the firm if they are to be maximally useful.

Three important generalizations emerge from this way of viewing management accounting:

1. Accounting is not an end in itself, but only a means to help achieve business success. There is thus no such thing as good accounting practice or bad accounting practice as such. Accounting techniques or systems must be judged in light of their impact on business success.

2. Specific accounting techniques or systems must be considered in terms of the role they are intended to play. A concept such as return on investment analysis may have little relevance for assessing the performance of middle-level managers in situations where investment decisions are made centrally. However, this concept may at the same time be critically important in assessing the attractiveness of different strategic investment options. Accounting analysis that is not useful for some purposes may be extremely useful for others. A working knowledge of management accounting thus involves knowledge of the multiplicity of roles accounting information can play.

3. In evaluating the overall accounting system for a business, mutual consistency among the various elements is critical. The key question is whether the overall fit with strategy is appropriate. For example, a target cost system with tight, engineered cost allowances may be an excellent tool for assessing manufacturing performance in a business following a strategy of being the low-cost producer.

However, developing such an accounting tool might be dysfunctional in a business pursuing a strategy of differentiation via product innovations.

Summarizing these three generalizations, the key managment questions to ask about any accounting idea are:

1. Does it serve an identifiable business objective? (For example, facilitate strategy formulation, assess managerial performance, etc.)

2. For the objective it is designed to serve, does the accounting idea enhance the chances of attaining the objective?

3. Does the objective whose attainment is facilitated by the accounting idea fit strategically with the overall thrust of the business?

For an accounting idea to be useful for a particular purpose in a particular business at a particular time, all three of these questions must yield an affirmative answer. This book is about accounting as a tool for strategic management. The ideas presented here yield affirmative answers to these three questions, with explicit attention to the strategic issues involved. In short, strategic cost management (SCM) is the managerial use of cost information explicitly directed at one or more of the four stages of strategic management.

ROAD MAP FOR THE READER

This book is organized around three key themes for managing costs effectively. The emergence of strategic cost management (SCM) results from a blending of the following three themes, each taken from the strategic management literature:

1. Value chain analysis

2. Strategic positioning analysis

3. Cost driver analysis

Cost management issues underlying each of these three themes are developed and illustrated in this book.

Synopsis of Chapters

In chapter 2, we present the overall framework for this book, which is that the emerging concept of SCM is a blending of the financial analysis elements of three themes from the strategic management literature—value chain analysis, strategic positioning analysis, and cost driver analysis.

In chapter 3, we present a short case (dealing with a private label opportunity for a bicycle manufacturer) that supports a strategic analysis as well as a relevant cost analysis. The chapter demonstrates that strategic cost analysis is often just a different application of the same sorts of financial tools we normally use today. But, even when the analysis is different only in its focus and not in its underlying structure (such as a value chain analysis), the insights can differ dramatically. What we emphasize is a need for managers to be aware that cost analysis must explicitly consider strategic issues and concerns.

Chapters 4 and 5 deal with value chain analysis—the first key to effective cost management. In chapter 4, we define the value chain concept, contrast it with the value-added notion, and highlight the strategic power of value chain analysis. We then discuss the methodology for constructing and using a value chain. Finally, we discuss two real world examples to illustrate the power of the value chain perspective. The first example contrasts the value chains of AT&T, NYNEX, and IBM in the telecommunications industry. The second example is drawn from the airline industry; here, we not only discuss the value chain of a major trunk airline but we also contrast the value chains of United Airlines and People Express (in its heyday).

While the two examples discussed in chapter 4 are based on published financial statements, chapter 5 presents an example of value chain analysis based on our field research in the packaging industry. Here, we show the methodology for constructing a value chain for a firm and highlight the insights that can be derived from such an analysis.

Chapter 6 through 9 turn to differentiated controls for differentiated strategies—the second key to effective cost management. In chapter 6, we define the concept of strategy and describe generic strategies that business units can adopt. We then discuss how to vary the form and structure of control systems in accordance with variation in generic business-level strategic contexts. We summarize the research findings in this area in terms of how to link the different elements of control systems with business-level strategies. Finally, we contrast our strategic perspective on controls with conventional management practices.

The focus of the discussion in chapter 6 is conceptual. We present practical examples of how to tailor controls to strategies in the next three chapters. Chapter 7 presents a short disguised case to emphasize how variance analysis—an important tool of performance evaluation and control—becomes most meaningful when it is tied explicitly to the strategic context of the business under evaluation.

Chapter 8 presents a live (but disguised) case to illustrate two key ideas in strategically based cost analysis and control: (1) The use of cost analysis to identify the differing strategic positions of three products of a large chemicals manufacturer, and (2) the use of differentiated management controls focusing on the differing key success factors for the differentiated strategies for the three products.

Chapter 9 examines the use of nonfinancial measures based on a field study of five high-tech manufacturers (mostly makers of semiconductors). Hence, we synthesize the results from these field studies and describe the rise of nonfinancial performance measures as a tool of strategic control. We also review why these firms felt that their prior accounting systems did not capture all measures that were important for success.

In chapters 10 through 14, we discuss cost driver analysis—the third key for effective cost management. Chapter 10 provides a framework for understanding how structural factors (such as scale, scope, and experience) and executional factors (such as quality, design, and continuous improvement) drive product costs.

In chapters 11 and 12, we discuss activity-based costing (ABC), which is a framework to operationalize complexity, one fundamental structural cost driver. Chapter 10 uses a simplified case to demonstrate how traditional and even modern approaches to product costing can be dramatically deceiving about product profitability. The hero is ABC, which we contrast with the villain—costing based on throughput or output volumes (volume-based costing, for short). We also point out the limitations of ABC. Here, we argue that the benefits of ABC in product line assessment and activity management can best be achieved by avoiding its formalization as part of a general ledger bookkeeping system.

Chapter 12 illustrates the limitations of ABC by presenting and analyzing two case studies. In spite of the very useful insights that emerge from the ABC analysis, we see this situation as an example of the negative role ABC can play in strategic cost management when it is seen as an issue in the design of formal cost accounting systems.

Chapter 13 presents the underlying cost analysis framework for one of the soft executional cost drivers, quality management. Here, we compare and contrast two quality paradigms—traditional view and total quality management (TQM). We then discuss how conventional management accounting panders to the traditional view on quality and prevents companies from implementing TQM. Finally, we describe ways that a cost analysis framework can support TQM.

In Chapter 14, we describe a framework to understand how technology—another fundamental structural cost driver—influences product costs. We illustrate the strategic power of our framework by presenting a field study of a major technological innovation faced by a large forest products company. This chapter concludes the book by illustrating how the SCM theme can provide important new insights on a crucial concern of management today: how to bring strategic concerns directly into the evaluation of technology options. The chapter reviews the theme of the book while showing its relevance for key managerial decisions.

Target Audience

This book is intended for the following users:

Corporate financial officers and controllers as well as management consultants who are concerned about designing managerial accounting systems with a strategic orientation.

Line managers—marketing, operations, technology, and human resource managers—who are responsible for making operating decisions based on sound cost analysis.

Accounting educators who have the responsibility for teaching about today's business world in classrooms.

We have successfully used the contents of this book for two types of programs, executive development programs and the MBA program. We have conducted over one hundred executive programs on strategic cost management during the past ten years. These programs have included both controllers—who design cost management systems—as well as line managers who use the information generated by such systems. Most of the materials in this book have been developed, tested, and refined based on our interactions with over 3,000 executives, both in the United States and abroad.

In the academic context, we currently teach the required Management Accounting course in the first year of the Amos Tuck School of Business Administration MBA program around the concepts and ideas contained in this book. In addition, we have developed two highly successful second-year electives at Tuck—Strategic Cost Management and Management Control Systems—that draw heavily upon the materials from this book. We hope the reader will find the ideas and techniques presented here to be as useful as they have proved to be in our classroom.

more than 25% wrong 95% of the time. When the inventory buffers are stripped away from a highly unpredictable production process, the manufacturing activities of the suppliers become a nightmare. For every dollar of manufacturing cost the assembly plants saved by moving toward JIT management concepts, the suppliers' plants spent much more than one dollar extra because of schedule instability.

Because of its narrow value-added perspective, the auto company had overlooked the impact of its changes on its suppliers' costs. Management had ignored the idea that JIT involves a partnership with suppliers. Management did not realize that a major element in the success of JIT for a Japanese auto assembly plant is schedule stability for its supplier firms. In fact, whereas the U.S. plants regularly missed schedules only one week ahead by 25% or more, the Japanese plants varied 1% or less from schedules planned four weeks in advance (Jones & Udvare, 1986).[1] The failure to adopt a value chain perspective doomed this major effort by a leading U.S. firm. The lack of awareness of supply chain cost analysis concepts on the part of this company's management accountants proved to be a very costly oversight. Should those management accountants have been exposed to value chain concepts somewhere in their accounting education?

In addition to starting too late, value-added analysis has another major flaw; it stops too soon. Stopping cost analysis at sales misses all the opportunities for exploiting linkages with the firm's customers. Customer linkages can be just as important as supplier linkages.

Exploiting customer linkages is the key idea behind the concept of *life cycle costing*. Life cycle costing deals explicitly with the relationship between what a customer pays for a product and the total cost the customer incurs over the life cycle of using the product. Forbis and Mehta (1981) describe how a life cycle costing perspective on the customer linkage in the value chain can lead to increased profitability. Explicit attention to postpurchase costs by the customer can lead to more effective market segmentation and product positioning. Or, designing a product to reduce postpurchase costs of the customer can be a major weapon in capturing competitive advantage. In many ways, the lower life cycle cost of imported Japanese autos helps to explain their success in the U.S. market.

Just as many cost management problems are misunderstood because of failure to see the impact on the overall value chain, many cost management opportunities are missed in the same way. Consider one further example.

In 1992, the U.S. suppliers of paper to envelope converters suffered a loss in profit because they were caught unaware by a significant shift in the value chain of the envelope converter. The shift from sheet-fed to roll-fed envelope finishing machines dramatically changes the raw material specifications for envelope paper. With sheet-fed machines, the envelope company buys large rolls of paper (forty to sixty inches wide) that are first cut into sheets, then cut into blanks in die-cutting machines, and finally fed by hand into the folding and gluing machines. With roll-fed machines, the envelope company buys very narrow rolls of paper (five to eleven inches wide) that are converted directly into envelopes in one combined operation. Roll-fed machines are much more expensive to buy but much less expensive to operate. For large orders, they represent substantial overall savings for the envelope converter. Roll-fed machines were only introduced in the United States about 1980, but they now produce more than 60% of all domestic envelopes.

The paper manufacturers do not want to complicate their primary manufacturing process by producing rolls that are only five to eleven inches wide directly on the paper machines. Instead, they use secondary machines called rewinder-slitters to convert the large rolls of paper from the paper machines into the narrower rolls the converters want. Thus, the transition from selling wide rolls to selling narrow rolls added an additional processing step for the paper manufacturers. The business issue here is how the change in the customers' value chain should be reflected in paper prices. Now that manufacturing costs along the value chain have changed (in response to changed customer requirements), how should prices change?

In the paper industry, where management accounting does not include value chain analysis or life cycle costing, rewinder-slitter costs are seen as just a small part of mill overhead, which is assigned to all paper production on a per-ton basis. For a large, modern paper mill, rewinder-slitter cost is no more than 1% or 2% of total cost. The impact on total average cost per ton is less than $10. Also, very little of this cost varies with incremental production because the mill always keeps excess capacity in such a small department. It is common sense to make sure that $300 million paper machines are never slowed down by a bottleneck at a $2 million rewinder-slitter.

The industry norm is to charge $11 per ton extra if the customer wants the rolls slit to the narrow widths (less than eleven inches). The savings to the envelope converter from roll-fed machines far exceed this extra charge. Unfortunately, the full cost to the paper mill of providing the incremental rewinding-slitting service also far exceeds this extra charge. It can cost more than $100 per ton to have an outside subcontractor slit rolls to narrow widths. An external value chain perspective would look at the savings from narrow rolls for the customer and the extra costs to the paper mill and set a price differential somewhere in between. An internal mill costing perspective, however, sees no cost issues at all. The lack of a value chain perspective contributed to the lack of concern about product costing issues. The eleven-dollar surcharge looked like pure extra contribution to profit. The result is an uneconomic price, the impact of which is buried in a mill management accounting system that ignores value chain issues. Should the management accountants in the paper companies have been exposed to value chain concepts somewhere in their management accounting education?

Cost analysis considerations underlying the value chain concept are discussed in more detail in chapters 4 and 5.

THE STRATEGIC POSITIONING CONCEPT

The second major theme underlying the work in strategic cost management concerns the perceived uses of management accounting information. Stated, again, in question form: What role does cost management play in the firm?

The theme of SCM can be stated very succinctly. In SCM, the role of cost analysis differs in important ways depending on how the firm is choosing to compete. Following Porter's (1980) delineation of basic strategic choices, a business can compete either by having lower costs (cost leadership) or by offering superior products (product differentiation). That these two approaches demand very different conceptual frameworks has been widely accepted in the strategy literature.[2] And, although strategic positioning does not involve simple either/or choices in practice, the implications for strategic management have been frequently amplified.[3] But, the implications of strategic positioning for management accounting are not as well explored. Since differentiation and cost leadership involve different managerial mindsets, they also involve different cost analysis perspectives. As one example of how strategic positioning can significantly influence the role of cost analysis, consider the decision to invest in more carefully engineered product costs. For a firm following a cost leadership strategy in a mature, commodity business, careful attention to engineered target costs is likely to be a very important ongoing management tool. But for a firm following a product differentiation strategy in a market-driven, rapidly growing, fast-changing business, carefully engineered manufacturing costs may well be much less important.

Chapter 8 provides an example in which a large chemical company uses cost variances extensively for some products and not at all for others depending on the strategic context. It is not surprising that monitoring of R&D productivity is much more important to a pharmaceuticals company like Merck than is manufacturing cost control. On the other hand, a system for better monitoring R&D costs would not gain much attention in a company like International Paper, but they have many accountants whose jobs involve tracking manufacturing cost on a monthly basis. Although cost information is important in all companies in one form or another, different strategies demand different cost perspectives.

Expanding upon the work by Gupta and Govindarajan (1984b) and Govindarajan (1986a), exhibit 2–1 summarizes some illustrative differences in control system or cost management emphases depending on the primary strategic thrust of the firm.

Govidarajan's widely cited work provides empirical evidence of major differences in cost management and control system design depending on the strategy being followed.

If is interesting to compare the SCM perspective on the role of cost

EXHIBIT 2–1

Differences in Cost Management Caused by Differences in Strategy

	Primary Strategic Emphasis	
	Product Differentiation	*Cost Leadership*
Role of engineered product costs in assessing performance	Not very important	Very import
Importance of such concepts as flexible budgeting for manufacturing cost control	Moderate to low	High to very high
Perceived importance of meeting budgets	Moderate to low	High to very high
Importance of marketing cost analysis	Critical to success	Often not done on a formal basis
Importance of product cost as an input to pricing decisions	Low	High
Importance of competitor cost anlysis	Low	High

information with the perspective that is more prevalent in management accounting today. Often, the theme in management accounting texts today is the same that it has been for thirty years. That theme was first articulated by Simon et al. (1954), who coined three phrases to capture the essence of management accounting: "Score keeping," "problem solving," and "attention directing." Although these specific words are not always preserved, these three objectives frequently still come through in today's textbooks as clearly as they did when the Controllers Institute (now the Financial Executives Institute) commissioned a team of faculty from Carnegie Tech (now Carnegie Mellon) to study the elements of effective controllership.[4] It is interesting and somewhat ironic that Carnegie Tech and the Controllers Institute have long since been modernized, but not this 1954 tripartite delineation of the roles of managerial accounting.

The point is not to deprecate this longstanding common starting point, but rather to emphasize how much our conception of what we do starts with our consensus about why we do it. Each of the three well-known roles involves a set of concepts and techniques that are implicitly assumed to apply to all firms—albeit in varying degrees. For example, standard cost variances are a key tool for attention-directing and contribution margin analysis is a key tool for problem solving.

Because the three roles are not seen as varying across firms depending on strategic context, the relevance of the related costs analysis tools also is not seen to vary across the firms. If agreement could be reached that why we do management accounting differs in important ways depending on the basic strategic thrust of the firm, it would be a much easier transition to see that how we do management accounting should also reflect the basic strategic thrust.

Even if management accounting in most companies today is still heavily involved with conventional tasks, it is important to realize that this focus need not be true in the future. Management accounting can adapt to the real business needs of the firm, if those needs are articulated.

THE COST DRIVER CONCEPT

In SCM it is acknowledged that cost is caused, or driven, by many factors that are interrelated in complex ways. Understanding cost behavior means understanding the complex interplay of the set of cost drivers at work in any given situation. At this level of generality, the idea is almost tautological. It is hardly contentious or counterintuitive until one contrasts it with the prevailing theme in traditional management accounting today. In management accounting, cost is a function, primarily, of only one cost driver, output volume. Cost concepts related to output volume permeate the thinking and the writing about cost: fixed versus variable cost, average cost versus marginal cost, cost-volume-profit analysis, break even analysis, flexible budgets, and contribution margin, to name a few. In SCM, output volume as such is seen to capture very little of the richness of cost behavior. Management accounting, in this regard, tends to draw upon the simple models of basic microeconomics. SCM, on the other hand, tends to draw upon the richer models of the economics of industrial organization (Scherer, 1980).

One other strategic cost driver, cumulative experience, has also received some attention among management accountants over the years as a determinant of unit costs.[5] References to the learning curve also appear in many managerial accounting texts.[6] However, rather than seeing experience as one of many cost drivers, the accounting literature sees it more narrowly as an explanation of how the relationship between cost and output volume changes over time as cumulative output increases for one particular product or process. That is, even in the learning curve literature in accounting, output volume is still the preeminent cost driver. Experience is seen as a phenomenon that can help explain the changing relationship between output volume and costs over time.

If output volume is a poor way to explain cost behavior, what is a better way? Porter (1985a) presents one attempt to create a comprehensive list of cost drivers, but his attempt is more important than his particular list. In the strategic management literature, better lists exist (Riley, 1987). Following Riley, the following list of cost drivers is broken into two categories. The first category comprises "structural" cost drivers, drawing upon the industrial organization literature (Scherer, 1980). From this perspective there are at least five strategic choices by the firm regarding its underlying economic structure that drive cost position for any given product group:

1. *Scale:* How big an investment to make in manufacturing, in R&D, and in marketing resources.

2. *Scope:* Degree of vertical integration. Horizontal integration is more related to scale.

3. *Experience:* How many times in the past the firm has already done what it is doing again.

4. *Technology:* What process technologies are used at each step of the firm's value chain.

5. *Complexity:* How wide a line or products of services to offer to customers.

Each structural driver involves choices by the firm that drive product cost. Given certain assumptions, the cost calculus of each structural driver can be specified.[7] Of the structural drivers, scale, scope, and experience have received a large amount of attention from economists and strategists over the years. Of these three, only experience has drawn much interest from management accountants, as noted previously. Technology choice is such a thorny topic area that it is not surprising that management accountants have pretty much ignored it. At the level of explicit analysis, so have most other people as well. Perhaps the most explicit work that deals with cost analysis for technology choices is in industrial economics. Gold et al. (1970) and Oster (1982) represent excellent examples of innovations in the steel industry. We present a framework for considering this topic in chapter 14.

Complexity, as a structural variable, has received the most attention among accountants recently. Some examples of the potential importance of complexity as a cost determinant are in the work on activity-based costing by Kaplan (1987), Cooper (1986), or Shank and Govindarajan (1988d). We consider this work and some extensions in chapters 11 and 12. We see ABC as a useful strategic analysis tool, but not as the primary tool.

The second category of cost drivers, executional drivers (Riley, 1987), are those determinants of a firm's cost position that hinge on its ability to execute successfully. Whereas structural cost drivers are not monotonically scaled with performance, executional drivers are. That is, for each of the structural drivers, more is not always better. There are diseconomies of scale, or scope, as well as economies. A more complex product line is not necessarily better or necessarily worse than a less complex line. Too much experience can be as bad as too little in a dynamic environment. For example, Texas Instruments emphasized the learning curve and became the world's lowest-cost producer of microchips that were no longer state of the art. Technological leadership versus followership is a legitimate choice for most firms.

In contrast, for each of the executional drivers, more is always better. The list of basic executional drivers includes at least the following:

Work force involvement (participation)—the concept of work force commitment to continual improvement.

Total quality management (beliefs and achievement regarding product and process quality).

Capacity utilization (given the scale choices on plant construction).

Plant layout efficiency. (How efficient, against current norms, is the layout?)

Product configuration. (Is the design or formulation effective?)

Exploiting linkages with suppliers and/or customers, per the firm's value chain.

While it may not always be true that a higher level of these executional factors improves cost position, examples of diseconomies are much less frequent.

Operationalizing each of these drivers also involves specific cost analysis issues, as illustrated later. Many strategy consultants maintain that the strategic cost analysis field is moving very quickly toward executional drivers because the insights from analysis based on structural drivers are too often old fashioned. It is somewhat ironic that the cost drivers concept is moving from one revolution to a second one before the accounting world has caught up with the first one.

As of this writing there is no clear agreement on the list of fundamental cost drivers. For example, two different lists are proposed in one single publication (Booz, Allen, & Hamilton, 1987). However, those who see cost behavior in strategic terms are clear that output volume alone does not typically catch enough of the richness. How unit cost changes as output volume changes in the short run is seen to be a less interesting question than how cost position is influenced by the firm's comparative position on the various drivers that are relevant in its competitive situation.

Whatever cost drivers are on the list, the key ideas are as follows:

• For strategic analysis, volume is usually not the most useful way to explain cost behavior.

* In a strategic sense, it is more useful to explain cost position in terms of the structural choices and executional skills that shape the firm's competitive position.
* Not all the strategic drivers are equally important all the time, but some (more than one) of them are very probably very important in every case.
* For each cost driver there is a particular cost analysis framework that is critical to understanding the positioning of a firm. Being a well-trained cost analyst requires knowledge of these various frameworks. This point is illustrated later in this chapter and discussed more fully in chapter 10.

The underlying cost analysis framework for one of the soft executional drivers, quality management, is described next to demonstrate how a cost driver can be looked at in terms of an underlying analytic framework. There is a very well developed literature on cost of quality (COQ) analysis.[8] This topic area is rich in measurement issues. Yet is is virtually ignored in the conventional accounting literature. The fact that COQ analysis is so well-developed and so rich and yet apparently so foreign to accounting authors makes it a good example for the reader who is still wondering whether SCM warrants more attention.

The basic managerial dilemma for COQ analysis is summed up by the following rather fundamental difference of opinion. On the one hand, some authors believe that COQ analysis is a complete waste of time (Deming, 1982). For Deming, time spent figuring out the costs of doing things wrong would be much better spent doing those things right the first time. Quite literally, Deming sees cost analysis for quality as a misguided waste of time. On the other hand, other authors believe that the overall cost of quality curve is U-shaped (Juran, 1985). For Juran, regular, ongoing COQ analysis is critical if management is to insure that the firm is operating in the relatively flat part of the COQ curve.

In one adopts Juran's perspective, the relevant analytic framework is to measure and monitor costs in terms of a four-part breakdown:

1. *Prevention:* Costs of preventing bad quality (such as worker quality circles).

2. *Appraisal:* Costs of monitoring the level of bad quality (such as scrap reporting systems).

3. *Internal failure:* Costs of fixing bad quality that is discovered before it leaves the factory (such as rework labor).

4. *External failure:* Costs of bad quality that is not discovered before it is shipped (such as warranty claims or customer ill will)

Within this perspective, as shown in exhibit 2–2, the first two categories reflect a positive slope if plotted against the level of quality (measured by product defects). That is, the more one spends on prevention and appraisal, the higher the level of quality. On the other hand, the last two categories reflect a negative slope when plotted against the level of quality. The lower the level of quality (the more defects), the higher the cost of product failures, whether discovered before or after the product is shipped. This contrast in slopes gives rise to the U-shape of the additive total cost curve. It also gives rise to the concept that effective strategic management of quality means choosing that quality level and mix of spending across the four categories that minimizes total quality cost.

If one accepts this perspective, COQ analysis becomes an important

EXHIBIT 2–2
The Relationship Between Quality and Costs

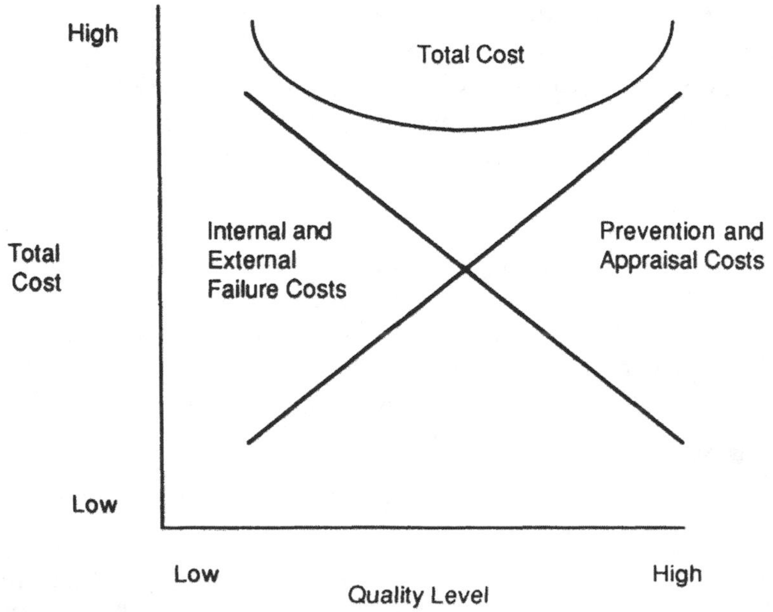

ongoing management control tool beyond just measuring quality in non-financial terms (first pass yield rates, defect rates, etc.). On the other hand, if one believes that it is conceptually and strategically impossible to have a quality level too high (Deming, 1982), COQ analysis is a misguided waste of time and money. Given the central prominence that discussions about quality play in the economy today, it seems puzzling that cost of quality analysis is absent from accounting curricula and accounting journals. This topic is discussed in much more depth in chapter 13.

From the multiple cost drivers perspective, reducing cost behavior to a question of fixed, variable, and mixed costs does not begin to explain costs in a way that is useful in making future strategic choices. Rather, focusing on fixed versus variable costs can be dangerous, strategically. According to Simpson and Muthler (1987) the misguided belief that profit was more a function of efficient plant operation (spread the fixed costs) than of minimizing product defects (a cost of quality issue) led Ford Motor Company to the brink of insolvency in 1980. In Ford's case, attention to the broader set of relevant cost drivers (such as quality, complexity, and product design) helped restore the firm to profitability even though these cost drivers were not explicitly a part of their management accounting system then. They are now.

STRATEGIC MANAGEMENT AND STRATEGIC COST ANALYSIS

As noted previously, the emerging concept of SCM blends the financial analysis elements of three themes from the strategic management literature: value chain analysis, strategic positioning analysis, and cost driver analysis. At each of the four stages of the strategic management cycle, these three themes recur regularly in a firm's efforts to achieve sustainable competitive advantage. For each of the themes, conventional managerial accounting has not provided the financial analysis support deemed necessary by writers about strategy, by strategy consultants, or by executives striving to implement strategic management in their firms. The financial analysis that is emerging to meet those needs is SCM.

Strategic Cost Management: A Paradigm Shift?

The power of paradigms to shape collective thinking is well documented. Kuhn's (1970) work in physics introduced this concept of a dominant belief structure to the physical sciences. Burrell and Morgan (1979) apply it to the social sciences. The concept has even been applied to the strategic management literature (Prahalad & Bettis, 1986). Also well documented is the slow adjustment of collective thinking to new ideas that are different enough to represent a shift in an underlying paradigm or schema (Weick, 1979). Reversing the old metaphor, Weick says that "believing is seeing." Our beliefs shape our perceptions. Thus, it is usually very difficult to get people to see the need to change their beliefs. As noted previously, strategic cost management may represent such a different mode of thought about management accounting that it represents a kind of paradigm shift. This is certainly not a shift in the same sense that Copernican astronomy replaced the Ptolemic view or that Einsteinian physics replaced the Newtonian view. Much more modest changes are at work here. Also, rather than being totally different, the SCM perspective is just more inclusive than the management accounting perspective.

Taken individually, most of the pieces of SCM require substantial change in the way we think about what we do and why we do it. Some pieces, however, such as activity-based costing, are not new at all. Rather, they stem from a reawakened awareness of "old wine." In the case of activity-based costing, the old wine is the traceability concept (Shillinglaw, 1961). The widespread attention to activity-based costing stems from widespread implementation problems in applying the traceability concept in complex product situations rather than form any theoretical shortcomings in the "old wine." On the other hand, many of the individual SCM concepts—such as technology costing, value chain analysis, or cost of quality—are sufficiently different from conventional ways of thinking that they cannot easily be accommodated into the list of key topic areas. It is as if one is thinking in terms of round, square, or triangular and then is asked to fit green into the list. Color does not fit a shape paradigm.

Further, accepting all of the concepts in SCM together requires rejecting some of the basic attitudes that shape current thinking about management accounting. One has to discard some elements of the old paradigm in favor of the new one. Contribution margin analysis, for example, plays almost no role in SCM, which adopts a long-run perspective in thinking about product cost. Sidney Davidson struggled in 1963 to explain J. M. Clark's concern for fully absorbed cost. Full cost was already outdated thinking in 1963. Davidson considered the old wine of contribution margin analysis from Clark to be much more relevant to modern management accounting in 1963 than the old wine of full-absorption costing that also heavily shaped Clark's thinking. In this case, the new thinking in 1993 is fully consistent with the old-old thinking of 1923, even though the 1993 thinking is inconsistent with the old-new thinking that has dominated the field from 1963 until the present.

Thus, SCM involves some ideas that are fully consistent with the management accounting paradigm but are not well implemented today (activity-based costing), some ideas that are largely outside the scope of the conventional paradigm (cost of quality), and some ideas that are in-

EXHIBIT 2–3
The Management Accounting Versus the Strategic Cost Paradigm

	The Management Accounting Paradigm	The Strategic Cost Management Paradigm
What is the most useful way to analyze costs?	In terms of: products, customers, and functions	In terms of the various stages of the overall value chain of which the firm is a part
	With a strongly internal focus	With a strongly external focus
	Value added is a key concept	Value-added is seen as a dangerously narrow concept
What is the objective of cost analysis?	Three objectives all apply, without regard to the strategic context: score keeping, attention directing, and problem solving	Although the three objectives are always present, the design of cost management systems changes dramatically depending on the basic strategic positioning of the firm: either under a cost leadership strategy, or under a product differentiation strategy
How should we try to understand cost behavior?	Cost is primarily a function of output volume: variable cost, fixed cost, step cost, mixed cost	Cost is a function of strategic choices about the structure of how to compete and managerial skill in executing the strategic choices: in terms of structural cost drivers and executional cost drivers

consistent with the conventional paradigm (full cost is preferable to variable cost). Is it overreaching to describe SCM as a new paradigm? Or, is it overreaching in the first place to argue that there is, in fact, an underlying paradigm of conventional management accounting at all?

With full cognizance of the limitation noted here, each of the three themes of SCM can be contrasted with a parallel theme from conventional management accounting. From this perspective, each of the three themes deals with a basic question for which SCM and management accounting pose answers that tend to differ substantially. That set of three basic questions, with two very different sets of answers, constitutes the crux of the paradigm shift idea. The exhibit 2–3 summarizes this view of the two paradigms.

Until managers who use accounting information are ready to look at these three basic questions from the extended perspective of SCM, they will continue to underestimate the significance of the turmoil surrounding management accounting in a great many companies today.

The winds of change are blowing, and they are no longer mild breezes. The time has come for management accounting to take heed.

CHAPTER 3

DEMONSTRATING STRATEGIC VERSUS CONVENTIONAL ANALYSIS

A Peek at the SCM Themes

In this chapter we present a short case (dealing with a private label opportunity for a bicycle manufacturer) that supports a strategic analysis as well as a relevant cost analysis. The chapter demonstrates the conventional analysis and then a strategic analysis drawing upon the three themes described in chapter 2. When the analysis is presented in the strategic terms, the managerial insights can differ dramatically. This case is an excellent example of the need for managers to be aware that cost analysis must explicitly consider strategic issues and concerns. This concept represents a very natural extension of the managerial accounting framework that became popular about thirty years ago (Anthony, 1956; Horngren, 1962). Managerial accounting replaced cost accounting as a framework for financial analysis for decision making by demonstrating that the cost accounting framework lacked decision relevance. The cost accounting framework failed to take into account the advances in decision analysis that had become popular in the 1950s. In the past twenty years there has been another dramatic extension of decision analysis to take explicit account of strategic issues.[1]

It is now time for management thinking about cost analysis to move forward again to incorporate this newly enriched decision analysis paradigm. Strategic accounting will supplant managerial accounting as a framework for decision making by demonstrating that managerial ac-

A modified version of this chapter appeared as "Making Strategy Explicit in Cost Analysis: A Case Study," by John K. Shank and Vijay Govindarajan; *Sloan Management Review*, 29, 3 (spring 1988), pp. 19–30.

counting lacks strategic relevance. These points are illustrated by the following case concerning the Baldwin Bicycle Company.

THE CASE OF BALDWIN BICYCLE COMPANY

In May 1983, Suzanne Leister, marketing vice president of Baldwin Bicycle Company, was mulling over the discussion she had had the previous day with Karl Knott, a buyer from Hi-Valu Stores, Inc. Hi-Valu operated a chain of discount department stores in the northwest. Hi-Valu's sales volume had grown to the extent that it was beginning to add house-brand (also called private-label) merchandise to the product lines of several of its departments. Mr. Knott, Hi-Valu's buyer for sporting goods, had approached Ms. Leister about the possibility of Baldwin's producing bicycles for Hi-Valu. The bicycles would bear the name "Challenger," which Hi-Valu planned to use for all of its house brand sporting goods.

Baldwin had been making bicycles for almost forty years. In 1983, the company's line included ten models, ranging from a small beginner's model with training wheels to a deluxe twelve-speed adult's model. Sales were currently at an annual rate of about $10 million. The company's 1982 financial statements appear in exhibit 3–1. Most of Baldwin's sales were through independently owned retailers (toy stores, hardware stores, sporting goods stores) and bicycle shops. Baldwin had never distributed its products through department store chains of any type. Ms. Leister felt that Baldwin bicycles had the image of being above average in quality and price, but not a top of the line product.

Hi-Valu's proposal to Baldwin had features that made it quite different from Baldwin's normal way of doing business. First, it was very important to Hi-Valu to have ready access to a large inventory of bicycles, because Hi-Valu had had great difficulty in predicting bicycle sales, both by store and by month. Hi-Valu wanted to carry these inventories in its regional warehouses, but did not want title on a bicycle to pass from Baldwin to Hi-Valu until the bicycle was shipped from one of its regional warehouses to a specific Hi-Valu store. At that point, Hi-Valu would regard the bicycle as having been purchased from Baldwin and would pay for it within thirty days. However, Hi-Valu would agree to take title to any bicycle that had been in one of its warehouses for four

The case study of Baldwin Bicycle Company was adapted from R. N. Anthony and J. S. Reece, *Accounting: Text and Cases* (Homewood, Ill.: Richard Irwin, 1983), pp. 742–44.

EXHIBIT 3–1
FINANCIAL STATEMENTS
(Thousand of dollars)

BALDWIN BICYCLE COMPANY
Balance Sheet
As of December 31, 1982

Assets		Liabilities and Owners Equity	
Cash	$ 342	Accounts payable	$ 512
Accounts receivable	1,359	Accrued expenses	340
Inventories	2,756	Short-term bank loans	2,626
Plant and equipment (net)	$3,635	Long-term Note payable	1,512
	$8,092	Total liabilities	$4,990
		Owners' equity	3,102
			$8,092

Income Statement
For the Year Ended December 31, 1982

Sales revenues	$10,872
Cost of sales	8,045
Gross margin	2,827
Selling and administrative expenses	2,354
Income before taxes	473
Income tax expense	218
Net income	$ 255

months, again paying for it within thirty days. Mr. Knott estimated that, on average, a bicycle would remain in a Hi-Valu regional warehouse for two months.

Second, Hi-Valu wanted to sell its Challenger bicycles at lower prices than the name brand bicycles it carried and yet earn approximately the same dollar gross margin on each bicycle sold. The rationale was that Challenger bicycle sales would take away from the sales of the name brand bikes. Thus, Hi-Valu wanted to purchase bicycles from Baldwin at lower prices than the wholesale prices of comparable bicycles sold through Baldwin's usual channels.

EXHIBIT 3–2
DATA PERTINENT TO HI-VALU PROPOSAL
(Notes Taken by Suzanne Leister)

1. Estimated first-year costs of producing Challenger bicycles (average unit costs, assuming a constant mix of models):

Materials	$39.80*
Labor	19.60
Overhead (@ 125% of labor)	24.50†
	$83.90

   * Includes items specific to models for Hi-Valu, not used in our standard models.
   † Accountant says about 40% of total production overhead cost is variable; 125% of DL$ rate is based on volume of 100,000 bicycles per year.

2. Unit price and annual voluem: Hi-Valu estimates it will need 25,000 bikes a year and proposes to pay us (based on the assumed mix of models) an average of $92.29 per bike for the first year. Contract to contain an inflation escalation clause such that price will increase in proportion to inflation-caused increases in costs shown in item 1, above; thus, the $92.29 and $83.90 figures are, in effect, constant-dollar amounts. Knott intimated that there was very little, if any, negotiating leeway in the $92.29 proposed initial price.

3. Asset-related costs (annual vairable costs, as percent of dollar value of assets):

Pretax cost of funds (to finance receivables or inventories)	18.0%
Record keeping costs (for receivables or inventories)	1.0
Inventory insurance	0.3
State property tax on inventory	0.7
Inventory-handling labor and equipment	3.0
Pilferage, obsolescence, breakage, etc.	0.5

4. Assumptions for Challenger-related added inventories (average over the year):

   Materials: two months' supply.
   Work in process: 1,000 bikes, half completed (but all materials for them issued).
   Finished goods: 500 bikes (awaiting next carload lot shipment to a Hi-Valu warehouse).

5. Impact on our regular sales: Some customers comparison shop for bikes, and many of them are likely to recognize a Challenger bike as a good value when compared with a similar bike (either ours or a competitor's) at a higher price in a nonchain toy or bicycle store. In 1982, we sold 98,791

bikes. My best guess is that our sales over the next three years will be about 100,000 bikes a year if we forego the Hi-Valu deal. If we accept it, I think we'll lose about 3,000 units of our regular sales volume a year, since our retail distribution is quite strong in Hi-Valu's market regions. These estimates do not include the possibility that a few of our current dealers might drop our line if they find out we're making bikes for Hi-Value.

The information about overhead in item 1 can be used to infer that fixed manufacturing overhead is about $1.5 million per year.

Finally, Hi-Valu wanted the Challenger bicycle to be somewhat different in appearance from Baldwin's other bikes. While the frame and mechanical components could be the same as used on current Baldwin models, the fenders, seats, and handlebars would need to be somewhat different, and the tires would have to have the name Challenger molded into their sidewalls. Also, the bicycles would have to be packed in boxes printed with the Hi-Valu and Challenger names. Ms. Leister expected these requirements to increase Baldwin's purchasing, inventorying, and production costs over and above the added costs that would be incurred for a comparable increase in volume for Baldwin's regular products.

On the positive side, Ms. Leister was acutely aware that the bicycle boom had flattened out, and this trend plus a poor economy had caused Baldwin's sales volume to fall during the past two years.[2] As a result, Baldwin currently was operating its plant at about seventy-five percent of one shift's capacity. Thus, the added volume from Hi-Valu's purchases possibly could be very attractive. If agreement could be reached on prices, Hi-Valu would sign a contract guaranteeing to Baldwin that Hi-Valu would buy its house-brand bicycles only from Baldwin for a three-year period. The contract would then be automatically extended on a year-to-year basis, unless one party gave the other at least three months' notice that id did not wish to extend the contract.

Suzanne Leister realized that she needed to do some preliminary financial analysis of this proposal before having any further discussions with Karl Knott. She had written on a pad the information she had gathered to use in her initial analysis; this information is shown in exhibit 3–2.

This short but very rich case is particularly useful for illustrating strategic accounting because the conclusions that emerge from a relevant cost analysis diverge so widely from the conclusions suggested by a strategic cost analysis. In order to contrast the two perspectives, we will first present the relevant cost analysis—an exercise in financial analysis for a potential extra chunk of business.

RELEVANT COST ANALYSIS OF THE HI-VALU OFFER

A relevant cost perspective would typically consider cost behavior as a starting point. From the facts of the case, it is not difficult to deduce that the incremental cost of producing a Challenger bicycle is about $69 (material, direct labor, and about $9+ of variable overhead). The idea here is to back out the allocated share of fixed manufacturing overhead from the unit cost. In terms of the management decision, the point is that a $92+ selling price provides much more incremental profit than the standard cost of $84+ might suggest. Since the fixed costs are already being covered by the regular business, they need not be covered again.

A second element of the relevant cost analysis typically would be the cost of carrying the incremental investment needed to support the incremental sales. This calculation has two components: the incremental working capital investment (no incremental fixed assets are required) and the annual carrying charge percentage. The extra investment can be estimated fairly readily as shown in exhibit 3–3.

The major judgment in this calculation is the number of bikes in the consignment inventory. We do not try to formalize that uncertainty any more carefully here because the issue is not central to the point of this chapter. However, choosing the annual carrying charge rate is clearly a major element in the analysis. Several basic ideas are involved:

Capital is not free.

The relevant charge is the cost of capital plus incremental carrying costs (insurance, handling, taxes, etc.).

Cost of capital is some form of weighted average across the debt and equity capital sources used by the firm.

Any specific number chosen is, at best, a rough approximation because the true cost of capital cannot be observed.

If incremental debt costs 18%, before tax, a first-cut weighted average cost of capital (after tax) might be 13% assuming $\frac{1}{3}$ debt and $\frac{2}{3}$ equity in the capital structure—$\frac{1}{3} \times (18\% \times 0.5) + \frac{2}{3} (15\%)$.

EXHIBIT 3–3
Calculating the Extra Investment Required to Support Incremental Sales

Raw Material (2 months' stock)	
~ 4,000 bikes × ~ $40 =	~$160,000
Work in process (1,000 units)	
"Half finished" implies about $55 semi finished cost	
(100% of material plus half of labor and variable overhead)	
~ 1,000 bikes × ~$55 =	~ $55,000
Finished units in the factory	
~ 500 bikes × ~ $69 =	~ $35,000
Finished units in the Hi-Valu warehouse	
Per case facts, about 2 months'	
supply, on average ~ 4,000 bikes × ~ $69 =	~$280,000
(The range here is probably from ~ $100,000 to ~ $550,000)	
Accounts receivable (30 days sales)	
~ 2,000 bikes × ~$92 =	~$185,000
(Less a trade credit offset	
Assume 45 days credit from the materials suppliers	
~ 3,000 bikes × ~$40 =	(~$120,000)
Net Extra Investment	
(Range = ~ $400,000 to ~$900,000)	~$595,000

Incremental carrying cost seems to be about 4% a year (before tax) for inventory and 0% for receivables, rejecting part of the case note as being just an allocation of common costs.

Combining carrying costs and cost of capital, an after-tax charge of 15% for inventory and 13% for receivables is a reasonable first cut.

Combining these two components (incremental working capital investment and annual carrying charge) of the carrying cost calculation produces an annual cost number somewhere between about $56,000 (for a $400,000) investment) and about $131,000 (for a $900,000 investment). A midrange estimate is about $100,000 or $4 per bike (over the estimated 25,000 Challenger bicycles). The range here is from about $2 to about $5 per bicycle. This amount is well below the $11.50 after-tax marginal contribution ([$92 − $69] × 5), even at the high end of the investment and carrying cost range.

A third element of the relevant cost analysis would typically be an erosion or cannibalization charge for the lost sales of regular Baldwin bikes as a direct result of Hi-Valu's entry into the market. The two main judgments here are how much the charge should be, assuming it is relevant and whether this is a relevant charge against the project. If a charge is to be assessed, it should be the lost profit contribution from the lost sales. It is possible to calculate that the regular business yields a contribution of about $44 per bicycle (sales price of ~$110 [$10.8M/99K] less variable cost of ~$66 [$8.0M – 1.5M*/99K]). Thus, if 3,000 units are lost, the impact on profit would be about $130,000. (3,000 × ~$44). Partly offsetting this, the incremental working capital investment (calculated earlier) would decline somewhat.

Whether or not an erosion charge is relevant is arguable. Assuming that 3,000 customers who otherwise would have bought a Baldwin bicycle buy a Challenger bicycle, the lost profit is certainly real to Baldwin. On the other hand, it probably is reasonable to assume that Hi-Valu will find someone to make Challenger bikes and that Baldwin's sales will drop somewhat as a result, regardless of what Baldwin does. Thus, the sales are lost once Hi-Valu enters the market, regardless of Baldwin's actions. Baldwin's base volume has become 96,000 units instead of 99,000 and the erosion charge is not incremental to the Challenger deal. The marketing dimension of a relevant cost analysis supports the idea that one cannot stop new products from eroding the sales of old products. A firm can only choose whether or not to sell the new products. In this context, focusing on the erosion is not only arrogant (our products are impervious to decline unless we cannibalize them) but also short-sighted (we lose the opportunity to sell new products but sales of the old products decline anyway). Thus, a strong argument can be made to exclude the erosion charge.

Summarizing the components of the cost analysis, we can calculate the incremental profitability as follows:

1. Incremental profit contribution for 25,000 bikes = ~$288,000, after tax:

$$(\$92 - \$69) \times 25,000 \times 0.5.$$

2. The incremental capital charge would be about $100,000, after tax.

3. Incremental residual income after tax is about $188,000 per year on a $600,000 investment. Thus, this is a very attractive return.

This calculation is clearly only a first approximation of the incremental return because it ignores the time value of money. A multiperiod, discounted cash flow approach would be preferable. Also, it leaves open the time period for the project. However, refining this calculation does not change the basic message that the Hi-Valu deal is very attractive from a short-run, incremental financial analysis perspective.

If there are caveats in the analysis, they center around the following issues:

The consigned inventory issue. (Does Baldwin have to tolerate this sort of imposition on normal business terms by Hi-Valu?)

The capacity issue. (Is it wise for Baldwin to tie up most of its excess capacity, unused though it currently is, for several years at well below normal prices?)

The long-run/short-run cost issue. (Is it really appropriate to ignore fixed overhead in a project that uses almost 20% of Baldwin's capacity over a three-year period?)

The uncertainty of Hi-Valu's demand. (What happens to the incremental analysis if Hi-Valu takes fewer than 25,000 bikes or more than 25,000?)

The incremental debt capacity issue. (Can Baldwin borrow an incremental $400,000–$900,000 to finance the project?)

Only the last one of these potential concerns requires additional analysis. The other four are more qualitative than quantitative. The debt capacity issue does require explicit attention.

The $2.6 million level of short-term debt is very high for a year-end balance sheet for a company like Baldwin. December 31 should be a point in the year of nearly maximum liquidity for a manufacturer of a seasonal, consumer durable product like bicycles. Production for the Christmas season should be shipped and paid for by that date, and the production buildup for spring should not be started. One clue to this liquidity crunch is the high level of inventory still on hand at this slack time of year. The $2.7M of inventory represents about 120 days' supply ($2.7/8.0 \times 365$) at a time of the year when very little stock should be on hand. Much of this inventory is likely to be slow moving or even obsolete product. And, it is all financed with short-term debt.

Even though the incremental residual income from the project looks very attractive, it is problematic whether the firm could justify borrowing another $600,000 or so for the Hi-Valu project. One imaginative thought in this regard is reworking some of these bicycles as Challengers. This approach would save much of the material cost per bicycle and also substitutes rework labor for new assembly labor. If the idea is feasible, it probably involves an incremental cost of much less than $69 per bicycle, so that the financing need is reduced. Our experience with the case indicates that managers who get this far in the analysis are sufficiently attracted by the high incremental profit to lead them to argue that the financing problem would not be unsurmountable, even if troublesome, and even if reworking existing inventory isn't deemed practical.

On balance, this analysis comes down to very attractive incremental short-run profits, coupled with some qualitative caveats that somewhat mitigate this attractiveness and a major financing concern that may or may not be deemed binding. The case is sufficiently rich that managers very seldom go outside this relevant cost framework in considering the decision. The case reinforces many basic managerial accounting themes such as:

Cost behavior analysis

Profit contribution analysis

Long-run versus short-run product and customer profitability

Inventory and receivables carrying cost

Working capital management

Project return on investment (ROA versus residual income)

Balancing quantitative and qualitative issues in a decision

Also, this case treats these themes in a context that involves sufficient marketing complexity (the erosion issue and the private label volume enhancement idea for makers of branded products) and sufficient uncertainty (the short-term debt crunch and the structure of the consigned inventory provision) to support excellent discussion with senior management groups. We have used the case more than sixty times in programs for a dozen major corporations and in the Amos Tuck Executive Program. The relevant cost framework emerges in virtually every discussion.

STRATEGIC ANALYSIS OF THE HI-VALUE OFFER

We are not aware of many cases in which the strategic cost analysis yields such totally different insights from the managerial accounting analysis. Because the two perspectives diverge so widely in this case, it is an excellent example of how dangerously narrow our conventional viewpoint can sometimes be. It is interesting to note that virtually none of the points mentioned in this section of the chapter have been raised by the more than 1,000 senior-level managers with whom we have used the case. This observation is not a criticism of these managers; rather, it is a comment on the prevailing narrow conception of cost analysis among U.S. businesses.

Our strategic analysis starts by looking at the value chain positioning of the Challenger bicycle in the marketplace. How much penetration is it likely to achieve? This question follows the fundamental logic of marketing strategy: segmentation and positioning. The case is silent on the segmentation issue and on the differing basic economics of two very different customer groups—a middle-America retailer (Baldwin's normal customer) versus a discount chain (Hi-Valu). But is is not difficult to speculate with reasonable accuracy about the implications for Baldwin of two very different value chain configurations regarding product distribution. The fact that the case is totally silent on these issues is further evidence of what contemporary managerial accounting authors see as relevant concerns. Based on general knowledge or retailers' profit margins and some estimating of freight costs, it is possible to construct the strategic cost comparison outlined in exhibit 3–4.

Going to the next stage in the value chain, is this difference of $67 reflective of a commensurate difference in value to the consumer? It

EXHIBIT 3–4
The Distribution Step in the Value Chain

	One of Baldwin's Current Dealers		Hi-Valu Stores	
Purchase cost		$110		$92
Freight cost		10	(Truckload shipping)	8
Delivered cost		120		100
Necessary margin as percent of sales price	(Independent retailer)	40%	(Discount merchandiser)	25%
Implied retail price		$200		$133

should be noted that the bicycles differ only in cosmetic ways. The basic elements that drive the value of the bicycle are identical (weight to strength relationship in the frame, derailleur, crankshaft, gears, and brakes). Other elements of real value (free assembly, point of sale merchandising, service) or perceived value (brand image, dealer image) obviously differ between the two products. But, do they differ by $67 on a $200 purchase? This is a real issue.

It is also possible to develop a simple market segmentation of the distribution stage in the value chain, based on general knowledge about bicycle retailing, as shown in exhibit 3–5. This segmentation immediately raises the issue of whether Hi-Valu's positioning of the Challenger will attract customers from the cheap bicycle segment or the value bicycle segment. This distinction is critical for Baldwin. Challenger sales taken from low-end dealers (customers who trade up in quality for the same price) are totally new sales for Baldwin, but Challenger sales taken from mid-range dealers (customers who trade down in price for comparable quality) constitute a direct attack on Baldwin's mainstream business and on its mainstream dealer network.

Drawing again upon general knowledge of trends in retailing over the past few decades, it is very likely that a big share of Challenger sales will come from people who otherwise would have shopped in a neighborhood toy store, hardware store, sporting goods store, or small department store. Forty years ago, virtually all bicycles sold in the United States were value bicycles. Specialty shops pushing premium-priced bicycles did not exist and discount chains pushing the cheap, low-end bikes were just emerging. Sears, Roebuck and J. C. Penney were already well established, but they were not yet perceived as a catastrophic threat to "mom and pop" retailers.

Our strategic analysis must also consider strategic positioning issues. Over the past thirty years the bicycle business has developed almost exactly as Porter's competitive strategy framework would predict (Porter, 1980). One can compete successfully by being different and commanding a premium price for that differentiation, such as BMW automobiles. Or, one can compete by being cheaper, and offering reasonable quality for the low price, such as Toyota automobiles. A manufacturer who is neither identifiably better nor demonstrably cheaper will wither away over time, such as AMC automobiles. Porter refers to such firms as being "stuck in the middle" because they do not have a sustainable competitive advantage. Such firms may survive for a long time if the business is sufficiently attractive (automobiles, for example) and if growth

EXHIBIT 3–5
Market Segmentation

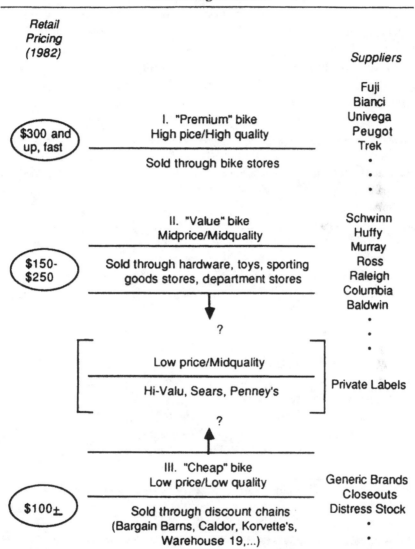

Retail Pricing (1982)

Suppliers

$300 and up, fast

I. "Premium" bike
High pice/High quality

Sold through bike stores

Fuji
Bianci
Univega
Peugot
Trek
•
•
•

II. "Value" bike
Midprice/Midquality

$150-$250

Sold through hardware, toys, sporting goods stores, department stores

Schwinn
Huffy
Murray
Ross
Raleigh
Columbia
Baldwin
•
•
•

?

Low price/Midquality

Hi-Valu, Sears, Penney's

Private Labels

?

III. "Cheap" bike
Low price/Low quality

$100±

Sold through discount chains (Bargain Barns, Caldor, Korvette's, Warehouse 19,...)

Generic Brands
Closeouts
Distress Stock
•
•

rates and investment rates do not force a quick shake out of the weaker players (as they have done in microcomputers, for example). But, firms that lack a sustainable competitive edge eventually will wither.

This focus on the value chain and strategic positioning highlights that, by putting Hi-Valu into the bicycle business, Baldwin is not only creating another direct competitor to its regular customers but also offering that competitor a much better price than it offers its regular customers. Baldwin can, of course, argue that the Challenger bicycle is different, but what will Hi-Valu tell its customers? And, what will the customers believe? In agreeing to this offer, Baldwin almost certainly would further erode the already declining market position of its regular customers. In all probability, this is not a short-run, tactical profit enhancement opportunity. It is very likely a strategic repositioning with major long-run implications.

Just because the Hi-Valu offer is a strategic opportunity to reconfigure the value chain rather than a tactical short-run profit boost does not mean it is necessarily unattractive for Baldwin. In fact, this sort of strategic repositioning may be just what Baldwin needs. As emphasized in the third element of the SCM framework, cost driver analysis can play a significant role in evaluating this strategic opportunity. Examining which cost factors drive the overall profitability of Baldwin is one way to assess the attractiveness of its current strategic niche. Exhibit 3–6 shows return on equity (profit/equity) in terms of margins (profit/sales), asset intensity (sales/assets), and leverage (assets/equity) and suggests that Baldwin currently is marginally profitable, at best.

Baldwin is earning only about half of the average of all manufacturing firms, even though it is much more heavily levered. A good case could be made that Baldwin presents too much basic business operating risk to justify such a high level of financial risk (leverage). Either Baldwin's lenders are inattentive or they have been forced into the current situation by supposedly short-term loans that become long term

EXHIBIT 3–6
Return on Equity

	Margins (P/S) ×	Asset Intensity (S/A)	Leverage (A/E)	=	Return
Baldwin, 1981	$255K/$10.8M	$10.8M/$8.0M (1.35)	$8.0M/$3.0M (2.67)	=	$255K/$3.0 0
Average of U.S. manufacturing (early 1980s	(2 + %) 5%	1.5	2	=	(8 + %) 15%
Baldwin with the HI-Valu deal in 1982, at best	~$400K/$12.8 (3%)	$12.8M/$8.6M (1.49)	$8.6M/$3.0M	=	13%

when inventory was not converted into sales. This strategic assessment of risk and return relationships makes it much harder to argue that Baldwin is a reasonable candidate for further loans.

Another use of cost driver analysis is to flesh out the likely results, over time, of Baldwin's move into the lower price segment of the market. The company's basic economic structure currently is as follows:

Contribution margin per unit $44 (40% of sales).

Fixed cost base (annually):
  Manufacturing: ~$1.5M }
  Selling and administration ~2.4M } $3.9M

Break-even point = 89K units ($3.9M/$44), is about two-thirds of one shift capacity.

Profit (before tax) at 99K units would be about $440K (10,000 × $44). This estimate is quite close to the $474K earned in 1981.

Profit (before tax) at one shift capacity of 133K units = 44,000 × $44 = $1.9M. This is an excellent return on equity.

Asset investment:
  Inventory = 120 days (obviously more an advocate of just in case than just in time)
  Accounts receivable = 45 days, which is typical
  Property turnover = 10.8/3.6 = 3x, which is reasonable

Fixed cost percentage of sales:
  Manufacturing = 1.5/10.8 = ~14%
  Selling and administrative = 2.4/10.8 = ~22%

Gross margin = ~26% of sales (2.8/10.8), a very low figure for a consumer durables manufacturer.

Selling and administrative cost = ~22% of sales, which seems very high for a low-margin manufacturer.

This analysis clearly suggests that Baldwin is geared up for a much higher level of sales than it is now achieving and that reasonable profit levels hinge on much higher volume levels. In SCM terms, Baldwin has committed to a strategy dependent on scale economies that are not being achieved. Bicycle sales in the United States reached a peak of 15 million units in 1973 and had declined to 10 million units in 1982, so it is not surprising that Baldwin looks like a company that sorely needs much more volume. Doesn't this requirement suggest that the extra volume provided by Hi-Valu would be an ideal option?

Not necessarily. The Hi-Valu project is very likely to alienate Baldwin's current dealers. It is usually unwise to try to be a significant supplier simultaneously in two price segments with a substantially identical product, although some industries try this ploy. The liquor companies seem to make it work. ("The only difference between $5 vodka and $10 vodka is $5 and a Russian-looking label.") But, this strategy has been a poor one for many other firms. Fram oil filters (Bendix) lost their ability to command a premium price when they became so readily available in discount chains. Chevrolet and Oldsmobile were totally different automobiles in the 1950s. Many people believe that much of General Motors' current decline can be traced to the decision to stop differentiating its cars in ways other than cosmetic trim and price. GM even lost a court case over Oldsmobile's use of Chevrolet engines in its cars. Oldsmobile saw this practice as a normal part of its common parts manufacturing strategy. Consumers saw it as breaking faith with the Oldsmobile tradition. The Toro Company almost went bankrupt in 1980 when it solved an excess inventory problem by flooding discount chains with its supposedly premium snow blowers. It almost lost its dealer network in the process.

Baldwin's dealers cannot stop the firm from supplying Hi-Valu, but they do not have to cooperate by offering the $200 Baldwin bicycle as the stalking horse for the $133 Challenger bicycle. If they normally stock two or three brands to give their customers a choice, they can add Huffy, Ross, Murray, or Schwinn and drop Baldwin from the set. This response would, in effect, drive Baldwin much more heavily toward the growing low-end bike segment and away from the declining mid-value segment. What would this change in Baldwin's sales mix do for its basic economics? In SCM terms, what cost drivers became critical in trying to serve the low-end segment?

- Contribution margin would only be $23 (25% of sales) instead of $44, and it would be likely to fall steadily because of competition from the Taiwanese and the Koreans.
- The break-even point would be 170K units ($3.9M/$23) or about 130% of one shift capacity. (Break-even point greater than capacity is one pretty sure strategic danger signal.)
- If there are good reasons to stay with a one shift operation and if

the firm wants to earn 15% ROE, on a $3M equity base, it must earn $450K after tax or $900K before tax. This requires ~39K bicycles (at $23 contribution each).

- This leaves ~94K bicycles to pay for fixed overhead (133K – 39K). At $23 per bicycle this allows ~$2.2M for overhead (94K × $23).
- Thus, the firm will have to cut its fixed costs by more than 40%, in the short run (from $3.9M to $2.2M) just to earn an average return on equity.
- As prices come under continuing pressure from foreign manufacturers, unless Baldwin can cut variable costs, margins will fall and overhead will have to be cut even more.

Can Baldwin realistically expect to compete as a supplier of low-cost bikes once the attraction of its mid-brand image has been eroded? What would be the possible source of its cost advantage? It could not plan to compete on scale advantages or learning curve advantages or technological leadership. Very few U.S. firms have learned to play this continual cost reduction game well, especially when starting from a weakened position such as Baldwin faces. Thus, the cold reality is that Baldwin is caught between the proverbial rock and hard place. Its position is summarized in exhibit 3–7.

Exhibit 3–8 summarizes the strategic options from a financial perspective. How can cost analysis help the firm to understand the relative attractiveness of the strategic alternatives?

Baldwin clearly cannot plan to stay in their current niche indefinitely nor can they move entirely to the Hi-Valu niche. What other strategic alternatives do they have? How could cost analysis help the firm to assess the relative attractiveness of these options? Two additional strategic alternatives would be:

1. Go entirely to the premium segment.

2. Try to find new product opportunities in the value niche (mountain bikes, etc.).

There is not enough information in the case for a strategic financial analysis of any of these options. Unless the firm can find a sustainable niche somewhere, its future is bleak. Some bicycle firms did find new prosperity in the mid-1980s with the emergence of the off-road bicycles, which sold almost 3 million units in 1986. But, the market research,

EXHIBIT 3–7
Baldwin's Situation

It is profitable, but only modestly so.
It is heavily leveraged—probably too heavily.
Its strategic niche is slowly eroding away.
A solution presents itself (the Hi-Valu offer).

Plus	Minus
Looks like great incremental return on investment.	Looks extremely profitable for Hi-Valu. Can Baldwin negotiate a better deal? (Probably yes, but should it try?)
Utilizes excess capacity.	Raises major ethical issues about Baldwin's responsibility to its current customers.
Opens new channel of distribution for Baldwin that is a growth market.	Barely break even on full cost basis.
	Major cash flow crunch: Can Baldwin borrow an additional $600K?
	At best, puts company ROE at average level.
	Strategically very risky.

What looks like a good opportunity from a short-run relevant cost perspective looks like a disaster from a strategic perspective.

product development, market development, and manufacturing retooling required to enter and succeed in this new niche probably would take far more money than Baldwin could muster. The firm has used up most of its slack in chasing fond hopes of resurgence in a gradually dying market segment. Strategically, it is dead in the water and it may not know it. Other strategic options for the firm could be developed here, but that is not the intent of this analysis.

The difficulty of finding an appropriate strategic response in this situation, even for a well-positioned firm, is demonstrated by the decline of the traditional market leader, Schwinn, into bankruptcy in 1992.

In summary, this strategic analysis, based heavily on concepts articulated in marketing strategy and in competitive strategy and using cost analysis designed to complement and reinforce the strategic view, presents a totally different perspective on the Baldwin Bicycle case. If we had access to the company's internal cost records and the records of its competitors and its customers, we could attempt a value chain analysis

EXHIBIT 3–8
Strategic Cost Analysis for Baldwin

Alternative #1. Do not accept the Hi-Value deal

ROE is inadequate (~8%).

Middle market is slowly shrinking.

Even if Baldwin rejects the Hi-Valu offer, someone else will do it, thereby further eroding Baldwin's current niche. So, even its current ROE of 8% is vulnerable.

Alternative #2. Current niche plus Hi-Value deal

ROE is still average (~13%) at best.

Great threat to the core business. If their dealers drop Baldwin products, the projected ROE of 13% is seriously open to question. Baldwin might be forced to go 100% to Hi-Valu's niche, where the basic economics are marginal, at best.

What if Baldwin's current dealers ask for a deal similar to Hi-Valu's?

Going private label is a strategic shift; what are the organizational implications of diluting the strategic thrust?

An ethical issue: Is the difference in price of $133 versus $200 reflective of a difference in value to the customer?

Alternative #3. Go 100% to Hi-Valu's niche

Basic economics are marginal, unless able to cut fixed costs by more than 40%, just in the short run.

Baldwin's ability to compete long run against foreign competition as a low-cost producer is very doubtful.

---

to see exactly where Baldwin got so far off the track, but that is not possible in this case.

What is possible, however, is to contrast this rudimentary strategic cost analysis with the relevant cost analysis to show how different the business problem looks from these two perspectives. Although the three elements of the SCM theme are all present here, the case is too limited to permit a careful exposition of any of them. A much more careful exposition of all three themes follows in chapters 4 through 14.

Cost analysis must be supplemented by strategic analysis, as the Baldwin case demonstrates, in order to understand the real business problem. This approach means that the cost analysis concepts must be explicitly tied to the strategic context of the business problem. In that sense, strategic cost analysis must now begin to go beyond managerial accounting just as managerial accounting wen beyond the cost accounting framework it replaced thirty years ago.

CHAPTER 4

THE VALUE CHAIN CONCEPT

The First Key to Effective Cost Management

The first major theme in strategic cost management concerns the focus of cost management efforts. As noted in chapter 2, in the SCM framework, managing costs effectively requires a broad focus, external to the firm, that Porter (1985a) has called the value chain. Each business is part, but only part, of a value chain running all the way from the periodic table of the elements to ultimate dust, and, in today's world, perhaps through recycling to the beginning of a new value chain cycle. Each firm must be understood in the context of the overall chain of value-creating activities of which it is only a part.

This chapter demonstrates that the strategic insights yielded by the value chain analysis are much different from—and are superior to—those suggested by conventional value-added analysis.

THE VALUE CHAIN CONCEPT

According to Porter (1980), a business unit can develop a sustainable competitive advantage based on cost or on differentiation or on both, as shown in exhibit 4-1.

The primary focus of the low-cost strategy is to achieve low cost relative to competitors. Cost leadership can be achieved through such approaches as:

Economies of scale of production.

Experience curve effects.

Parts of this chapter appeared in two journal articles: *Journal of Cost Management*, 5, 4 (1992b), pp. 5–21, and *Journal of Management Accounting Research* 4 (1992a), pp. 179–97. Reproduced with permission.

EXHIBIT 4–1
Developing Competitive Advantage

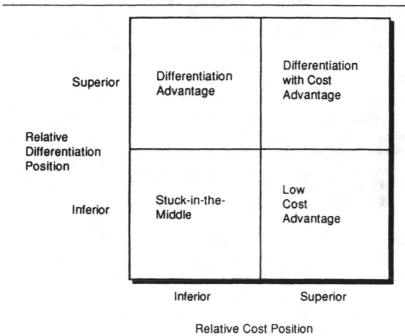

Superior	Differentiation Advantage	Differentiation with Cost Advantage
Inferior	Stuck-in-the-Middle	Low Cost Advantage

Relative Differentiation Position

Relative Cost Position

Inferior / Superior

Tight cost control.

Cost minimization in areas such as R&D, service, sales force, or advertising.

Examples of firms following the low-cost strategy include Texas Instruments in consumer electronics, Emerson Electric in electric motors, Hyundai in automobiles, Briggs and Stratton in gasoline engines, Black and Decker in machine tools, Commodore in business machines, K-Mart in retailing, BIC in pens, and Timex in wrist watches.

With a strategy of differentiation, the primary focus is on differentiating the product of the business unit by creating something that is perceived by customers as unique. Approaches to product differentiation include brand loyalty (Coca Cola in soft drinks), superior customer service (IBM in computers), dealer network (Caterpillar Tractors in construction equipment), product design and features (Hewlett Packard in electronics), and/or technology (Coleman in camping equipment). Other examples of firms following a differentiation strategy include Mercedes-

Benz in automobiles, Stouffer's in frozen foods, Neiman Marcus in retailing, Cross in pens, and Rolex in wristwatches.

Whether or not a firm can develop and sustain differentiation or cost advantage or differentiation-with-cost advantage (as the Japanese have demonstrated) depends fundamentally on how the firm manages its value chain relative to the value chains of its competitors. Both intuitively and theoretically, competitive advantage in the market place ultimately derives from providing better customer value for equivalent cost (i.e., differentiation) or equivalent customer value for a lower cost (i.e., low cost). Thus, value chain analysis is essential to determine exactly where in the chain customer value can be enhanced or costs lowered. Ignoring linkages upstream from the firm as well as downstream is too restrictive a perspective.

The Dangers of Ignoring Value Chain Linkages

The value chain framework is a method for breaking down the chain—from basic raw materials to end-use customers—into strategically relevant activities in order to understand the behavior of costs and the sources of differentiation. We are aware of no firm that spans the entire value chain in which it operates.

A firm such as Chevron in petroleum spans wide segments of the value chain in which it operates, from oil exploration to service stations, but it does not span the entire chain. Fifty percent of the crude oil it refines comes from other producers, and more than one-third of the oil it refines is sold through other retail outlets. Also, Chevron is not in the auto business at all—the major user of gasoline. More narrowly, a firm such as Maxus Energy is only in the oil exploration and production business. The Limited Stores have downstream presence in retail outlets but own no manufacturing facilities. Reebok is a famous shoe brand, but the firm owns very few retail outlets. Reebok does, however, own its factories.

To recapitulate, typically a firm is only a part of the larger set of activities in the value delivery system. Since no two firms, even in the same industry, compete in exactly the same set of markets with exactly the same set of suppliers, the overall value chain for each firm is unique.

Suppliers not only produce and deliver inputs used in a firm's value activities but they importantly influence the firm's cost/differentiation position. For example, developments by steel minimills lowered the operating costs of wire products users who are the customers of the customers of the minimill—two stages down the value chain. Similarly, customers' actions can have a significant impact on the firm's value activities. For example, when printing press manufacturers create a new three-meter-wide press, the profitability of paper mills is affected because paper machine widths must match some multiple of printing press widths. Mill profit is affected by customer actions even though the paper mill is two stages upstream from the printer who is a customer of the press manufacturer. As we discuss more fully later, gaining and sustaining a competitive advantage requires that a firm understand the entire value delivery system, not just the portion of the value chain in which it participates. Suppliers and customers and suppliers' suppliers and customers' customers have profit margins that are important to identify in understanding a firm's cost/differentiation positioning, because the end-use customers ultimately pay for all the profit margins along the entire value chain.

Exhibit 4–2 presents a conceptual value chain for the paper industry. The distinct value activities—such as timber, logging, pulp mills, paper mills, and conversion plants—are the building blocks by which this industry creates a product valuable to buyers.

It is possible to quantify the economic value created at each stage by identifying the costs, revenues, and assets for each activity. We argue that every firm in exhibit 4–2—A, B, C, D, E, F, and G—must construct a value chain for the total paper industry that breaks the total value in the chain into its fundamental sources of economic value. Such an analysis has potential strategic implications for every competitor in this industry.

For instance, consider three firms in the paper products industry. Weyerhaeuser participates in most parts of the value chain, with the exception of logging. James River has very limited timberlands but participates in the remainder of the value chain. Finally, TetraPak does not own trees, or pulp mills, or paper mills but makes cartons from paperboard purchased on the market. Every one of these three firms can benefit by constructing the entire value chain, even though they do not participate in every stage of the chain.

Value Chain Insights for Different Competitors

If competitor A (a fully integrated company) in exhibit 4–2 calculates the return on assets (ROA) at each stage of the chain by adjusting all

EXHIBIT 4–2
Value Chain in the Paper Products Industry

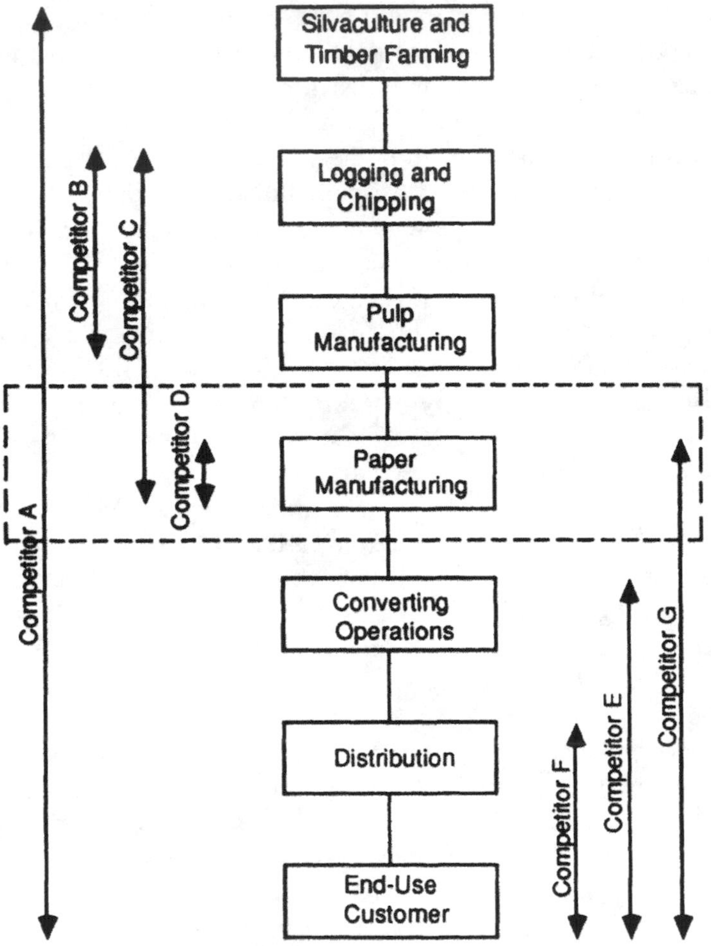

transfer prices to competitive market levels, it could highlight potential areas where the firm could more economically buy from the outside instead of making (the strategic choice of make or buy). For example, most of the fully integrated forest product companies (e.g., Weyerhaeuser, International Paper) still use independent loggers to cut their trees on the way to their mills.

With a complete value chain, competitors B, C, D, E, F, and G in exhibit 4–2 might be able to identify possibilities to forward or backward integrate into areas that can improve their performance. Westvaco has stopped manufacturing envelope paper although it still owns a large envelope converter. Champion International has sold its envelope converting business but still produces envelope paper. Both choices, although apparently inconsistent, could be plausible given the specific strategies of Westvaco and Champion.

Each value activity has a set of unique cost drivers that explain variations in costs in that activity (Shank, 1989). Thus, each value activity has its unique sources of competitive advantage. Companies are likely to face a different set of competitors at each stage. Some of these competitors would be fully integrated companies and some of them would be more narrowly focused specialists. For instance, firm D in exhibit 4–1 faces competition from firms, A, C, and G in the paper mill stage. Yet, firms A, C, and G bring very different competitive advantage to this stage of the value chain vis-à-vis firm D. It is possible for firm D to compete effectively with firms A, C, and G only by understanding the total value chain and the cost drivers that regulate each activity. For example if scope (vertical integration) is a key structural driver of paper mill cost, firm A has a significant advantage and firm D a significant disadvantage in this marketplace.

Because each firm illustrated in exhibit 4–2 is both a buyer and a seller somewhere within the chain, calculating the profit (and ROA) earned at each stage can help in understanding the relative power of buyers versus sellers at that stage. For example, comparing the returns for firm E versus firm F can help identify the relative power within the chain of the converting stage for which E is a supplier but F is a buyer. This comparison then could help the firms in identifying ways to exploit their linkages with their suppliers as well as with their customers to reduce costs or enhance differentiation or both.

Parenthetically, we might note that the concept of value chain we have described so far includes but goes beyond the traditional view that a firm's value chain represents the collection of activities that the firm performs in the different functional areas. This traditional view was diagrammatically represented by Porter (1985a) as shown in exhibit 4–3.

A firm's value chain in embedded in a larger system that includes suppliers' and customers' value chains. A firm can enhance its profitability not only by understanding its own value chain—from design to distribution—but also by understanding how the firm's value activities fit into suppliers' and customers' value chains.

EXHIBIT 4–3
Value Activities Within a Firm

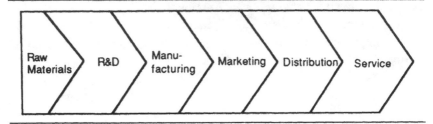

Value Chain Versus Value Added

The value chain concept can be contrasted with the internal focus that is typically adopted in management accounting. Management accounting usually takes a value-added perspective, as noted earlier. From a strategic perspective, unlike the value-added concept, the value chain concept highlights four profit improvement areas:

1. Linkages with suppliers.

2. Linkages with customers.

3. Process linkages within the value chain of a business unit.

4. Linkages across business unit value chains within the firm.

Linkages with Suppliers

The value-added concept starts too late. That is, beginning cost analysis with purchases misses all the opportunities for exploiting linkages with the firm's suppliers. The word exploit does not imply that the relationship with the supplier is a zero-sum game. Quite the contrary, as implied by exhibit 4–4, the link should be managed so that both the firm and its supplier can benefit. Such opportunities can be dramatically important to a firm. In chapter 2, we presented an example from the U.S. automobile industry that demonstrated the strategic benefits in explicitly considering supplier linkages.

Another example of how beneficial linkages with suppliers (i.e., linkages with suppliers that are managed so that all parties benefit) can be tracked more accurately with value chain analysis than with value-added analysis comes from the chocolate industry:

EXHIBIT 4-4
Develop Competitive Advantage Through Linkages with Suppliers

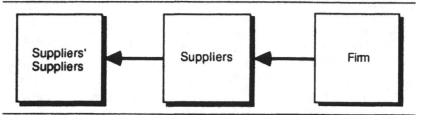

When bulk chocolate began to be delivered in liquid form in tank cars instead of ten pound molded bars, an industrial chocolate firm (i.e., the supplier) eliminated the cost of molding bars and packing them and a confectionery producer saved the cost of unpacking and melting. (Hergert & Morris, 1989)

Linkages with Customers

In addition to starting too late, value-added analysis has another major flaw: it stops too soon. Stopping cost analysis at sales misses all the opportunities for exploiting linkages with the firm's customers. As indicated in exhibit 4–5 customer linkages can be just as important as supplier linkages. Here, again the relationship with the customer need not be a zero-sum game, but one in which both parties can gain.

There are many examples in which the linkage between a firm and its customer is designed to be mutually beneficial and in which the relationship with the customer is viewed not as a zero-sum game but as a mutually beneficial one. For example:

Some container producers have constructed manufacturing facilities next to beer breweries and deliver the containers through overhead conveyers directly onto the customers' assembly line. This results in significant cost

EXHIBIT 4-5
Develop Competitive Advantage Through Linkages with Customers

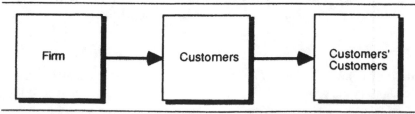

reductions for both the container producers and their customers by expediting the transport of empty containers which are bulky and heavy. (Hergert & Morris, 1989).

The value chain framework highlights how a firm's products fit into the buyer's value chain. For instance, under this framework, it is readily apparent what percentage the firm's product costs are in the customer's total costs. The fact that paper constitutes over forty percent of the total costs of a magazine is very useful in encouraging the paper mill and the publisher to work together to reduce costs. The *San Francisco Chronicle* adopted the Just in Time concept for paper delivery to its printing plant, a program only possible with close supplier cooperation. Since the value-added concept ignores activities after the product leaves the firm, it often does not highlight the degree of buyer power.

Process Linkages Within the Value Chain of a Business Unit

Unlike the value-added concept, value chain analysis explicitly recognizes the fact that the individual value activities within a firm are interdependent rather than independent (exhibit 4–6). For instance, at McDonald's, the timing of promotional campaigns (one value activity) significantly influences capacity utilization in production (another value activity). These linked activities must be coordinated if the full effect of the promotion is to be realized. As another example, Japanese VCR producers were able to reduce prices from $1,300 in 1977 to $298 by 1984 by emphasizing the impact of an early step in the chain (product design) on a later step (production) by drastically reducing the number of parts in VCRs (Hergert & Morris, 1989).

Conventional management accounting approaches tend to emphasize across-the-board cost reductions. However, by recognizing inter-linkages, the value chain analysis admits to the possibility that deliberately increasing costs in one value activity can bring about a reduction in total costs. The expense incurred by Proctor & Gamble to place its order entry computers directly in Wal-Mart stores significantly reduces overall order entry and processing costs for both firms.

Linkages Across Business Unit Value Chains Within the Firm

In sharp contrast to the value-added notion, the value chain analysis also recognizes the profit potential accruing from exploiting linkages among value activities across business units (exhibit 4–7). For example, within

EXHIBIT 4-6
Develop Competitive Advantage Through Process Linkages Within the Value Chain of a Business Unit

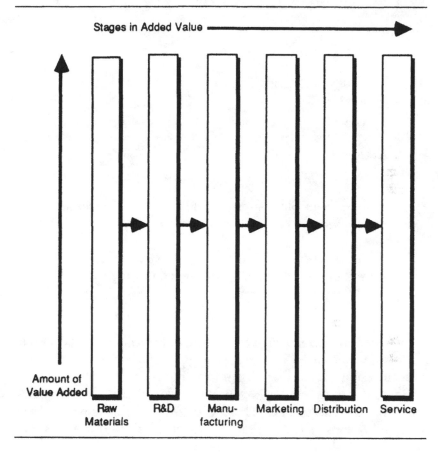

Stages in Added Value ⟶

Amount of
Value Added

| Raw Materials | R&D | Manu-facturing | Marketing | Distribution | Service |

EXHIBIT 4-7
Develop Competitive Advantage Through Linkages Across Business Unit Value Chains Within the Firm

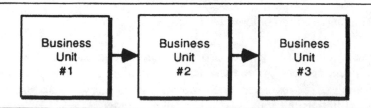

Business Unit #1 → Business Unit #2 → Business Unit #3

Procter & Gamble, the cost position of the disposable diaper business unit is enhanced by its ability to share in distribution with other business units whose products (such as soaps and paper towels) also go through supermarkets.

VALUE CHAIN METHODOLOGY

The methodology for constructing and using a value chain involves the following steps:

1. Identify the industry's value chain and assign costs, revenues, and assets to value activities.

2. Diagnose the cost drivers regulating each value activity.

3. Develop sustainable competitive advantage, either through controlling cost drivers better than competitors or by reconfiguring the value chain.

These steps are considered in detail in the following sections.

Identify the Value Chain

Competitive advantage cannot be meaningfully examined at the level of the industry as a whole. The value chain disaggregates the industry into its distinct strategic activities. Therefore, the starting point for cost analysis is to define an industry's value chain and assign costs, revenues, and assets to value activities. These activities are the building blocks by which firms in the industry create a product valuable to buyers. Activities should be isolated and separated if:

They represent a significant percentage of operating costs; or

The cost behavior of the activities (or the cost drivers) is different; or

They are performed by competitors in different ways; or

They have a high potential for creating differentiation.

Each value activity incurs costs, generates revenues, and ties up assets in the process. After identifying the value chain, one must assign operating costs, revenues, and assets to individual value activities. For intermediate value activities, revenues should be assigned by adjusting internal transfer prices to competitive market prices. With this information, it should be possible to calculate return on assets for each value activity.

Diagnose Cost Drivers

The next step is to identify the cost drivers that explain variations in costs in each value activity. In conventional management accounting, cost is a function, primarily, of only one cost driver, output volume. Although cost concepts related to output volume dominate the conventional cost management literature, in the value chain framework, output volume as such is seen to capture very little of the richness of cost behavior. Rather, multiple cost drivers are usually at work. Further, cost drivers differ across value activities.

Porter's (1985a) attempt to create a comprehensive list of cost drivers is more important than his particular list. In the strategic management literature better lists exist (Riley, 1987). Following Riley, the cost drivers are broken into two categories:

1. Structural cost drivers.

2. Executional cost drivers.

These distinctions are explained and illustrated in chapter 2.

Operationalizing individual drivers also involves specific cost analysis issues. As pointed out in chapter 2, the SCM field is moving very quickly toward executional drivers because the insights from analysis based on structural drivers are too often old fashioned.

Whatever items are on the list of cost drivers, the key ideas are:

* Value chain analysis is the broader framework; the cost driver concept is a way to understand cost behavior in each activity in the value chain. Thus, ideas such as ABC are only a subset of the value chain framework.
* For strategic analysis, volume is an uninteresting way to explain cost behavior.
* What is more useful in a strategic sense is to explain cost position in terms of the structural choices and executional skills that shape the firm's competitive position. For example Porter (1986b) analyzes the classic confrontation between General Electric and Wes-

tinghouse in steam turbines in 1962 in terms of the structural and executional cost drivers for each firm.

- Not all the strategic drivers are equally important all the time, but some (more than one) of them are very probably very important in every case. For example, Porter (1986a) develops a strategic assessment of Dupont's position in titanium dioxide based primarily on scale and capacity utilization issues.
- For each cost driver, a particular cost analysis framework is critical to understanding the positioning of a firm.
- Different value activities in the value chain are usually influenced by different cost drivers. For instance, the relevant cost driver for advertising is market share, whereas promotional costs are usually variable. Coca Cola, for example, can realize economies of scale in advertising because of its large market share. A price-off, by contrast (an example of a sales promotion activity), is strictly a variable cost per unit.

Cost drivers are discussed in more depth in chapter 10.

Develop Sustainable Competitive Advantage

Once the firm has identified the value chain and diagnosed the cost drivers of each value activity, the firm can gain sustainable competitive advantage in one of two ways:

1. By controlling those cost drivers better than competitors.

2. By reconfiguring the value chain.

Control Cost Drivers Better Than Competitors

For each value activity, the key questions are:

Can we reduce costs in this activity, holding value (revenues) constant?

Can we increase value (revenues) in this activity, holding costs constant?

Can we reduce assets in this activity, holding costs and revenues constant?

By systematically analyzing costs, revenues, and assets in each activity, the firm can achieve differentiation-with-cost advantage—something which Japanese manufacturers have been able to achieve. An effective way to accomplish differentiation-with-cost advantage is to compare the value chain of the firm with the value chains of one or two of its major competitors and identify the actions needed to manage the firm's value chain better than those of its competitors. In short, competitive advantage is purely relative. What matters is not how fast the firm runs but whether or not the firm is running faster than its competitors. The dynamics of competition automatically lead to continuously shifting benchmarks. The firm can be assured that its average competitors will be smarter tomorrow than they are today. As such, ongoing competitor cost analysis is crucial to developing and sustaining competition advantage.

Reconfigure the Value Chain

While continuing the focus on managing the firm's existing value chain better than competitors, greater efforts need to be spent on redefining the value chain where payoffs could be even more significant. For instance, in the mature and tough meat-packing industry, Iowa Beef Processors has performed exceptionally well by controlling their processing, distribution, and labor costs. They accomplished these cost reductions by redefining the traditional value chain in this industry. To quote Stuart (1981, pp. 67–73):

> Earnings per share [of Iowa Beef Processors] have soared at a compound annual rate of over 23 percent since 1973. The company has achieved this remarkable record by never wavering from its strategy and obsession—to be the low-cost producer of beef.
>
> To that end, it rewrote the rules for killing, chilling, and shipping beef. It built plants on a grand scale, automated them to a fare-thee-well, and now spends up to $20 million a year on renovation to keep them operating efficiently. The old-line packers shipped live animals to the abattoirs at such rail centers at Chicago, but Iowa Beef brought the plant to the cattle in the sprawling feedlots of the High Plains and Southwest. This saved on transportation and avoided the weight loss that commonly occurs when live animals are shipped. Iowa Beef also led the industry in cleaving and trimming carcasses into loins, ribs, and other cuts, and boxing the pieces at the plant, which further reduced transport charges by removing excess weight.

The company has fought tenaciously to hold down labor costs. Though some of its plants are unionized, it refused to pay the wages called for in the United Food & Commercial Workers' expensive master agreement, which the elders of the industry have been tied to for 40 years. Iowa Beef's wages and benefits average half those of less hard-nosed competitors.

Calculational Difficulties

We do not wish to imply that constructing a value chain for a firm is easy. There are several thorny problems to confront: calculating value (revenues) for intermediate products, isolating key cost drivers, identifying linkages across activities, computing supplier and customer margins, and constructing competitors's cost structures.

The analysis starts by segmenting the chain into those components for which some firm makes a market, even if other firms do not. This approach will catch the segments outlined in exhibit 4–2 for the paper industry, for example. One could start the process by identifying every point in the chain at which an external market exists, thereby achieving a good first cut at identifying the value chain segments. One can always find some stage narrow enough that an external market does not exist. An example would be the progress of a roll of paper from the last press section of a paper machine to the first dryer section on the same machine. Obviously, there is no external market for paper halfway through a continuous-flow paper machine. Thus, seeing the press section and the dryer section of the paper machine as separate stages in the value chain is probably not operational.

Part of the art of strategic analysis is deciding which stages in the value chain can meaningfully be decoupled conceptually and which cannot. Unless some firm has decoupled a stage by making a market at that stage, one cannot independently assess the economic profit earned at that stage. But the opportunities for meaningful analysis across a set of firms that have defined differently what they make versus what they buy and sell are often very significant.

Despite the calculational problems, we contend that every firm should attempt to estimate its value chain. Even the process of performing the value chain analysis, in and by itself, can be quite instructive. Such an exercise forces managers to ask how their activity adds value to the chain of customers who use their products (or services) and how their cost structure compares with those of their competitors.

THE STRATEGIC POWER OF VALUE CHAIN ANALYSIS: CASE STUDIES

In the next two sections, we present examples to illustrate further the value chain perspective and how it differs from conventional management accounting analysis. The first example is drawn from the telecommunications industry; this example describes the value chains of three competitors in this industry in qualitative terms. The second example is drawn from the airline industry; here, we contrast the cost/differentiation positioning of United Airlines and People Express by comparing the cost per seat mile of these two airlines in the different components of their value chains.

The Telecommunications Industry

Exhibit 4–8 contains the value chains of AT&T, NYNEX, and IBM in the telecommunications industry. To quote Hax and Majluf (1991, pp. 80–81):

> AT&T is a dominant firm in U.S. telecommunications, NYNEX is one of the leading Bell operating companies serving the New York and New England area, and IBM is a growing force in this industry.
>
> The telecommunications industry is in a state of flux, due to the rapid progress in technology and changes in the regulatory and competitive environment. The increasing technological sophistication in many telecommunications networks has expanded the range of products being offered. It has also increased the pressures on major players to maintain their technological edge as a competitive tool. There are three classes of products: public networks (for example, telephone lines, satellites), customer-premise equipment (CPE, ranging from answering machines to sophisticated PBXs), and value-added network services (VANs, like electronic mail, videotext, voice messaging).
>
> The comparative value chains of AT&T, NYNEX, and IBM [exhibit 4–8] highlight their different competitive strategies in this industry. AT&T has a nation-wide presence, a strong technological and procurement leadership through Bell Labs and Western Electric, the strongest telecommunications network, and a great reputation for high-quality service. NYNEX enjoys a regional monopoly, freedom to use any suppliers, proximity to the customer, as well as a service image. IBM is attempting to position itself in this important industry using its enormous worldwide reputation for excellence in computers, that gives it easy access to

EXHIBIT 4–8
Value Chain Configurations: The Telecommunications Industry

Value Chain Elements	Strategic Differences		
	AT&T	*NYNEX*	*IBM*
Procurement	Owns manufacturing branch (Western Electric)	Free to use any supplier it wants	Owns Rolm, CPE manufacturer
Technology development	Technological leadership through Bells Labs	Focus on software products	Strong R&D in computer hardware and software technologies
Operations	National presence High quality of equipment through heavy capital expenditure Similar communications standards nationwide Strongest national telecommunications network	Regional monopoly Innovative equipment from outside suppliers High-quality regional network through heavy capital investment	Global presence Leading computer technology Partnership with MCI
Marketing and sales	New emphasis on marketing (still weak) High name recognition Long-term relationship with clients Recruits computer executives	Use of Bell logo Focus on top 1,000 corporate customers Sales and distribution centers close to customers	Strong reputation for marketing excellence Already sells to most major corporations Experienced sales force

Source: Extracted from Hax and Majluf (1991), pp. 79–82.

most major corporations. Its alliance with ROLM and MCI, and its strong capabilities in software and hardware technologies, provide IBM a solid foundation to launch a competitive assault in telecommunications.

It is hard to predict the final competitive position of these three corporations in the telecommunications industry. It will depend eventually on a variety of outside factors, such as government regulation, technological development, evolution of customers' expectations, and most importantly the exact scope of the market in which the three firms compete. There are two trends which seem to define this scope: the blurring of the computer and communications industry into a still nebulous information society, and the trend toward globalization of major markets.

In the case of the telecommunications industry, the value chain differences among AT&T, NYNEX, and IBM were explained in qualitative terms. In the next section, we describe the value chains of competitors in the airline industry, both qualitatively and in dollar terms.

The Airline Industry

At a very general level, one can say that all commercial airlines provide value to customers a three stages:

1. Providing reservation information and ticketing services.

2. Operating the aircraft from point A to point B.

3. Providing service to the passenger before flight, during flight, and after arrival.

Each element in the value chain utilizes specific assets and has a specific cost function. Overall return on investment is a result of all three linked stages.

Yet, conventional financial reports reveal nothing about the separate value-creating activities in which the airline is engaged. Exhibit 4–9 is a disguised and condensed version of the published financial statements of one of the major trunk airlines, which we call Ajax Airlines. The statements clearly reveal much that is interesting about the company—but nothing about the value chain. Combining the financial statements with a DuPont analysis (exhibit 4–10) can yield conventional insights, but not much about business strategy.

What does this analysis tell us? For one, profit margins improved along with sales. The airline was able to sell more tickets while operating expense declined per dollar of sales. Asset utilization also improved, a critical factor in the airline industry. This change is reflected in the improved asset turnover from 0.857 to 0.917 (exhibit 4–10). At the same time, financial leverage remained constant. It appears that Ajax was able

EXHIBIT 4–9
Ajax Airlines Financial Data

Statements of Income	1988	1987
Sales	$8,800	$7,200
Expenses		
Salaries and benefits	2,900	2,400
Aircraft fuel	1,100	1,000
Fleet operations cost		
(leases and depreciation)	3,900	$3,200
Total operating expense	7,900	6,600
Operating income	900	600
Interest expense	230	200
Tax	335	200
Net income	$335	$200
Balance Sheets		
Current Assets	$2,600	$2,100
Property and equipment	7,000	6,300
Total assets	$9,600	$8,400
Current liabilities	$2,700	$2,000
Long-term debt	3,000	3,000
Equity	3,900	3,400
Total liabilities	$9,600	$8,400

EXHIBIT 4–10
Ajax Airlines: DuPont Analysis

	$\dfrac{\text{Net Income}}{\text{Sales}}$		$\dfrac{\text{Sales}}{\text{Assets}}$		$\dfrac{\text{Assets}}{\text{Equity}}$		$\dfrac{\text{Net Income}}{\text{Equity}}$
1988	$\dfrac{335}{8,800}$	×	$\dfrac{8,800}{9,600}$	×	$\dfrac{9,600}{3,900}$	=	$\dfrac{335}{3,900}$
	0.038	×	0.917	×	2.46	=	0.086
1987	$\dfrac{200}{7,200}$	×	$\dfrac{7,200}{8,400}$	×	$\dfrac{8,400}{3,400}$	=	$\dfrac{200}{3,400}$
	0.028	×	0.857	×	2.47	=	0.059

to improve both margins and asset utilization while holding financial risk constant. Management apparently has done a good job and should continue with what looks like a successful growth strategy.

But how has Ajax grown? And how have they been able to earn greater margins at a higher level of sales? Where has Ajax added to capacity in order to improve the asset utilization? And what is the strategy Ajax is pursuing? Financial statements do not answer these questions.

Traditional managerial accounting provides additional information about Ajax, but still without a value chain perspective. Traditional cost accounting would suggest that in a high fixed cost industry like airlines, contribution analysis is the key. The argument would be that because fleet cost and compensation for pilots, flight attendants, and ground personnel are not volume dependent in the short run, the airline strategy should be to fill up capacity by aggressive pricing. Once the break-even point is met, most of every incremental dollar of revenue goes straight to the bottom line. Incremental variable cost is probably only fuel and food.

Given some additional information that is usually supplied in the annual report of major carriers, one can construct the traditional contribution analysis for Ajax that is shown in exhibit 4–11 using seat miles as the per-unit metric.

Because, in the short run, incremental cost is very low, traditional managerial accountants would tell us to fill up that unused capacity (as shown in exhibit 4–11) at almost any price. The supplementary financial data shows that Ajax did not. Ajax was able to charge significantly more for each set mile, but they did not improve utilization of the available seat miles. Seat mile capacity utilization stayed constant at 64%. We also now have some conflicting data from the DuPont analysis in exhibit 4–10. DuPont analysis told us that asset utilization improved, but traditional management accounting is telling us that it remained constant for the seat mile metric. Is there a conflict?

The managerial analysis in exhibit 4–11 tells us that for the same capacity utilization, Ajax was able to charge a higher price per seat mile flown while paying more for compensation and equipment (compensation per seat mile flown rose from $0.042 to $0.045, while fleet operations cost per seat mile flown rose form $0.056 to $0.06). This leads to the logic that by improving the quality of service and equipment, Ajax was able to charge higher prices. This may be what was happening, but

EXHIBIT 4–11
Ajax Airlines: Contribution Analysis

	Additional Information	
	1988	*1987*
Seat miles flown	65,000	57,000
Available seat miles	102,000	89,000
Asset utilization (load factor realized)	64%	64%
Revenue/seat mile	13.5¢	12.6¢
Compensation/seat mile	4.5¢	4.2¢
Fuel/seat mile	1.7¢	1.8¢
Fleet operations cost/seat mile	6.0¢	5.6¢
Total	12.2¢	11.6¢
Operating profit/seat mile	1.3¢	1.0¢
Contribution margin/seat mile	11.8¢	10.8¢
Break-even level:	$6,800 = 57,600	$5,600 = 51,900
	$.118	$.108
Break-even percent of available capacity	56.5%	58.5%

can we be certain that this strategy was being pursued? We don't believe it was. Also, how does one explain the contradictory asset utilization numbers from the two analyses? Also, both financial and managerial analyses seem to tell management that by filling those unused seats, extra revenue will flow straight to the bottom line. Should that policy be implemented? Does this picture accurately reflect what was going on at Ajax?

Very different insights can be gleaned from a value chain perspective, as shown in exhibit 4–12. Clearly, Ajax invested heavily in ticketing and reservations, most likely in improvements to their computerized reservations system. And, in spite of a 14% increase in seat miles flown (i.e., from 57,000 in 1987 to 65,000 in 1988, as exhibit 4–11 shows), ticketing and reservations (T&R) cost per seat mile was held constant at $0.005 (see the "Costs" section near the bottom of exhibit 4–12), though T&R cost is hardly fixed. Presumably, Ajax was willing to increase T&R costs and assets as a strategic investment in better service.

Also, the cost of operating the aircraft is as purely fixed as traditional management accounting thought suggests. While the number of miles flown increased 14%, the operating expenses of those miles flown increased 28% (i.e., from $3,900 to $4,980, as the first line item, "Aircraft operations," in exhibit 4–12 shows). This cost hardly seems fixed.

EXHIBIT 4–12
Ajax Airlines: A Value Chain Analysis

	1988	1987
Sales	$8,800	$7,200
Expenses		
Tickets and reservations	320	300
Aircraft operations	4,980	3,900
Customer service	2,600	2,400
Total expenses	$7,900	$6,600
Identifiable property, plant, and equipment assets		
Tickets and reservations	$2,000	$1,000
Aircraft operations	5,000	5,300
Customer service	0	0
Total	$7,000	$6,300

	Per seat mile flown		Per available mile	
	1988	**1987**	**1988**	**1987**
Costs				
Tickets and reservations	$0.005	$0.005	$0.003	$0.003
Aircraft operations	0.077	0.069	$0.049	0.044
Customer service	0.040	0.042	$0.025	0.027
Total	$0.122	$0.116	$0.077	$0.074
Assets				
Tickets and reservations	$0.031	$0.018	$0.020	$0.011
Aircraft	0.077	0.093	0.049	0.060
Customer service	0	0	0	0
Total	$0.108	$0.111	$0.069	$0.071

Clearly, cost drivers other than capacity utilization were at work, and management appears not to have controlled them. The reduction in the asset base (see the line item "Aircraft operations" in exhibit 4–12 under the category "Identifiable property, plant and equipment assets") presumably reflects one more years' depreciation on the aging fleet, rather than a strategic change in fleet configuration. Also, it is interesting that aircraft operations cost per seat mile flown rose 12% (i.e., from $0.069 to $0.077—see the line item "Aircraft operations" in exhibit 4–12 under the category "Costs" near the bottom of the exhibit). This element in the value chain seems not to translate easily into value to the customer—it simply involves getting from point A to point B.

Apparently, Ajax raised the price per seat mile flown mostly to compensate for an increase in fleet operating expenses; the action had no clear strategic justification.

Customer service expense per seat mile flown dropped from $0.042 to $0.040. As a straight fixed cost, this should have dropped to 0.037 (0.042 ÷ 1.14, where 1.14 adjusts for the 14% increase in seat miles flown), so Ajax was spending a little more in this activity, as adjusted for volume.

Strategically, Ajax seemed to be hoping that a small increase in aggregate (but not per-unit) customer service expenditures and a better ticketing and reservation system would justify higher prices in an aging fleet. But increased aircraft operations costs wiped out most of the profit impact of the increase in revenue per seat mile flown from $0.126 in 1987 to $0.135 in 1988 (see "Revenue per seat mile flown" in exhibit 4–11). This result hardly seems to fit the success story told by the conventional financial analysis. Value chain analysis can yield very different insights. The linking of financial analysis to strategic positioning in this way is a critical element in effective financial analysis.

Value Chains of United Airlines Versus People Express

Value chain analyses that are comparative across competing firms further enhance the value of the technique. As one simple example of the comparative value chain perspective, consider the chart prepared from publicly available information for two very different major airlines, United Airlines and People Express in its heyday (see exhibit 4–13).

Structured in this way, the difference in strategies between the two airlines becomes apparent. The no frills concept of People Express shows clearly. Specifically, strategic decisions in five areas listed in the "Value Chain Elements" column of exhibit 4–14 account for the $13,100 difference in the cost per 100,000 seat miles between these two airlines.

In this example, the value chain technique confirms what we already know about these two airlines. We turn in the next chapter to a field study which illustrates how value chains are prepared and used. Here the insights which emerge were not already known. The real power of the value chain technique is in framing cost issues to yield strategic insight.

EXHIBIT 4–13
Value Chain Configurations: A Comparison Between People Express and United Airlines

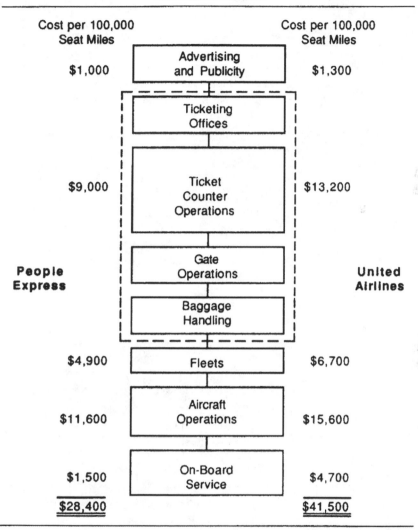

EXHIBIT 4–14
Strategic Inferences from the Value Chains of People Express and United Airlines

Value Chain Elements	People Express Less Than United Airlines (Cost per 100,000 Seat Miles	Strategic Differences	
		People Airlines	*United Airlines*
Advertising and publicity	$300	Heavy promotion to tout low-price, no-frills airline	Heavy promotion of full-service airline
Ticketing and reservations	$3,200	No ticket offices No separate computer reservation system	Ticket offices in downtown locations Extensive computer reservation system
		Secondary airports and terminals	Full service
		No ticket counters (check-in only)	
		Purchase tickets on board the aircraft or from machines	
		No interline tickets	
		Few fare options	
		First come, first served seating	Full service
		No ticketing at gates	
		Provide carry-on space	Free baggage checking
		Charge for checked baggage	
		No interline baggage	
Fleet costs	$1,800	Used aircraft ("budget" airplanes)	New aircraft
Flight operations	$4,000	High-density seating Nonunion pilots Smaller crews and more flying hours per day Flight crews paid on dramatically lower scale Flight crews double on ground duties	Union pilots Bigger crews Crews paid on higher scale
Cabin operations	$3,200	Nonunion flight attendants Lower pay scale No first class No meals Charge for snacks and drinks served	Full service

CHAPTER 5

COST ANALYSIS CONSIDERATIONS AND MANAGERIAL APPLICATIONS OF VALUE CHAINS

An Extended Field Study

A firm's value chain traditionally is viewed as the collection of activities that the firm performs in the different functional areas (see exhibit 4–3 in chapter 4). Our concept of value chain, discussed more fully in chapter 4, extends this traditional view and argues that a firm's value chain is embedded in a larger system that includes suppliers' and customers' value chains (exhibit 4–2 in chapter 4). This chapter further illustrates the power of this extended concept of value chain—that is, the power of seeing each firm in the context of the overall chain of value-creating activities of which it is only a part, from basic raw material components to end-use customers. While the two examples in the preceding chapter are based on published financial statements, the extended example in this chapter is drawn from our field research in the packaging industry. Here, we show the methodology for constructing a value chain for a firm and also highlight the insights that can be derived from such an analysis. In the case of the airline industry example, the value chain analysis confirms what we already knew about United Airlines and People Express. However, the real power of the concept comes from applying it to draw insights in situations where we do not know what we will find. That is the case for the field study presented here. The name of the company and the financial data are disguised.

A modified version of this chapter appeared in the *Journal of Management Accounting Research* 4, (1992a), pp. 179–97. Reproduced with permission.

NORTHAM PACKAGING COMPANY

The Business Setting

NorthAm Packaging Company produced 206,000 tons of coated paperboard in 1989. This paperboard was sold to consumer product firms (processors) who formed the paperboard into cartons, then filled and sealed them for shipment to retail outlets. NorthAm served two market segments. In 1989, 146,000 tons of the company's output went to commodity product firms for whom the carton was just a box. For these firms, price was the major purchase characteristic, assuming normal quality and service. The company had 40% market share in this segment. These processors' products were considered commodities because they did not have an ability to achieve a price premium for the brand name. These processors were typically smaller in size. NorthAm sold to over 300 customers in this segment. Overall sales in this segment had declined 3% per year over the last five years, but were believed to have stabilized in 1989.

The second customer segment, to whom NorthAm sold 60,000 tons of paperboard in 1989, was high quality, differentiated processors for whom the carton was an important element of the marketing strategy. NorthAm had a 15% market share in this segment. These processors were typically larger in size. NorthAm sold to only six customers in this segment. This segment was growing at approximately 10% per year and was projected to grow even faster in the future. The quality of the packaging material (strength, durability, and printability) was particularly important for this segment because the carton was a point-of-sale merchandising aid for the differentiated products. NorthAm's market share in this segment had declined over time. Customers attributed the decline to NorthAm's inability to consistently produce the high-quality board this segment demanded.

NorthAm was one of four major competitors in the coated paperboard industry. Because of the scale, technology, and integration economies of these firms, new entrants were effectively shut out.

Substitutes

Plastic was the major substitution threat to the manufacturers of coated paperboard. Shell Chemical and Hoover International (now Johnson Controls) had changed the consumer packaging industry overnight in

1965 when they combined to introduce the plastic resin pellet and the blow molding machine to manufacture plastic cartons. At first, the polyethylene pellets, supplied by Shell Chemical, were quite expensive. But the blow molding machine was so easy to use that plastic made steady inroads into the consumer packaging industry. However, there were several reasons why coated paperboard continued to be used.

First, although plastic was more economical when the price of plastic resin was low, high plastic resin prices made coated board look good. Predicting future levels of ethylene gas prices (the basic driver of polyethylene price) was notoriously difficult. Second, processors did not want to be totally at the mercy of oil companies. By using dual suppliers, processors created a hedge against the volatile price of plastic resin. For instance, in 1988, a fire in a Shell refinery in Louisiana destroyed thirty percent of the polyethylene pellet supply in the United States overnight and forced many processors who had largely converted to plastic back to coated board. Third, as new uses of the plastic resin were created (industrial and consumer uses of plastic containers), the input price went up. Fourth, because plastic was just a byproduct for the oil companies, there was no real assurance of supply. Finally, environmental indignation over plastic jugs was heating up. These containers were being outlawed in many states because of problems with burning them or dumping them in landfills. The most populous county in the United States, Suffolk County on Long Island, passed legislation in 1987 banning plastic cartons from its landfills.

Cost Structure

One way to understand NorthAm's position is to analyze and discuss the process flow from basic raw material sources through to the end-use product delivered into the final customers' hands. However, in order to keep this chapter to manageable length, we focus our discussion on the paper mill, extrusion, and conversion stages of the chain that relate to NorthAm. The timber, logging, chipping, and pulp mills stages are deemphasized because they are not critical to the issues addressed here. Obviously, the full value chain would consider these stages as well.

Step 1: Paperboard Manufacturing—The Mill

NorthAm's primary manufacturing facility bought pulp on the open market for $319 per ton and converted the pulp into uncoated paperboard at an additional cost of $105 per ton. The $105 is an average actual, full cost figure. We believe the analysis should use full cost because the focus is long run. We use average, actual cost as the best proxy for future cost.

The company sold some of the uncoated board to outside customers to an average price of $483 per ton, plus freight to the customer. On these shipments the mill earned a profit of $59 (483 − 319 − 105), as shown in exhibit 5–1. But the major customer for the uncoated board was NorthAm's own plastic extruding plant.

Step 2: Adding the Plastic Coating: Extrusion

The uncoated board was then trucked to a nearby coating plant at an average cost of $3 per ton. Polyethylene coating was applied to both sides of the board by two extruders at an average full cost of $91 per ton. At this stage, the product cost is $518 (319 + 105 + 3 + 91). But, using market price to value the transfer, the economic cost is $577 (483 + 3 + 91).

Coated board was currently sold in the market for an average price of $605, plus freight. On these shipments, the extruding plant earned an economic profit of $28 per ton (605 − 577), as shown in exhibit 5–1. The uncoated board from the mill is valued here at the external market price in order to measure segment profit.

Step 3: Carton Conversion

After extrusion, the coated board was shipped to NorthAm's carton converting plant at an average freight cost of $35 per ton. In the first stage of the converting operation, rolls of coated paperboard are spliced together to form a long, continuous web. Next, each particular processor's name, logo, and design is printed on one side. Then, the carton (container) blanks are stamped out and stacked on shipping pallets for loading. The total cost of the conversion operation averaged $234 per ton. The converting plant also paid an average of $10 per ton for freight to the end-use customers. Industry statistics showed that one ton of board yielded an average of 14,400 containers (the size of the container is half a gallon). All carton conversion costs are shown in exhibit 5–1.

Step 4: The Filling Plants—Processors of Consumer Products

The blank cartons (containers) were set up, filled, and then sealed in the processor's factory. The processors delivered their products to conve-

EXHIBIT 5–1
A Process Flow Value Chain
(Per Ton of Paperboard)

	Commodity Segment		Differentiated Segment	
Supermarket				
Price to customer (14,400 × 1.16, 1.89)	$16,704		$27,216	
–Price to store	–14,976		–20,448	
= Store gross margin	= 1,728		= 6,768	The part
		Link in the chain		of the chain
Processor of consumer products				external to
Price to store (14,400 × 1.04, 1.42)	4,976		20,448	NorthAm
–Cost of processing	–12,528		–15,984	
(14,400 × 0.87, 1.11)				
–Cost of carton (14,400 × 0.08, 0.07)	–1,152		–1,008	
= Processor profit	= 1,296		= 3,456	
		Link in the chain		
Carton converter (14,400 cartons per ton)				
Price to processor	1,152		1,008	
–Freight to processor	–10		–10	
–Converting cost	–234		–234	
–Price to converter	–640		–640	
= Converter profit	= 268		= 124	
		Link in the chain		
Extruding plant				
Price to converter	640		640	NorthAm's
–Freight to converter	–35		–35	part of the
–Extruding cost	–91		–91	chain
–Price to extruder	–486		–486	
= Extruder profit	= 28		= 28	
		Link in the chain		
Paperboard mill				
Price to extruder	486		486	
–Freight to extruder	–3		–3	
–Production cost	–105		–105	
–Pulp cost	–319		–319	
= Mill profit	= 59		= 59	

The stages further upstream from the paperboard mill are not shown in this example, but might be very important in other contexts.

nience stores and supermarkets. Without recycling, the cycle was complete when consumers purchased the products and eventually threw away the disposable cartons. The processors who produced an undifferentiated product usually paid $.08 per carton. The other costs of such processors were, on average:

Product cost, $0.75 per carton.

Converting, distribution, and shrinkage, $0.12 per carton.

They sold a carton of the commodity product for an average of $1.04 to supermarkets. Their profit per carton was $.09 (1.04 − 0.08 − 0.75 − 0.12), which converts to $1.296 per ton of coated paperboard (14,400 cartons/ton × $0.09), as shown in exhibit 5–1.

The differentiated processors, on the other hand, had a very different cost structure. Their cost structure was as follows:

Average container cost, $0.07.

Product cost, $0.64 per carton.

Converting, distribution, and shrinkage, $0.11 per carton.

National selling and advertising, 25% of the $1.42 per carton wholesale price to supermarkets, or $0.36 per carton.

The branded processor thus earned a profit per carton of $.24 (1.42 − 0.07 − 0.64 − .11 − 0.36). This figure converts to $3,456 per ton of paperboard (0.24 × 14,400), as shown in exhibit 5–1.

It is an anomaly of this industry that the higher-quality differentiated carton sells for less than the commodity carton ($0.07 versus $0.08). This is because of substantial quantity discounts in the differentiated segment. In this segment, 60,000 tons are spread over 6 customers, whereas 146,000 tons are spread over 300 customers in the commodity segment.

Step 5: The Retailer—The Supermarkets

A typical supermarket sells the undifferentiated product for $1.16 and the branded product for $1.89. The entire value chain (all five steps) is summarized in exhibit 5–1. This exhibit shows only gross margin for the supermarket, without an allocation of store operating expenses. Such an allocation is not relevant for the purposes of this example. The first three steps in the chain relate to NorthAm. The final two steps relate to the processors of consumer products and the supermarkets to whom they sell.

The assets invested at each stage of the process were estimated as follows. The righthand column shows assets valued using current replacement cost and assuming full utilization of the item. This calculation included allocation of common assets based on full utilization where several products were involved.

Paperboard mill	$2,800
Extruding plant	$190
Carton converter	$830
Commodity processor	$5,400
Differentiated processor (lower investment per ton	
because of scale economies)	$2,890
Supermarket	$1,800

This five-step value chain approach to cost reporting is very unusual in management accounting, but we believe the inferences it suggests, as shown later, justify this framework.

Data Sources

In generating the cost and asset numbers for processors and supermarkets, we followed multiple approaches: we interviewed NorthAm executives about their customers' cost structures; we visited several processors and supermarkets and interviewed managers about their costs and investments. The resulting estimates, though not precise, are near enough to draw meaningful inferences.

We turn now to the business decisions NorthAm was facing.

Strategic Options

NorthAm Packaging has some major decisions to make. Specifically, the company had to decide the following.

Which market segment should they emphasize?

Where should they invest capital dollars?

The strategic positioning and capital spending decisions facing NorthAm in 1989 would shape its future for many years.

On the choice of market segments, NorthAm considered two specific alternatives:

1. The company could continue to emphasize the commodity processors whose total market had been declining 3% a year but who had always been their main customers.

2. NorthAm could aggressively try to build market share with differentiated processors whose market was growing at 10% or more and who would pay top dollar for board (holding quantity discounts constant) but who demanded a consistent high quality.

In analyzing these questions, NorthAm recognized its weaknesses vis-à-vis the differentiated segment. Its primary manufacturing was technologically obsolescent, because most of the plant and equipment had been bought in the 1960s. The company experienced nagging problems with the quality of its paperboard because of the lack of up-to-date machinery. Similarly, NorthAm Packaging lacked high-quality printing—which would have been very expensive to acquire—in the conversion plant. The company also had limited extrusion capacity.

NorthAm's 15% market share in the differentiated segment reflected their status as largely a backup supplier. Major capital investments (a total of $61.5 million) had to be made if NorthAm seriously wanted to rebuild market share in this fast-growing segment. Three specific new investments would be:

1. About $43 million to upgrade its primary manufacturing facility to improve board strength, printability, and smoothness.

2. About $17 million to add a new extruder to compete in multilayered polymer coating applications. Differentiated processors required multiple coatings to extend the shelf life of products and to hold difficult products (liquids, for example).

3. About $1.5 million to purchase a rotogravure printing press. At that time, NorthAm printed the cartons with flexographic presses that used rubber printing rolls. This method is inexpensive but produces low-quality images. After the initial capital investment, the rubber plates cost about $150 each, with six needed for a standard six-color process. Although the quality was not as good as rotogra-

vure printing, high-quality printing had never been required by the commodity processors. Rotogravure printing uses etched metal printing rolls and gives an extremely precise and high-quality finish, but it is expensive. After the initial capital expense, each etched metal printing plate costs $2,500. With a six-color process, $15,000 must be spent for only one run. Once that run is complete, those etched cylinders probably will never be used again.

This completes the descriptive part of the field study. In the next section, we compare the results of several different ways of analyzing the strategic options.

CONVENTIONAL ANALYSIS OF THE STRATEGIC OPTIONS

How should NorthAm's senior executives evaluate the marketing and investment options open to them? Conventional capital expenditure requests, using discounted cash flow analyses, had been prepared to justify the proposed investments. These requests focused solely on projected value added for NorthAm. Using assumptions recommended by the marketing group, these discounted cash flow (DCF) analyses showed acceptable returns for NorthAm for investing $61.5 million to build market share in the differentiated segment (exhibit 5–2).

Another way to address these options would be through a simple two-by-two growth/share matrix, as originally introduced by the Boston Consulting Group (BCG) (Henderson, 1979). Exhibit 5–3 displays NorthAm's strategic options on this familiar portfolio grid using the dimensions of market growth (a proxy for market attractiveness) and market share. NorthAm historically had emphasized the commodity segment. Even though volume had been shrinking at 3% per year over the past five years, the firm had maintained market share at 40% in this large segment (350,000 tons per year). This segment appears to be the classic "cash cow" in the BCG terminology—"high market share in a low-growth segment." The strategic inference from the BCG grid would be that NorthAm should harvest this commodity segment.

NorthAm, on the other hand, had a relatively modest 15% of the market in the differentiated package segment. The overall market in this segment was growing at 10% per year, with projections to grow even faster in the future. NorthAm had a low market share in this high-growth segment. The strategic inference from the BCG grid would be that

EXHIBIT 5–2
NorthAm Packaging Company: Capital Investment Analysis
of the Differentiated Segment

Capital investments needed in year 0:

Primary manufacturing	$43 million
Third extruder	17 million
Rotogravure printing	1.5 million
Total	$61.5 million

Annual cash flows:	Per ton
Revenue (assumes a 10% price increase due to a better quality board, 7.7¢ x 14,400)	$1,109
Costs (per exhibit 5–1) (319 + 105 + 3 + 91 + 35 + 234 + 10)	(797)
Plus additional printing costs (due to rotogravure printing)	(10)
Profit per ton	302
Total market (differentiated segment)	= 400,000 tons (our volume of 60,000 tons is 15% of the market)
Projected market growth	= 14%
Additional volume next year (400,000 x 14%)	= 56,000
Assume we can capture 50% of this additional volume	= 28,000
Plus a 5% increase in our share of the existing market (400,000 x 5%)	= 20,000
Additional volume	48,000 tons*

Annual cash profits (48,000 x $302):	= $14.5 million
After-tax profits (40% tax rate)	= $8.7 million
Plus depreciation tax shield (straight-line depreciation for 10 years) $6.15 million x 40%	= $2.46 million
Total annual cash flows	$11.16 million
Time horizon for the project	= 10 years
Salvage value of the plant and equipment in year 10 (after tax)	= $3 million

All cash flows are in real dollars; inflation is not incorporated.
Internal rate of return = 13% (after tax, real return).
*We ignore additional growth beyond year 1, to be conservative.

EXHIBIT 5–3
Boston Consulting Group Grid

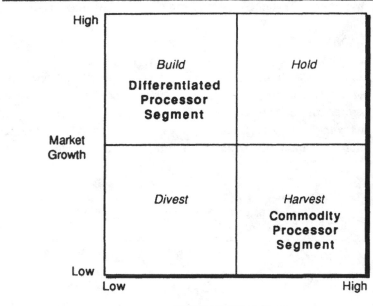

NorthAm should aggressively build market share in this segment by making the $61.5 million in new investments. This sentiment also prevailed within NorthAm. This point of view was supported by formal financial analysis using DCF techniques (exhibit 5–2), as indicated previously. A 13% real return certainly argues for investing $61.5 million to build share in the differentiated segment.

An alternative way of viewing NorthAm's problem, using different input assumptions, might yield different analytic inferences. For instance, value chain analysis, as we show later, casts severe doubt on the assumptions that underlie the analysis in exhibit 5–2. (For examples, the differentiated segment will give NorthAm a 10% price increase; at the higher price level, NorthAm can gain an additional sales volume of 48,000 tons or an additional 11% market share.)

STRATEGIC ANALYSIS: A VALUE CHAIN PERSPECTIVE

Organizing the information in the value chain framework (exhibit 5–1) provides a fundamentally different view of the marketing and invest-

ment options facing NorthAm. Exhibits 5–4 through 5–6 summarize the
inferences from the value chain framework. To recap, the methodology
we used in creating the value chain is reviewed in the following para-
graphs.

Identify value chain stages. We identified the mill, extruder, converter, processor, and supermarket as the key building blocks in the
value chain. A conventional management accounting system tends to
ignore the value created by the processors and supermarkets because
they are beyond the scope of profitability to the firm.

Identify strategic options. Because the value chain analysis was done
to draw inferences about two strategically distinct market segments, we

EXHIBIT 5–4
Profit per Ton of Board
(Data Taken from Exhibit 5–1)

	Commodity Segment	Differentiated Segment
Supermarket	$1,728	$6,768
Processor	$1,296	$3,456
North Am		
Converter	$268	$124
Extruder	$28 $355	$28 $211
Mill	$59	$59
Total Profit	$3,379	$10,435
NorthAm % of Total Profit	10.5%	2.0%

EXHIBIT 5–5
Return on Assets per Ton of Paperboard
(Based on Current Replacement Cost and Full Capacity Utilization

	Commodity Segment			Differentiated Segment		
	Profit	Assets	ROA	Profit	Assets	ROA
Supermarket	$1,728	$1,800	96%	$6,768	$1,800	376%
Processor	1,296	5,400	24%	3,456	2,890	120%
Converter	268	830	32%	124	830	15%
Extruder	28	190	15%	28	190	15%
Mill	59	2,800	2%	59	2,800	2%
Total	$3,379	$11,020	31%	$10,435	$8,510	123%

EXHIBIT 5–6
North Am Packaging Company: A Value Chain Perspective

Commodity Segment				Differentiated Segment		
Profit	% of the Total Profit	ROA		Profit	% of the Total Profit	ROA
59	3%	2%	Mill	59	.5%	2%
28	1%	15%	Extruder	28	.25%	15%
268	7%	32%	Convertor	124	1.2%	15%
1,296	40%	24%	Processor	3,456	33%	120%
1,728	49%	96%	Supermarket	6,768	65%	376%
$3,379	100%			$10,435	100%	

prepared separate value chains for the commodity and differentiated processor segments.

Assign costs and revenues to value chain stages. After identifying the value chain activities and strategic options, the next step was to assign operating costs and revenues to these activities (exhibit 5–1). All costs and revenues have been calculated for one ton of paperboard, using estimated average actual full cost.

Estimate market value transfer prices. NorthAm's converting operations have a true market price for sales to the processors. But how can we approximate value for intermediate products? Uncoated board is transferred internally from the mill to the extruder, and coated board is transferred internally from the extruder to the converter. Because uncoated and coated paperboards are also traded in external markets, we used the competitive market prices for the intermediate products. Calculating profit per ton for each value activity based on the competitive market price, as opposed to arbitrary accounting transfer prices, helps to identify the fundamental sources of economic value and allows each stage to be evaluated independently. Exhibit 5–4 summarizes the profit earned at each stage in the linked value chain.

Estimate asset investment. We then estimate the assets per ton of board at each value activity, using current replacement costs and assuming full utilization of capacity (see earlier discussion). Current replacement costs were estimated from discussions with plant engineers and equipment vendors. Tons of production at full capacity were estimated from discussions with manufacturing management and equipment vendors. With profit and assets, we calculated Return on Assets for each value stage, as summarized in exhibit 5–5.

Calculational accuracy. We should emphasize that the computations in exhibits 5–1, 5–4, 5–5, and 5–6 do not involve the same level of precision that one is likely to encounter in audited financial statements. Profit margins for processors and supermarkets are based on estimates that average away substantial, continual day-to-day volatility in net prices. As the analysis proceeds and particular activities become critical in answering strategic questions, greater effort at precision can be made.

New Insights?

Does the information based on value chain analysis lead to new insights? We believe it does. Dramatically different strategic insights emerge when one considers the value chain analysis summarized in exhibit 5–6.

Of the total profit of $3,379 per ton of paperboard created in the commodity processor segment. NorthAm realized $355 (10.5% of the total value). In sharp contrast, in the differentiated processor segment, NorthAm's share of the total profit in the chain was only 2%. The buyer power in the differentiated segment was extremely strong. As we noted earlier, the average customer in the differentiated segment is much larger than the average commodity segment customer. Even though the carton is of higher quality and is much more a marketing tool in the differentiated segment, volume discounts and overall buyer power hold units prices below those for the commodity carton. Thus, NorthAm did more work here with more assets for a lower sales price, on a per-unit basis.

Moreover, there is no reason to believe that 10.5% of the overall profit in the commodity segment was a reasonable or unreasonable share for the carton manufacturer versus the processor or the retailer. But whatever the share for the carton manufacturer in the commodity segment, the share should have been higher in the differentiated segment where the carton is more expensive to make and is much more important as a point-of-sale marketing tool. Although NorthAm did not separate commodity end-use carton stock from differentiated end-use carton stock as it was produced, the differentiated end-use product must run slower to produce smoothness, thus yielding fewer tons per hour and higher cost per ton. For the share of overall profit to drop from 10.5% to 2% is dramatic evidence of the lack of seller power for NorthAm in the higher-value segment. The $0.07 carton price in the differentiated segment assumes a product that meets quality standards. That is, there is no way to charge more than $0.07 (the prevailing price in this segment) once the quality improvements are achieved.

The unattractiveness of the differentiated segment is further reinforced when ROA is examined. NorthAm's return on assets in the commodity segment is 2% at the mill, 15% at the extruder, and 32% at the converter. On the other hand, in the differentiated segment, the ROAs are 2%, 15% and 15% for the mill, extruder, and converter, respectively.

From the BCG grid (exhibit 5–3), the differentiated processor segment looked extremely attractive; but based on the value chain analysis, this market looks much less attractive. The differentiated processors had enormous leverage (buyer power). Why invest over $60 million to build market share in the differentiated segment where NorthAm was currently able to extract only 2% of the total value created in the chain? This insight is neither apparent in the BCG type strategic analysis nor in a conventional management accounting approach relying on DCF-based project returns to NorthAm. The value chain analysis calls into question the sales volume and selling price assumptions used in the DCF analysis contained in exhibit 5–2. Further, conventional management accounting is of little help in quantifying buyer power since it ignores the total value created in the chain. Because of the buyers' tremendous bargaining power, it is highly unlikely that NorthAm would be able to extract any more than 2% of the total value in the differentiated segment, even after it matched it's leading competitor's investment (unless the differentiated processors were willing to share some of their profit in order to entice an investment by NorthAm). The company would be at a disadvantage because:

There are very few buyers in the differentiated segment—fewer than 10 versus more than 1,000 in the commodity segment.

Buyers are very large.

The average order size tends to be quite large.

Differentiators typically keep two or more sources of supply. Poor service, quality, or uncompetitive prices are punished by cuts in order size.

Plastic has several attractive features as packaging materials: break resistance, design versatility, eye appeal, printability. Plastic poses a more significant threat to coated board in the differentiated segment because this segment more highly values the marketing appeal of the package. This substitution threat sets a cap on paperboard carton prices and a corresponding cap on investment returns, once the overwhelming buyer power is factored into the analysis.

Overall, the value chain perspective yields a much different picture of this industry. The closer one gets to the end-use customer and the more one creates product differentiation, the more money will be made (exhibit 5–6). NorthAm loses on both counts. They lack the ability to forward integrate into the processor and supermarket segments. Further, we have already argued that NorthAm lacks the product quality to successfully compete as a supplier to the differentiated processor segment. What should they do? NorthAm's position is similar to having failed to improve your hand in the draw in a poker game. Do you put more money in the pot, even though you know you have a bad hand? Do you fold? Or do you stay in as long as possible without adding much to the pot?

NorthAm, instead of deemphasizing the commodity segment as would be recommended by the BCG analysis, needs to find ways to effectively compete in the commodity segment by being the low-cost producer. Here, again, the value chain framework can provide important insights. NorthAm needs to understand the structural and executional drivers of cost behavior for the major cost items in the mill, extruder, and converter operations, as discussed in chapters 2 and 10. NorthAm then needs to manage these drivers better than its competitors. Staying in the commodity segment is the only logical choice for NorthAm. The attractiveness of this option is further enhanced by possible significant growth in commodity carton demand in export markets. Their manufacturing system is geared to this market, and their reputation has been made in this market. Also, they have a low investment base to support this business, because most of the plant and equipment was bought before 1970. Major new investments are not required to compete here.

Looking at the economics of the mill, extruder, and converting operations, the profitability at the mill and extruder stages is well below satisfactory levels. A cost driver analysis at the mill and extruder stages might go a long way in identifying profit improvement opportunities. However, such analysis is beyond the scope of this chapter.

VALUE CHAIN ANALYSIS—A KEY COST MANAGEMENT TOOL

Traditional cost analysis has focused on the notion of value added (selling price less cost of purchased raw materials) under the mistaken impression that this is the only area in which a firm can influence costs. But value chain—not value added—is the more meaningful way to explore competitive advantage. Value added can be quite misleading, for at least three reasons:

1. It arbitrarily distinguishes between raw materials and many other purchased inputs. Purchased services such as maintenance or professional consulting services are treated differently than raw materials purchased.

2. Value added does not point out the potential to exploit the linkages between a firm and its suppliers or between a firm and its customers with a view to reducing costs or enhancing differentiation.

3. Competitive advantage cannot be fully explored without considering the interaction between purchased raw materials and other cost elements (e.g., purchasing higher-quality, higher-priced raw material could reduce scrap significantly and thus lower total cost).

The focus of the value chain analysis, in contrast, is external to the firm and sees each firm in the context of the overall chain of value-creating activities of which it is very probably only a part. We are aware of no firm that spans the entire value chain in which it operates. Value chain analysis is relevant for all firms.

The methodology for constructing and using a value chain involves the following steps:

1. Define the industry's value chain and assign costs, revenues, and assets to each activity.

2. Investigate the cost drivers regulating each value activity.

3. Examine possibilities to build sustainable competitive advantage either through controlling cost drivers better than competitors or by reconfiguring the value chain.

Efforts at simultaneously reducing costs and enhancing differentiation are possible by carefully considering costs, revenues, and assets at each value activity vis-à-vis competitors.

Chapters 4 and 5 present examples of value chain analysis in the telecommunications, airline, and packaging industries. These examples illustrate that the insights derived from value chain analysis are much different from those suggested by more conventional management accounting tools. A summary of the key differences between value chain and conventional management accounting is shown in exhibit 5–7.

- Because virtually no two companies compete in exactly the same set of value activities, value chain analysis is a critical first step in understanding how a firm is positioned in its industry. Building sustainable competitive advantage requires a knowledge of the full linked set of value activities of which the firm and its competitors are a part.

- Once the value chain if fully articulated, critical strategic decisions regarding make/buy and forward/backward integration become clearer. Investment decisions can be viewed from the perspective of their impact on the overall chain and the firm's position within it.

- Once the chain is explicated, the next steps involve understanding what factors drive competitive success at the key value chain stages.

- The value chain analysis helps to quantify supplier power by calculating the percentage of total profits that can be attributed to suppliers. This knowledge could help the firm to identify ways to exploit linkages with suppliers.

- The value chain framework highlights how a firm's product fits

EXHIBIT 5–7
A Summary of Value Chain Versus Conventional
Management Accounting

	Traditional Management Accounting	Value Chain Analysis in the SCM Framework
Focus	Internal	External
Perspective	Value added	Entire set of linked activities from raw material suppliers to ultimate end-use customers
Cost driver concept	A single fundamental cost driver pervades the literature—cost is a function of volume Applied too often only at the overall firm level	Multiple cost drivers Structural drivers (e.g., scale, scope, experience, technology, complexity) Executional drivers (e.g., participative management, total quality management) Each value activity has a set of unique cost drivers
Cost containment philosophy	Cost reduction approached via responsibility centers or product cost issues	Cost containment is a function of the cost driver(s) regulating each value activity Exploit linkages with suppliers Exploit linkages with customers Exploit process linkages within the firm
Insights for strategic decisions	None are readily apparent. This is a major reason why the strategy consulting firms typically throw away the conventional reports as they begin their cost analyses	Identify cost drivers at the individual activity level; develop cost/differentiation advantage either by controlling those drivers better than competitors or by reconfiguring the value chain (e.g., Federal Express in mail delivery, MCI in long-distance telephone services) For each value activity, ask strategic questions pertaining to make versus buy and forward versus backward integration Quantify and assess supplier power and buyer power; exploit linkages with suppliers and buyers

into the buyer's value chain; under this framework, it is readily apparent what percentage the firm's product costs are in the buyer's total costs. This information could be very useful in encouraging the firm and the buyer to work together in cost reduction activities.

• In the final analysis, the simultaneous pursuit of low cost and differentiation depends upon a sophisticated understanding of the drivers of costs, revenues, and assets at each value activity and the interlinkages across value activities.

CHAPTER 6

EXPLICIT ATTENTION TO STRATEGIC POSITIONING

The Second Key to Strategic Cost Management

The role of accounting information within a business is to facilitate the development and implementation of business strategies. Its explicit attention to the strategic management context distinguishes SCM from managerial accounting.

Many factors jointly influence the management control process in a company. Researchers have attempted to examine these factors by applying what is called *contingency theory;* the name simply means that management controls are contingent on various external and internal factors. Research studies have identified important factors that influence the design of control systems, some of them being size, environment, technology, interdependence, and strategies. Given the overall framework of this book—that cost management and control become most meaningful in the context of the particular strategy being followed—we suggest in this chapter how different strategies influence the management control process. Strategies differ in different types of organizations, and controls should be tailored to the requirements of specific strategies. The logic for linking controls to strategy is based on the following line of thinking:

1. For effective execution, different strategies require different task priorities; different key success factors; and different skills, perspectives, and behaviors.

2. Control systems are measurement systems that influence the behavior of those people whose activities are being measured.

Parts of this chapter have appeared in the *Journal of Cost Management* 6, 3, (1992), pp. 14–25. Reproduced with permission.

3. Thus, a continuing concern in the design of control systems should be whether the behavior induced by the system is the one that is consistent with the strategy.

Two general observations are important. First, the suggestions made in this chapter on linking controls to strategies are presented as tendencies, not hard-and-fast principles. Second, systems designers need to take into consideration the influence of other external and internal factors (environment, technology, size, culture, geographical location, management style) while designing control systems.

In the first part of this chapter, we define the concept of strategy and describe generic strategies that business units can adopt. In the second part, we discuss how to vary the form and structure of control systems in accordance with variations in generic business-level strategic contexts.

THE CONCEPT OF STRATEGY

Strategy has been conceptualized by Andrews (1971), Ansoff (1965), Chandler (1962), Hofer and Schendel (1978), Miles and Snow (1978), and others as the process by which managers, using a three- to five-year time horizon, evaluate external environmental opportunities as well as internal strengths nd resources in order to decide on goals as well as a set of action plans to accomplish these goals. Thus, a business unit's strategy depends upon two interrelated aspects: (1) its mission or goals, and (2) the way the business unit chooses to compete in its industry to accomplish its goals—the business unit's competitive advantage.

Mission. Turning first to mission, consulting firms such as the Boston Consulting Group (Henderson, 1979), Arthur D. Little (Wright, 1975), and A. T. Kearney (Hofer & Davoust, 1977) as well as academic researchers such as Buzzell and Wiersema (1981) and Hofer and Schendel (1978) have proposed the following three missions that a business unit can adopt:

1. *Build:* This mission implies a goal of increased market share, even at the expense of short-term earnings and cash flow. A business unit following this mission is expected to be a net user of cash in that the cash throw off from its current operations would usually be insufficient to meet its capital investment needs. Business units

with low market share in high-growth industries typically pursue a build mission (e.g., Apple Computer's Macintosh business, Monsanto's Biotechnology business).

2. *Hold:* This strategic mission is geared to the protection of the business unit's market share and competitive position. The cash outflows for a business unit following this mission would usually be more or less equal to cash inflows. Businesses with high market share in high-growth industries typically pursue a hold mission (e.g., IBM in mainframe computers).

3. *Harvest:* This mission implies a goal of maximizing short-term earnings and cash flow, even at the expense of market share. A business unit following such a mission would be a net supplier of cash. Businesses with high market share in low-growth industries typically pursue a harvest mission (e.g., American Brands in tobacco products).

Competitive advantage. In terms of competitive advantage, Porter (1980) proposed the following two generic ways in which businesses can develop sustainable competitive advantage:

1. *Low cost:* The primary focus of this strategy is to achieve low cost relative to competitors. Cost leadership can be achieved through approaches such as economies of scale of production, learning curve effects, tight cost control, and cost minimization in areas such as R&D, service, sales force, or advertising. Examples of firms following this strategy include Texas Instruments in consumer electronics, Emerson Electric in electric motors, Chevrolet in automobiles, Briggs and Stratton in gasoline engines, Black and Decker in machine tools, and Commodore in business machines.

2. *Differentiation:* The primary focus of this strategy is to differentiate the product offering of the business unit, creating something that is perceived by customers as being unique. Approaches to product differentiation include brand loyalty (Coca Cola in soft drinks), superior customer service (IBM in computers), dealer network (Caterpillar Tractors in construction equipment), product design and product features (Hewlett Packard in electronics), and/or product technology (Coleman in camping equipment).

BUSINESS UNIT MISSION

The planning and control requirements of business units pursuing different strategies are quite different. In this part of the chapter, we discuss how control systems should be designed so that they implement diverse business unit missions. We discuss differentiated controls for differentiated competitive advantages in the next section.

As noted earlier, the mission for ongoing business units could be build, hold, or harvest. These missions constitute a continuum, with pure build at one end and pure harvest at the other end. For effective implementation, there should be congruence between the mission chosen and the types of controls used. We develop the control–mission fit using the following line of reasoning.[1]

> The mission of the business unit influences the uncertainties that its general manager faces and the short-term versus long-term tradeoffs that he or she makes.

> Management control systems can be systematically varied to help motivate the manager to cope effectively with uncertainty and make appropriate short-term versus long-term tradeoffs.

> Thus, different missions often require systematically different management control systems.

Mission and Uncertainty

Build units tend to face greater environmental uncertainty than harvest units. Build strategies typically are undertaken in the growth stage of the product life cycle, whereas harvest strategies typically are undertaken in the mature/decline stage of the product life cycle. Factors such as manufacturing process, product technology, market demand, relations with suppliers, buyers, and distribution channels, number of competitors, and competitive structure change more rapidly and are more unpredictable in the growth than the mature/decline stage of the product life cycle

The uncertainty faced by a build business unit is also greater because one of its objectives is to increase market share. Since the total market share of all firms in an industry is 100%, the battle for market share is a zero-sum game; thus, a build strategy puts a business unit into greater conflict with its competitors than does a harvest strategy. Competitors' actions are likely to be unpredictable and thus contribute to the uncertainty faced by build business units.

Both on the input and output sides, build managers tend to be more dependent on external individuals and organizations than do harvest managers. For instance, a build mission signifies additional capital investment (greater dependence on capital markets), expansion of capacity (greater dependence on the technological environment), increase in market share (greater dependence on customers and competitors), increase in production volume (greater dependence on raw material suppliers and labor market), and so on. The greater the external dependencies that the business unit faces, the greater the uncertainty it confronts.

Finally, environmental uncertainty can be increased because build business units are often in new and evolving industries. The experience of build managers in their industries is likely to be less than that of their counterparts in established businesses. This inexperience also contributes to the greater uncertainty faced by managers of build units in dealing with external constituencies.

Mission and Time Span

The choice of build versus harvest strategies has implications for short-term versus long-term profit tradeoffs. The share-building strategy includes price cutting, major R&D expenditures (to introduce new products), and major market development expenditures. These actions are aimed at establishing market leadership, but they depress short-term profits. Thus, many decisions that the manager of a build unit makes today may not result in profits until some future period. A harvest strategy, on the other hand, demands attention to tasks with a view to maximizing short-term profits.

Strategic Planning

While designing a strategic planning process, several design issues need to be considered. There are no single answers on these design choices; rather, the answers depend upon the mission being pursued by the business unit (exhibit 6–1).

The Importance of the Strategic Planning Process

When the environment is uncertain, the strategic planning process is especially important. Management needs to give much thought to how to

EXHIBIT 6–1
Different Strategic Missions: Implications for Strategic Planning

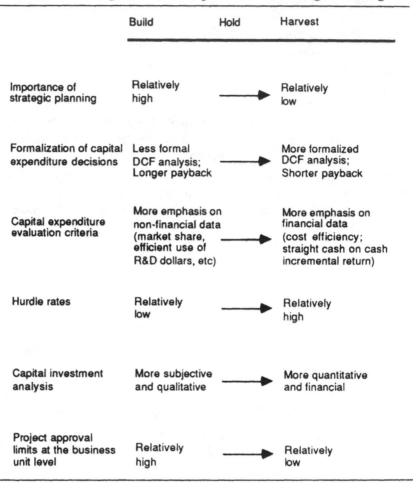

	Build	Hold	Harvest
Importance of strategic planning	Relatively high	⟶	Relatively low
Formalization of capital expenditure decisions	Less formal DCF analysis; Longer payback	⟶	More formalized DCF analysis; Shorter payback
Capital expenditure evaluation criteria	More emphasis on non-financial data (market share, efficient use of R&D dollars, etc)	⟶	More emphasis on financial data (cost efficiency; straight cash on cash incremental return)
Hurdle rates	Relatively low	⟶	Relatively high
Capital investment analysis	More subjective and qualitative	⟶	More quantitative and financial
Project approval limits at the business unit level	Relatively high	⟶	Relatively low

cope with the uncertainties and usually requires a longer-range view of planning than is possible in the annual budget. If the environment is stable, there may be no strategic planning process or only a broad-brush strategic plan. Thus, the strategic planning process is more critical and more important for build, as compared to harvest, business units. Nevertheless, strategic plans for the harvest business units may be necessary because the company's overall strategic plan must encompass all of its businesses in order to effectively balance cash flows.

Capital Deployment

In screening capital investments and allocating resources, the systems may be more quantitative and financial for harvest units. A harvest business unit operates in a mature industry and does not offer tremendous new investment possibilities. Hence, the required earnings rate for such a business unit may be relatively high so as to motivate the manager to search for projects with truly exceptional returns. Since harvest units tend to experience stable environments (with predictable products, technologies, competitors, and customers), discounted cash flow (DCF) analysis often can be used with confidence. The required information used to evaluate investments from harvest units is primarily financial. A build unit, on the other hand, is positioned on the growth stage of the product life cycle. The corporate office wants to take advantage of the opportunities in a growing market, and they may therefore set a relatively low discount rate, thereby motivating build mangers to forward to corporate office more investment ideas. Given the product/market uncertainties, financial analysis of some projects from build units may be unreliable. For such projects, nonfinancial data are more important.

Budgeting

Implications for designing budgeting systems to support varied missions are contained in exhibit 6–2.

Reliance on Budgets in Performance Evaluation

A key issue is how much importance should be attached to meeting the budget while evaluating the business unit managers's performance. The greater the uncertainty, the more difficult it is for superiors to regard subordinates' budget targets as firm commitments and to consider unfavorable budget variances as clear indicators of poor performance (see Govindarajan, 1984). There are several reasons for this.

First, performance evaluation presupposes the establishment of accurate profit targets. To arrive at targets that can serve as valid standards for subsequent performance appraisal, one must be able to predict the conditions that will exist during the coming year. If these predictions are incorrect, the profit objective will also be incorrect. Obviously, these conditions can be predicted more accurately under stable conditions than under changing conditions. The basic effect of uncertainty is to

EXHIBIT 6–2
Different Strategic Missions: Implications for Budgeting

	Build	Hold	Harvest
Role of the budget	More a short term planning tool	⟶	More a control tool ("document of restraint")
Business unit manager's influence in preparing the annual budget	Relatively high	⟶	Relatively low
Revisions to the budget during the year	Relatively easy	⟶	Relatively difficult
Role of standard costs in assessing performance.	Relatively low	⟶	Relatively high
Importance of such concepts as flexible budgeting for manufacturing cost control	Relatively low	⟶	Relatively high
Frequency of informal reporting and contacts with superiors	More frequent on policy issues; Less frequent on operating issues	⟶	Less frequent on policy issues; More frequent on operating issues
Frequency of feedback from superiors on actual performance versus the budget	Less often	⟶	More often
"Control limit" used in periodic evaluation against the budget	Relatively high (i.e., more flexible)	⟶	Relatively low (i.e., less flexible)
Importance attached to meeting the budget	Relatively low	⟶	Relatively high
Output versus behavior control	Behavior control	⟶	Output control

limit the ability of managers to plan or make decisions about activities in advance of their occurrence. Thus, the greater the uncertainty, the more difficult it is to prepare satisfactory targets that could then become the basis for performance evaluation.

Second, because efficiency refers to the amount of output per unit of input, an evaluation of a manager's efficiency depends on a detailed knowledge of the outcomes associated with given management actions—that is, knowledge about cause–effect relationships. Better knowledge about cause–effect relationships exists under stable conditions than under uncertain conditions. Therefore, judgments about efficiency are more difficult under uncertain conditions.

Third, the emphasis of financial performance indicators is on outcomes rather than on process. Managers control their own actions, but they cannot control the states of nature that combine with their actions to produce outcomes. In a situation with high uncertainty, therefore, financial information does not adequately reflect managerial performance.

Since build units tend to face higher uncertainty than harvest units, less reliance is usually placed on budgets in build units than in harvest units. For example, in the late 1970s, the SCM Corporation adopted a two-dimensional yardstick to evaluate business units: bottom-line performance against budget was one dimension and performance against specific objectives was another. The ratios of the two were made to vary according to the mission of the business unit. For instance, pure harvest units were evaluated 100% on budget performance; pure hold, 50% on budget and 50% on completion of objectives; pure build, 100% on completion of objectives (Hall, 1987).

Other Differences in the Budget Process

Two additional differences in the budget process are likely to exist between build and harvest units. First, in contrast to harvest units, budget revisions are likely to be more frequent to build units because of the more frequent changes in their product/market environment. Also, build unit managers may have relatively greater input and influence in the formulation of the budget than harvest unit managers because build managers operate in rapidly changing environments and have better knowledge of these changes than does senior management. For harvest units, with stable environments, the knowledge of the manager is less important.

Incentive Compensation System

In designing an incentive compensation package for business unit mangers, some of the following questions need to be resolved:

1. What should be the size of incentive bonus payments relative to the general manager's base salary? Should the incentive bonus payments have upper limits?

2. What measures of performance (e.g., profit, return on investment, sales volume, market share, product development) should be employed as the basis for deciding the general manager's incentive bonus awards? If multiple performance measures are employed, how should they be weighted?

3. How much reliance should be placed on subjective judgments in deciding on the bonus amount?

4. With what frequency (semiannual, annual, biennial, etc.) should incentive awards be made?

Decisions on these design variables are influenced by the mission of the business unit (exhibit 6–3).

EXHIBIT 6–3
Different Strategic Missions: Implications for Incentive Compensation

	Build	Hold	Harvest
Percent compensation as bonus	Relatively high	⟶	Relatively low
Bonus criteria	More emphasis on non-financial criteria	⟶	More emphasis on financial criteria
Bonus determination approach	More subjective	⟶	More formula-based
Frequency of bonus payment	Less frequent	⟶	More frequent

Bonus to Base Salary Ratio

When considering the first question, many firms use the principle that the riskier the strategy, the greater the proportion of the general manager's compensation in bonus compared to salary (the risk/return principle). they maintain that because managers in charge of more uncertain task situations should be willing to take greater risks, they should have a higher percentage of their remuneration in the form of an incentive bonus. Thus, reliance on a bonus is likely to be higher for build managers than for harvest managers.

Which Performance Measure to Use

As for the second question, the behavior of an individual whose rewards are tied to performance according to certain criteria is influenced by the desire to optimize performance with respect to those criteria.

Some performance criteria (cost control, operating profits, cash flow from operations, and return on investment) focus more on the short-term performance, whereas other performance criteria (market share, new product development, market development, and people development) focus on long-term profitability. Thus, linking an incentive bonus to the former set of criteria tends to promote a short-term focus on the part of the general manager, whereas linking an incentive bonus to the latter set of performance criteria is likely to promote long-term focus.

Given the relative differences in the time horizons of build and harvest managers, it may be inappropriate to use a single, uniform financial criteria (such as return on investment) to evaluate the performance of every business unit. Rather, it may be desirable to use multiple performance criteria, with differential weights for each criterion depending upon the mission of the business unit, as implemented by the following companies:

General Electric Company and Westinghouse Electric Corporation, for example, are tailoring compensation packages to the different "missions" of their individual businesses.

Both GE and Westinghouse have mature as well as young businesses. In the mature businesses, short-term incentives might dominate the compensation packages of managers, who are charged with maximizing cash flow, achieving high profit margins, and retaining market share. In the younger businesses, where developing products and establishing marketing strategies are most important, nonfinancial measures geared to the execution of long-term performance might dictate the major portion of managers' remuneration.[2]

Use of Subjective Judgments

To address the third question, in addition to varying the importance of different criteria, superiors must also decide on the approach to take in determining a specific bonus amount.

At one extreme, a manager's bonus might be a strict formula-based plan with the bonus tied to performance on quantifiable criteria (e.g., $X\%$ bonus on actual profits in excess of budgeted profits); at the other extreme, a manager's incentive bonus amounts might be based solely on the superior's subjective judgment or discretion. Alternatively, incentive bonus amounts might also be based on a combination of formula-based and subjective (nonformula) approaches.

Performance on most long-term criteria (market development, new product development, and people development) is clearly less amenable to objective measurement than is performance along most short-run criteria (operating profits, cash flow from operations, and return on investment). Because, as already noted, build managers—in contrast to harvest managers—should focus more on the long rather than the short run, build managers typically are evaluated more subjectively than harvest managers.

Frequency of Bonuses

Finally, frequency of bonus awards influences the time horizon of managers. More frequent bonus awards encourage concentration on short-term performance because they motivate managers to focus on facets of the business that they can affect in the short run. Less frequent calculation and payment of bonuses encourages the manager to take a long-term perspective. Thus, build managers tend to receive bonus awards less frequently than harvest managers. For example, Premark International (formed in 1986 in a spinoff from Dart & Kraft, Inc.) used a similar logic in designing the incentive bonus for the general manager of its Tupperware division, whose mission was to build market share. "If you award the bonus annually, Tupperware could reduce advertising and promotional activities and you can look good in profits that year. Then, the franchise starts to go to hell. If you're shooting for an award after three years, there's less tendency to do things short time."[3]

BUSINESS UNIT COMPETITIVE ADVANTAGE

A business unit can choose to compete either as a differentiated player or as a low-cost player. The choice of a differentiation approach rather than a low-cost approach increases uncertainty in a business unit's task environment for three reasons.

First, product innovation is likely to be more critical for differentiation business units than for low-cost business units. This tendency is partly due to the fact that a low-cost business unit, with its primary emphasis on cost reduction, typically prefers to keep its product offerings stable over time, whereas a differentiation business unit, with its primary focus on uniqueness and exclusivity, is likely to engage in greater product innovation. A business unit with greater emphasis on new product activities tends to face greater uncertainty because the business unit is betting on unproven products.

Second, low-cost business units typically tend to have narrow product lines in order to minimize inventory carry costs as well as to benefit from scale economies. Differentiation business units, on the other hand, tend to have a broader set of products in order to create uniqueness. Product breadth creates high environmental complexity and, consequently, higher uncertainty.

Third, low-cost business units typically produce no-frill, commodity products, and these products succeed primarily because they have lower prices than competing products. On the other hand, products of differentiation business units succeed if customers perceive that the products have advantages over competing products. Because customer perception is difficult to learn about and because customer loyalty is subject to change resulting from actions of competitors or other reasons, the demand for differentiated products is typically more difficulty to predict than the demand for commodities.

The specifics of the control systems for low-cost and differentiation business units are similar to the ones described earlier for harvest and build business units. This is so because the low-cost and differentiation business units face levels of uncertainty similar to those facing harvest and build business units, respectively. for example, Digital Equipment Corporation (DEC) followed a differentiation strategy, whereas Data General followed a low-cost strategy. The control systems in these companies differed accordingly. DEC's product managers primarily were evaluated on the basis of the quality of their interaction with their customers (a subjective measure), whereas Data General's product managers were evaluated on the basis of results, or profits. Further, DEC's sales representatives were on straight salary, but Data General's salesmen received fifty percent of their pay on a commission basis. Salaried compensation indicates behavior control and commission compensation, outcome control.[4]

As is discussed more fully in chapter 8, a broad-based chemicals manufacturer used differentiated management controls focusing on the differing key success factors for its yellow dye unit (which followed a cost leadership strategy) and its red dye unit (which followed a differentiation strategy). The manager in charge of yellow dye was tightly held against continuous improvement targets tied to theoretical ideal costs rather than to currently achievable standard costs. The results of this tight financial control were remarkable: within a period of two years, actual cost for yellow dye decreased from $5.72 to $3.84 per pound, giving the yellow dye unit a major cost advantage. The key strategic issue for red dye was product differentiation, not cost leadership. The management control reports for the red dye unit, therefore, focused on product leadership variables (e.g., milestone reporting on the development project for hot spray dyeing) rather than cost control variables.

ADDITIONAL CONSIDERATIONS

Although tailoring controls to strategies has a sound logic, control systems designers need to be cognizant of several problems involved in doing so.

The Changing Environment

First, a business unit's external environment inevitably changes over time, and a change might imply the need for a shift in strategy. This consideration raises an interesting issue. Success at any task requires commitment. The strategy–control fit is expected to foster such a commitment to the current strategy. However, if the control system is too closely related to the current strategy, it could result in overcommitment, thereby inhibiting the manager from shifting to a new strategy when it becomes necessary.

The radio industry illustrates the problems of overcommitment when there is a close fit between strategy and controls:

> Financially oriented U.S. manufacturers once treated the radio as essentially a dot on the product portfolio matrix. Convinced that every product

has a life cycle, they viewed the radio as having passed its peak and being a prime candidate for "milking". Starved for investment funds and resources and being subject to tight financial controls, the radio died in a self-fulfilling prophecy. On the other hand, Japanese radio manufacturers such as Matsushita (Panasonic) and Sony—ignoring or unaware of product life cycle and portfolio theories—obstinately believed in their product's value. The division heads of these firms had no option but to extend the life of the product since to do otherwise would mean dissolving their divisions, which was an untenable option. So they pressed their engineers, component manufacturers, and marketing people for new ideas. . . . Today the portable radio-cassette and Sony Walkman stories are part of business folklore.[5]

Other examples are Yamaha in the musical instrument market in the United States, and Honda, Kawasaki, Suzuki, and Yamaha in the motorcycle market in the United States and in Europe. These companies successfully destroyed the dominance of incumbent manufacturers who concentrated on milking their products for profit in a stagnant market.[6]

Thus, there is an ongoing dilemma: How to design control systems that can simultaneously maintain a high degree of commitment to as well as a healthy skepticism regarding current strategies.

There are many examples of declining industries that have transformed into growth industries (e.g., the major growth of Arm & Hammer baking soda, which was once in the decline stage of the product life cycle; the 1980s surge in demand for the fountain pen, which once was considered an obsolete product).

Simultaneous Consideration of Mission and Competitive Advantage

We have discussed mission and competitive advantage as separate characteristics; however, business units have both a mission and a competitive advantage that, in some combinations, may result in a conflict regarding the type of controls to be used. As exhibit 6–4 demonstrates, the ordinal classification of mission and competitive advantage yields four distinct combinations. There is an unconflicting design in cells 2 and 3. Both of these cells have a similar level of uncertainty, and this suggests a similar control system design. Cells 1 and 4, however, have conflicting demands, and designing a control system that fits both is difficult. Several possibilities exist. It might be possible to change the mission or

EXHIBIT 6–4
Fits and Misfits in Control System Design

	Low Cost	**Differentiation**
Build	1 Potential Misfit	2 Fit
Harvest	3 Fit	4 Potential Misfit

Mission

Competitive Advantage

competitive advantage so that they do not conflict from the standpoint of systems design (i.e., move the business unit to cell 2 or cell 3). If this is not feasible, it might be that either mission or competitive advantage is more critical for implementation and would, therefore, dominate the choice of the appropriate type of control. If mission and competitive advantage are equally important, control system design becomes especially difficult. Here, control systems cannot be designed for the mission or competitive advantage in isolation without incurring costs.

Administrative Problems and Dysfunctional Effects

Explicitly differentiated controls across business units might create administrative awkwardness and potential dysfunctional effects, especially for managers in charge of harvest units.

Many harvest managers believe that their career prospects within the company are somewhat limited. While corporate managers in most diversified firms may find it rational to harvest one or more of their businesses, every company wants to grow at the overall firm level. Thus, as one goes higher in the corporate hierarchy, skills at successfully executing a build strategy become more important than those of successfully executing a harvest strategy. From a career perspective, this likelihood tends to favor managers currently in charge of build businesses. For example, the following speculation regarding who might succeed Walter Wriston as the next CEO of Citicorp appeared in *The Wall Street Journal* nearly three years before the actual announcement of his successor: "Ironically, Mr. Theobald may not get to the top precisely because he runs a division that has always been a big money maker for Citicorp, its institutional division. Unlike his two competitors, who are charting new courses for Citicorp, Mr. Theobald is simply carrying forward a tradition of profiting handsomely from making loans to corporations and governments, domestically and abroad."[7] Subsequent events confirmed these speculations. Given these possibilities, harvest managers may perceive their roles as being less important. Explicitly designing tight controls over harvest strategies compounds this problem.

System designers might consider two possibilities to mitigate this problem. First, as part of the planning process, they might consider not using harshly graphic and negative terms such as "cash cow," "dog," "question mark," and "star" but instead use terms such as "build," "hold," and "harvest." The former are static terms that do not, in any case, indicate missions as well as do dynamic action-oriented terms such as build, hold, and harvest.

Second, to the extent possible, a harvest manager should be given one or more products with high growth potential. This strategy would prevent a manager from getting typecast solely as a harvester. Corning Glass Works follows this policy of assigning a growth-oriented product to a manager in charge of a harvest business.[8]

SUMMARY

The role of management control really depends upon the strategy being followed, and effective cost management systems are differentiated, depending on strategy. For instance, for a firm such a Champion International following a cost leadership strategy in a mature, commodity-oriented business, carefully engineered product target costs are likely to be a very important ongoing management control tool. But, for a firm following a product differentiation strategy in a market-driven, rapidly growing, fast-changing business, carefully engineered manufacturing costs are much less important. Nike, in fact, does not own its manufacturing facilities.

As noted in chapter 2, it is not surprising that monitoring of R&D productivity is much more important to a company like Merck than is manufacturing cost control. On the other hand, a system for better monitoring R&D costs would not gain much attention in a company such as Clorox, which has a mature process technology, but they have many accountants whose jobs involve marketing cost analysis on a regular monthly basis. Although cost information is important in all companies in one for or another, different strategies demand different control perspectives.

Designers of management control systems should take explicit notice of the strategic context in which the controls are being applied. Business units have missions that can be classified as build, hold, or harvest, and their managers can also decide to build competitive advantage based on low cost or differentiation. The appropriate management control process is influenced by which of these strategies a given business unit selects.

The discussion in this chapter on linking controls to strategies should not be used in a mechanistic manner; the suggestions made here are tendencies, not universal truths. Control systems should be designed in the context of each organization's unique external environment, technology, strategy, organization structure, culture, and top management style.

CHAPTER 7

PROFIT VARIANCE ANALYSIS

A Strategic Perspective on a Common Cost Management Tool

This chapter presents a disguised case—United Instruments, Inc.—to illustrate how variance analysis, an important component in the cost management process, can be, and should be, explicitly linked to the strategic context of the manager under evaluation. In the context of this book, the purpose of the case is to demonstrate that effective cost management systems are explicitly adapted, depending on strategic positioning.

Profit variance analysis is the process of summarizing what happened to profits during the period to highlight the salient managerial issues. Variance analysis is the formal step leading to determining what corrective actions are called for by management. Thus, it is a key link in the overall management control process.

Historically, variance analysis involved a simple methodology in which actual results were compared with the budget, line by line (Phase I thinking). One step forward was provided by Shank and Churchill (1977), who proposed a management-oriented approach to variance analysis. Their approach was based on the dual ideas of profit impact as unifying theme and a multilevel analysis in which complexity was added gradually, one level at a time (Phase II thinking). Though Shank and Churchill's approach represents the only comprehensive framework in the literature so far, their approach needs to be modified in important ways to take explicit account of strategic issues. Our framework (Phase III thinking) argues that variance analysis becomes most meaningful when it is tied explicitly to strategic analysis.

A modified version of this chapter appeared in the *Issues in Accounting Education*, 4, 2 (1991), pp. 396–410. Reproduced with permission.

THE CASE OF UNITED INSTRUMENTS, INC.

In 1987, for the second year in succession, United Instruments, Inc., had exceeded its profit budget (see exhibit 7–1). Their latest financial results showed that they had exceeded profit targets by $622,000. Although obviously very happy with the 1987 results, the management wanted a better feel for the relative contributions of the R&D, manufacturing, and marketing departments to this overall success. To gain a clearer understanding of this favorable profit variance, the company prepared an analysis of the contributions of each of these three areas. The data in exhibit 7–2 shows the results of this analysis.

United Instruments' products can be grouped into two main lines of business: electric meters (EM) and electronic instruments (EI). Both EM and EI are industrial measuring instruments and perform similar functions. However, these products differ in their manufacturing technology and their end-use characteristics. EM is based on mechanical and electrical technology, whereas EI is based on microchip technology. EM and EI are substitute products in the same sense that a mechanical watch and a digital watch are substitutes.

PHASE I THINKING: THE ANNUAL REPORT APPROACH TO VARIANCE ANALYSIS

A straightforward, simple explanation of the difference between actual profit ($3,150) and the budgeted profit ($2,528) is given in exhibit 7–3.

EXHIBIT 7–1
United Instruments, Inc.
Income Statement for the Year 1987

		Budget (1,000s)		Actual (1,000s)
Sales		$16,872		$17,061
Cost of goods sold		9,668		9,865
Gross margin		$7,204		$7,196
Less: Other operating expenses				
Marketing	$1,856		$1,440	
R&D	1,480		932	
Administration	1,340	4,676	1,674	4,046
Profit before taxes		$2,528		$3,150

EXHIBIT 7–2
Additional Information

	Electric Meters	Electronic Instruments
Selling prices per unit		
Average standard price	$40.00	$180.00
Average actual prices, 1987	30.00	206.00
Variable product costs per unit		
Average standard manufacturing cost	$20.00	$50.00
Average actual manufacturing cost	21.00	54.00
Volume information		
Units produced and sold, actual	141,770	62,172
Units produced and sold, planned	124,800	66,000
Total industry sales, 1987, actual	$44 million	$76 million
Total industry variable product costs, 1987, actual	$16 million	$32 million
United's share of the market (percent of physical units)		
Planned	10%	15%
Actual	16%	9%

	Planned	Actual
Firmwide fixed expenses (1,000s)		
Fixed manufacturing expenses	$3,872	$3,530
Fixed marketing expenses	1,856	1,440
Fixed administrative expenses	1,340	1,674
Fixed R&D expenses		
(exclusively for electronic instruments)	1,480	932

EXHIBIT 7–3
The Annual Report Approach to Variance Analysis

	Budget (1,000s)		Actual (1,000s)	
Sales		$16,872 (100%)		$17,061 (100%)
Cost of goods sold		9,668 (58%)		9,865 (58%)
Gross margin		$7,204 (42%)		$7,196 (42%)
Less: Other expenses				
Marketing	$1,856 (11%)		$1,440 (8%)	
R&D	1,480 (9%)		932 (6%)	
Administration	1,340 (8%)	4,676 (28%)	1,674 (10%)	4,046 (24%)
Profit before tax		$2,528 (14%)		$3,150 (18%)

This type of variance analysis is what one usually sees in published annual reports (where the comparison is typically between last year and this year). If we limit ourselves to this type of analysis, we will draw the following conclusions about United's performance:

Good sales performance (slightly above plan).

Good manufacturing cost control (margins as per plan).

Good control over marketing and R&D costs (costs down as a percent of sales).

Administration overspent a bit (slightly up as a percent of sales).

Overall evaluation: nothing of major significance; profit performance above plan.

How accurately does this summary reflect the performance of United? This chapter demonstrates that the analysis is misleading. The plan for 1987 has embedded in it certain expectations about the state of the total industry and about United's market share, its selling prices, and its cost structure. Results from variance computations are more actionable if changes in actual results for 1987 are analyzed against each one of these expectations. The Phase I analysis simply does not break down the overall favorable variance of $622,000 according to the key underlying causal factors.

PHASE II THINKING: A MANAGEMENT-ORIENTED APPROACH TO VARIANCE ANALYSIS

The analytical framework proposed by Shank and Churchill (1977) to conduct variance analysis, Phase II thinking, incorporates the following key ideas:

1. Identify the key causal factors that affect profits.

2. Break down the overall profit variance by these key causal factors.

3. Focus always on the profit impact of variation in each causal factor.

4. Try to calculate the specific, separable impact of each causal factor by varying only that factor while holding all other factors constant.

5. Add complexity sequentially, one layer at a time, beginning at a very basic common-sense level.

6. Stop the process when the added complexity at a newly created level is not justified by added useful insights into the causal factors underlying the overall profit variance.

Exhibits 7–4 and 7–5 contain the explanation for the overall favorable profit variance of $622,000 using the above approach. In the interest of brevity, most of the calculational details are omitted. If we consider the variance analysis summarized in exhibit 7–5, we gain a number of insights into the performance of United, as shown in exhibit 7–6.

Thus, exhibit 7–6 reveals that the overall evaluation of the general manager under Phase II thinking would probably be good, though there

EXHIBIT 7–4
Variance Calculations Using Shank and Churchill's Management-Oriented Framework

Key Causal Factors:						
Total market	Expected	Actual	Actual	Actual	Actual	Actual
Market share	Expected	Expected	Actual	Actual	Actual	Actual
Sales mix	Expected	Expected	Expected	Actual	Actual	Actual
Selling price	Expected	Expected	Expected	Expected	Actual	Actual
Costs	Expected	Expected	Expected	Expected	Expected	Actual
Profit Calculation:						
Sales	$16,872	$15,836	$18,034	$16,862	$17,060	$17,060
Variable costs	5,796	5,440	6,195	5,944	5,944	6,334
Contribution	$11,076	$10,396	$11,839	$10,918	$11,116	$10,726
Fixed costs	8,548	8,548	8,548	8,548	8,548	7,576
Profit	$ 2,528	$ 1,848	$ 3,291	$ 2,370	$ 2,568	$ 3,150

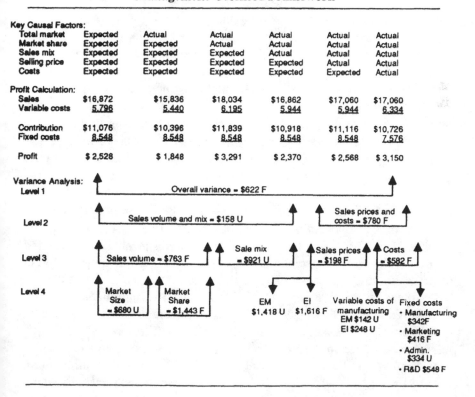

EXHIBIT 7–5
Variance Summary for the Phase II Approach

Overall market decline	$680U
Share of market increase	1,443F
Sales mix change	921U
Sales prices improved	198F
EM $1,418U	
EI $1,616F	
Manufacturing cost control	48U
Variable costs $390U	
Fixed costs $342F	
Other	
R&D	548F
Administration	334U
Marketing	416F
Total	$622F

are specific areas (such as manufacturing cost control or administrative cost control) that need attention. The summary in exhibit 7–6 is quite different from—and clearly superior to—the one presented under Phase I thinking. But, we can do better. The framework needs to be modified in important ways to accommodate the following ideas.

Sales volume, share of market, and sales mix variances are calculated on the presumption that United is essentially competing in one industry—that is, as a single-product firm with two different varieties of the product. Thus, the target customers for EM and EI are the same, and the two products are substitutable. Is United a single product firm, with two product offerings or does the firm compete in two different markets? In other words, does United have a single strategy for EM and EI, or does the firm have two different strategies for the two businesses? As we argue later, EM and EI have very different industry characteristics and compete in very different markets, thereby requiring quite different strategies. It is, therefore, more useful to calculate market size and market share variances separately for EM and EI. Just introducing the concept of a sales mix variance implies that the average standard profit contribution across EM and EI together is meaningful.

For an ice cream manufacturer, for example, it is probably reasonable to assume that the firm operates in a single industry with multiple product offerings, all targeted at the same customer group. It would, there-

EXHIBIT 7–6
Performance Evaluation Summary
(1,000s)

Functional Areas	Comments	Variance	Overall Evaluation
Marketing	Market share (SOM) increase benefitted the firm	$1,443F	
	But, unfortunately, sales mix was managed toward the lower margin product	921U	
	Control over marketing expenditure benefitted the firm (especially in the face of an increase in SOM)	416F	Very good
	NET	$938F	performance
	Uncontrollables:		
	Unfortunately, the overall market declined and cost the firm	$680U	
Manufacturing	Manufacturing cost control cost the firm	$48U	Marginally satisfactory performance
R&D	Savings in R&D budget	$548F	Good cost control
Administration	Administration budget overspent	$334U	Poor performance

fore, be meaningful to calculate a sales mix variance because vanilla ice cream and strawberry ice cream, for instance, are substitutable and more sales of one implies less sales of the other for the firm. (For an elaboration on these ideas, refer to the Midwest Ice Cream Company case, in Shank, 1982, pp. 157–73.) On the other hand, for a firm such as General Electric, it is much less clear whether a sales mix variance across jet engines, steam turbines, and light bulbs makes sense. This situation is more nearly the case for United, because one unit of EM (which sells for $30) is not really fully substitutable for one unit of EI (which sells for $206).

An important issue in the history of many industries is to determine when product differentiation has progressed sufficiently so that what was a single business with two varieties is now two businesses. Some examples include the growth of the electronic cash register for NCR, the growth of the digital watch for Bulova, or the growth of the industrial robot for General Electric.

Performance evaluation (in Phase II thinking) did not relate the variances to the differing strategic contexts facing EM and EI.

PHASE III THINKING: VARIANCE ANALYSIS USING A STRATEGIC FRAMEWORK

We argue that performance evaluation—which is a critical component of the management control process—needs to be tailored to the strategy being followed by the business units.

We pointed out earlier that a business unit's strategy can be considered along two dimensions: its mission (build, hold, harvest) and its competitive advantage (low cost, differentiation). This framework allows us to explicitly consider the strategic positioning of the two product groups—electric meters and electronic instruments. Though they both are industrial measuring instruments, they face very different competitive conditions that probably call for different strategies. Exhibit 7–7 summarizes the differing environments and the resulting strategic issues.

How well did the electric meters and electronics instruments groups perform, given their strategic contexts? The relevant variance calculations are given in exhibits 7–8 and 7–9. These calculations differ from Phase II analysis (given in exhibit 7–4) in one important respect. Exhibit 7–4 treated EM and EI as two varieties of one product, competing as substitutes, with a single strategy. Thus, a sales mix variance was computed. Exhibits 7–8 and 7–9 treat EM and EI as different products with dissimilar strategies. Therefore, there is no attempt to calculate a sales mix variance. The basic idea is that even though a sales mix variance can always be calculated, the concept is only meaningful when a single business framework is applicable. For the same reason, Exhibits 7–8 and 7–9 report the market size and market share variances for EM and EI separately, while Exhibit 7–4 reported these two variances for the instruments business as a whole. Obviously there is a high degree of subjectivity involved in deciding whether United is in one business or two. The fact that the judgment is to a large extent subjective does not negate its importance.

Exhibit 7–10 summarizes the managerial performance evaluation that would result if we were to evaluate EM and EI against their plausible strategies, using the variances reported in exhibits 7–8 and 7–9.

EXHIBIT 7–7
Strategic Contexts of the Two Businesses

	Electric Meters	Electronic Instruments
Overall market (units)		
Plan	1,284,000	440,000
Actual	886,080	690,800
	Declining market	Growth market
	(29% decrease)	(57% increase)
United's share		
Plan	10%	15%
Actual	16%	9%
United's prices		
Plan	$40	$180
Actual	30	206
	Apparently cut price to build share	Apparently raised price to ration the high demand
United's margin		
Plan	$20	$130
Actual	9	152
Industry prices		
Actual	$50	$110
	Well below market	Well above market
Industry prices		
Actual	$18	$46
Product/market characteristics	Mature	Evolving
	Lower technology	Higher technology
	Declining market	Growth market
	Lower margins	Higher margins
	Low unit price	High unit price
	Industry prices holding up	Industry prices falling rapidly
United's apparent strategic mission	Build	Skim or Harvest
United's apparent competitive strategy	The low price implies trying for low-cost position	The high price implies trying for a differentiation position
A more plausible strategy	Harvest	Build
Key success factors (arising from the plausible strategy)	Hold sales prices vis-à-vis competition	Competitively price to gain SOM

(continued)

EXHIBIT 7-7
Strategic Contexts of the Two Businesses (Continued)

	Electric Meters	Electronic Instruments
	Do not focus on maintaining and improving SOM	Product R&D to create differentiation
	Aggressive cost control	Lower costs through experience curve effects
	Process R&D to reduce unit costs	

EXHIBIT 7-8
Variance Calculations Using a Strategic Framework

Key Causal Factors:

Total market	Expected	Actual	Actual	Actual	Actual
Market share	Expected	Expected	Actual	Actual	Actual
Selling price	Expected	Expected	Expected	Actual	Actual
Variable costs	Expected	Expected	Expected	Expected	Actual

Electric Meters (EM):

Sales	$ 4,992	$ 3,544	$ 5,671	$ 4,253	$ 4,253
Variable costs	2,496	1,772	2,835	2,835	2,977
Contribution	$ 2,496	$ 1,772	$ 2,836	$ 1,418	$1,276

Market Size = $724 U	Market Share = $1,064 F	Sales price = $1,418 U	Manufacturing cost = $142 U

Electronic Instruments (EI):

Sales	$11,880	$18,652	$11,191	$12,807	$12,807
Variable costs	3,300	5,181	3,109	3,109	3,357
Contribution	$ 8,580	$13,471	$ 8,082	$ 9,698	$ 9,450

Market Size = $4,891 F	Market Share = $5,389 U	Sales price = $1,616 F	Manufacturing cost = $248 U

Firmwide Fixed Costs (by responsibility centers)

	Budget	Actual	Variance
Manufacturing	$3,872	$3,530	$342 F
Marketing	1,856	1,440	416 F
Administration	1,340	1,674	334 U
R&D	1,480	932	548 F

EXHIBIT 7–9
Variance Summary for the Phase III Approach

Electric meters	
Market size	$ 724U
Market share	1,064F
Sales price	1,418U
Variable manufacturing cost	142U
Electric instruments	
Market size	4,891F
Market share	5,389U
Sales price	1,616F
Variable manufacturing cost	248U
R&D	548F
Firmwide fixed costs	
Manufacturing	342F
Marketing	416F
Administration	334U
Total	$ 622F

The overall performance of United would probably be judged as unsatisfactory. The firm has not taken appropriate decisions in its functional areas—marketing, manufacturing, R&D, and administration—either for its harvest business (EM) or for its build business (EI). This summary indicates a dramatically different picture of United's performance than the one discussed under Phase II thinking. This result is to be expected because Phase II thinking does not tie variance analysis to strategic objectives. Neither Phase I nor Phase II analyses explicitly focus on ways to improve performance en route to accomplishing strategic goals. This observation implies that rewards ought not to be tied to performance assessment undertaken using Phase I or Phase II frameworks. Yet, Phase II analysis represents the best current thinking on variance analysis—at least as documented in the literature.

VARIANCE ANALYSIS: A STRATEGIC FOCUS

Variance analysis represents a key link in the management control process. It involves two steps. First, one needs to break down the overall profit variance by key causal factors. Second, one needs to put the pieces back together most meaningfully, with a view to evaluating man-

EXHIBIT 7–10
Performance Evaluation Summary for Phase III Approach

	Electric Meters Harvest Versus Build	Electronic Instruments Build Versus Skim
Marketing comments	If we held prices and share, decline in this mature business would have cost us $ 724U But, we were further hurt by price cuts made in order to build our SOM (our price was $30 versus the industry price of $50) $1,418U 1,064F Net effect $1,078U This market declined 29%. Why are we sacrificing margins to build market position in this mature, declining lower-margin business? We underspent the marketing budget $ 416F But why are we cutting back here in the face of our major marketing problems?	We raised prices to maintain margins and to ration our scarce capacity (our price was $206 versus the industry price of $110). In the process, we lost significant SOM that cost us (netted against $1,616F from sales prices) $3,773U This booming market grew 57% during this period. Why did we decide to improve margins at the expense of SOM in this fast-growing, higher-margin business? Fortunately, growth in the total market improved our profit picture. $4,891F We underspent the marketing budget $ 416F Why are we cutting back here in the face of our major marketing problems?
Overall evaluation	Poor performance	Poor performance
Manufacturing comments	Manufacturing cost control was poor and cost the firm $142U If we are trying to be a cost leader, where are the benefits of our cumulative experience or our scale economies? (Industry unit costs of $18 versus our costs of $21)	Variable manufacturing costs showed an unfavorable variance of $248U. (Industry costs of $46 versus our costs of $54.) Does the higher manufacturing cost result in a product perceived as better? Apparently not, based on market share data
Overall evaluation	Poor performance	Poor performance
R&D comments	Not applicable	Why are we not spending sufficient dollars in product R&D? Could this explain our decline in SOM?
Overall evaluation		Poor performance

(continued

EXHIBIT 7–10
Performance Evaluation Summary for Phase III Approach (Continued)

	Electric Meters Harvest Versus Build	Electronic Instruments Build Versus Skim
Administration comments	Inadequate control over overhead costs, given the need to become the low-cost producer ($334U)	Administration budget overspent $334U
Overall evaluation	Poor performance	Not satisfactory

agerial performance. Putting together the bits and pieces most meaningfully is just as crucial as computing the pieces. This function is managerial, not computational.

Phase I, Phase II, and Phase III thinking yield different implications for this first step. That is, the detailed variance calculations differ across the three approaches. Their implications differ even more for the second step. The computational aspects identify the variance as either favorable or unfavorable. However, a favorable variance does not necessarily imply favorable performance; similarly, an unfavorable variance does not necessarily imply unfavorable performance. The link between a favorable or unfavorable variance, on the one hand, and favorable or unfavorable performance, on the other, depends upon the strategic context of the business under evaluation.

Judgments about managerial performance can be dramatically different under Phase I, Phase II, and Phase III thinking (as the United Instruments case illustrates). Moving toward the third-generation thinking (i.e., analyzing profit variances in terms of the strategic issues involved) represents progress in adapting cost analysis to the new era in which strategic analysis is a major element in business thinking. This new perspective is one important way that effective cost management involves tailoring systems to the choices management has made about strategic positioning.

CHAPTER 8

DIFFERENTIATING COST MANAGEMENT SYSTEMS BASED ON STRATEGIC POSITIONING

A Field Study

This chapter presents a disguised case to further illustrate the concept of strategically adapted cost analysis and control. The primary rationale for cost analysis has always been decision relevance, as evidenced by the well-worn catch phrase "relevant cost analysis." As thinking evolves about the strategy formulation and implementation process, relevant cost analysis must take strategic positioning more fully into account. This strategic cost management emphasis is stressed in this book.

In particular, this case illustrates two ideas: (1) the use of cost analysis to help identify the differing strategic positions of three products of a large chemicals manufacturer, and (2) the use of differentiated management controls focusing on the differing key success factors for the differentiated strategies for the three products. Thus, this chapter blends the role of cost analysis in identifying strategic position with the role of cost management in implementing the strategies chosen.

MONARCH CHEMICALS: THE TRUBRITE DYEING SYSTEM

Textile manufacturing, viewed in aggregate, is a well-known example of a U.S. industry that is well past its prime. Once known in world markets for product dominance, manufacturing innovations, cost and price leadership, and substantial profits, the industry is now growing at less than 1% per year, is only marginally profitable, and is operating sub-

A modified version of this chapter appeared in *Journal of Cost Management,* 2, 3 (Fall 1988), pp. 25–32. Reproduced with permission. The case of Monarch Chemicals was made possible by the cooperation of a major multinational firm that prefers to remain anonymous.

stantially below capacity. Foreign competition continues to erode the markets for U.S.-produced textile products. Nevertheless, the industry is still huge, accounting for 700,000 jobs and $51 billion in sales in 1983. Monarch Chemicals is a leading firm in dyestuffs sold to domestic textile manufacturers.

Monarch, a broad-based chemicals manufacturer, had considered divestiture of its entire dyestuffs business as recently as 1980 because of the obsolescent technologies used, the vast industry overcapacity, the severe price competition, the limited profitability, the possibility of latent toxicology problems, and the fact that Monarch did not have sufficient strength in any segment of the industry. Long-run viability required the development either of a product leadership position or a cost leadership position in selected segments as a basis for building sales volumes large enough to generate an acceptable return on the invested capital. Rather than divest the U.S. business, Monarch made the commitment in 1981 to become the low-cost producer in selected segments to permit capturing leading sales volume positions. Two major positive features of the dyestuffs business are that the product is essential in textile manufacturing (no substitutes) and is a small factor in final product cost (only a few cents per square yard of fabric). The goal for dyestuffs was cash generation for investment in other, more dynamic, businesses. This case concerns the firm's programs to achieve acceptable profitability in one segment of the dyestuffs business that was still experiencing at least modest growth in the early 1980s—Trubrite fabric dyes.

Trubrite Dyes

In 1976, Monarch had introduced a new system of fabric dyeing in the product niches it served. The new system used a dramatically different chemical formulation that was patentable. Other firms had collaborated with Monarch in parts of the research and thus were included in some of the patents. This new system was given the brand name Trubrite by Monarch. The Trubrite dyes not only exhibited much better color fastness, but they also were technologically superior in terms of diffusion rate, migration rate, absorption rate, and solubility, all very important features to textiles manufacturers.

All shades of fabric color are achieved by blending appropriate proportions of the three primary color dyes; red, blue, and yellow. The new Trubrite dye system worked best when all three Trubrite dyes were used together. This characteristic presented a dramatic opportunity to sell manufacturers all of the dyestuff required for all three blending colors instead of selling each color separately, as had been the practice in the past. Because Trubrite was such a major technological innovation, it achieved widespread market acceptance even though Monarch priced the Trubrite three-color system at more than twice the prices for competing dyes. As a result, the achieved margins for the new dyes were very high initially.

All manufacturing of Trubrite dyes was done in one plant, which was among the largest dyestuffs manufacturing facilities in the United States. This plant had been built in 1956 as a joint venture of three chemical firms, Monarch, Trojan, and Ajax.

Yellow Trubrite Dye

During the late 1970, yellow Trubrite (Yellow TB) dye accounted for a steady 65% of total sales of yellow dye to customers in this niche. All three of the joint venture partners—Monarch, Ajax, and Trojan—shared rights to the yellow TB dye. Thus, all three were selling an identical product produced at the same factory and purchased at the same price. Monarch had about one-half of this business originally. However, by the end of 1980, price cutting by both Ajax and Trojan had reduced Monarch's penetration to about 25% of the business, and the downward trend was continuing.

Early in 1981, Monarch undertook a special blitz sales campaign, offering customers who would sign up immediately for a one-year contract, a price of $5.50 per pound versus its previous price of $6.50 (competitors were at about $6.00). Monarch gained a 68% share of the business with this ploy, which took the competitors completely by surprise. A few months later Monarch announced that it had bought out Ajax and Trojan from the joint venture manufacturing plant. This plant then became Monarch's only dyestuffs plant. Ajax gave up on the yellow fabric dyes business soon after. After the one-year contracts expired, Trojan moved aggressively to regain the business it had lost. In 1982, Trojan began to manufacture yellow fabric dye at its own facility, a newly constructed plant in which, presumably, they also were trying to achieve cost leadership via large volumes. By 1983, the yellow fabric dye business had become primarily a two-competitor race between Trojan and Monarch, both using price very aggressively and each possessing about 50% of the business. Data on price, volumes, and profitability for this segment between 1976 and 1983 are summarized in exhibit 8–1.

EXHIBIT 8–1
Yellow Dye

	Industry Volume	Monarch Volume	Monarch Share	Monarch Selling Price	Monarch Variable Cost
	(1,000 lbs)	*(1,000 lbs)*	*(%)*	*(Per lb)*	*(Per lb)*
1976	225	113	50	$7.14	$3.00
1977	310	154	50	7.58	2.72
1978	500	251	50	8.00	2.80
1979	880	353	40	7.48	2.62
1980	1,850	554	30	6.96	3.20
1981	2,214	443/920*	20/42*	6.30/5.50*	3.48
1982	2,065	1,164	56	4.40	3.70
1983	2,637	1,285	49	4.24	3.30

*The numbers to the left of the diagonal for 1981 represent the projected figures for the year if price had not been cut at mid-year. The numbers to the right of the diagonal are the actual numbers for the year, reflecting the price cuts at mid-year. In the fourth quarter of 1981, penetration achieved 68%.

Blue Trubrite Dye

The market for blue fabric dye is split depending on whether or not sensitivity to light is important. For that portion of the business for which this feature is not important, Monarch is not a factor. For the major and growing portion of the business for which light sensitivity is important, the major competitors have been Monarch, Ajax, and Spartan. Between 1976 and 1981, Monarch and Ajax shared the rights to Blue TB and thus were selling exactly the same product manufactured at the same (joint venture) plant. Trojan, the third partner in this plant, had chosen not to compete in the blue dyes business because of patent access complications. The Spartan product (Blue 79) is similar to Blue TB, but somewhat lower in quality. Also, its patent protection is not as secure. Blue 79 is somewhat cheaper to produce (about 10% less than Blue TB). Through 1980, Blue TB captured about half the business and Blue 79 about half. Monarch and Ajax were roughly comparable on price for Blue TB ($19 per pound), and Spartan was about $1 below for Blue 79 ($18 per pound). When Monarch acquired Ajax's share of the joint venture factory in 1981, Monarch was confident that Ajax was dropping out of the Blue TB business. Monarch decided to follow a strategy of meeting Spartan's prices in the marketplace head-on, trying to push technical superiority to achieve 60% penetration. In late 1981, Monarch cut price to $18 per pound to meet the Blue 79 price. Spartan nudged the price a little below $18 and the two-way struggle seemed to be underway, but still at a profitable price level. Then the roof fell in.

Ajax, which had lost out to Monarch in the yellow dye business in 1981, did not drop out of the blue dye business when it sold its share of the joint venture manufacturing plant. Instead, it took advantage of the softer patent protection on Blue 79 to begin manufacturing it at another plant. To take away Blue 79 business from Spartan, Ajax used very aggressive price cuts. They cut the price to $14.50 per pound in late 1981, but Spartan matched them. At this point, Monarch held Blue TB at $18. By 1983, Ajax had cut Blue 79 all the way to $9 per pound and Spartan had followed. Monarch had cut Blue TB to $16.40 per pound by 1983. From a 49% penetration in 1981, Blue TB had dropped all the way to 22% in 1983. Blue TB sales volume was stable and even growing somewhat, but the much lower price for Blue 79 had generated dramatic sales growth in which Monarch was not sharing. At these lower prices, users who didn't require light sensitivity began switching to the light sensitive segment anyway. Everyone likes this feature, even though it is not critical in all applications. At a low enough price, even those who don't require it will buy it. Data on price, volumes, and profitability for this segment for 1981–1983 are summarized in exhibit 8–2 below.

Red Trubrite Dye

Trubrite is clearly the superior red product for fabric dyeing. The patents are owned separately by Monarch, so neither Trojan nor Ajax ever had access to red dye manufacturing at the joint venture plant. Up through

EXHIBIT 8–2
Blue Dye (Light-Sensitive Segment Only)

	Industry Volume (1,000 lbs)	Monarch Volume (1,000 lbs)	Monarch Share (%)	Monarch Selling Price (Per lb)	Ajax Selling Price (Per lb)	Monarch Variable Cost (Per lb)
1981	907	449	49	$18.00	$14.50	$6.04
1982	1,322	476	36	16.60	11.00	6.06
1983	2,586	573	22	16.40	9.00	7.22

1982, Red TB was the high-price, high-quality, high-margin leading product in this business segment.

The main difficulty with Red TB stems from a change in dyeing technology that has been underway since the late 1970s. By 1983, only about 30% of fabric in the relevant niche was still being dyed by batch processing. Continuous spray dyeing machines were used for 70% of the applications. It was believed in the industry that batch dyeing would remain the preferred method for perhaps 25% of the fabric sold. The continuous spray dyeing machines operate at much lower temperatures. They substitute pressurized spraying for cooking as the way to fully impregnate the fabric with the dye. At these lower temperatures, the technical superiority of the red Trubrite dye is not achieved. Not only are competing products such as Red 66 dye technically comparable in the cold spray continuous dyeing machines, they also were priced much lower ($6.60 per pound in October 1983 versus $16.70 for Red TB). Even more troublesome was a new red dye (Red XL) introduced by Spartan in 1983 that seemed to be not just equal but technically superior to Red TB in some lower-temperature continuous spray dyeing applications. Spartan appeared to be willing to stay close to Monarch's price umbrella, as they had for blue dyes. Spartan introduced this new Red XL at $16 per pound. This figure was still $0.70 below the price of Red TB.

Red Trubrite was still the leading product for both batch and continuous dyeing applications in late 1983, with more than 40% penetration. Monarch had successfully defended patent infringement suits against both Ajax and Spartan for Red TB, indicating the superiority of this product. However, its penetration was beginning to erode for the continuous applications. A new technology using high temperature spray dyeing (gaining the joint benefits of heat and pressure) was emerging in 1983. Were it to gain acceptance, this process could reassert the technical superiority of Red TB, and Monarch was experimenting with a hot spray dyeing process in its research labs. Equipment manufacturers were also touting new hot spray processes. It thus was not clear that Red TB was in a state of decline. However, implementing a strategy of high volume to achieve cost leadership suggested that pricing for Red TB needed to be carefully evaluated. Complicating this picture was the fact that lower prices did not necessarily move the short-run price–volume–profitability tradeoff in the direction of higher distributable cash generation for the product. Price, volume, and profitability data for red fabric dyes for 1981–1983 are summarized in exhibit 8–3.

EXHIBIT 8–3
Red Dye

	Industry Volume (1,000 lbs)	Monarch Volume (1,000 lbs)	Monarch Share (%)	Monarch Selling Price (Per lb)	Red 66 Selling Price	Red XL Selling Price (Per lb)	Monarch Variable Cost
1981	2,053	732	36	17.50	$8.00	$—	$5.22
1982	1,914	867	45	16.60	7.80	—	5.78
1983	2,409	1,036	43	16.70	6.60	16.00	6.14

Trubrite Manufacturing Costs

Another factor to consider in pricing the Trubrite dyes was manufacturing cost performance. In 1983, Monarch's only dyestuffs plant (though fully utilized) was very inefficient by modern standards. Most of the equipment was more than twenty years old. Even though it was generally well maintained, the basic production process had not changed since 1956 and was out of date. During 1983, however, a major consolidation, renovation, and modernization program was initiated that was designed to improve yields substantially, to double the output per equipment hour, to cut labor costs dramatically, and to reduce inventory levels significantly. Overall, this program involved a time-phased expenditure of $35 million to generate $14 million per year in savings by 1985. It was felt that this program would give Monarch a cost leadership edge for approximately four to seven years, and perhaps for eight to ten years if competitors did not react quickly and could not match the inherent advantages from the large size of Monarch's plant. Still, it had to be acknowledged that the plant would never overcome the cost problems typical of any multipurpose chemicals factory. In 1983, the plant produced and sold 400 different compounds using 100 different basic chemicals drawn from 25 different chemical reaction types. Also, costing individual products was made very difficult by the fact that two-thirds of manufacturing cost (excluding raw material) was joint across the entire product line.

Cost data for the three major Trubrite dyes for 1981–1983 are summarized in exhibit 8–4 below. Variable product cost data were already shown in earlier exhibits. The total cost data add a share of fixed manufacturing expenses allocated on a machine hours basis.

EXHIBIT 8–4
Trubrite Products Costs (Dollars per Pound)

	Yellow		Blue		Red	
	VC	*TC*	*VC*	*TC*	*VC*	*TC*
1981	$3.48	$5.28	$6.04	$17.02	$5.22	$8.96
1982	3.70	5.72	6.06	14.52	5.78	9.20
1983	3.30	4.94	7.22	10.00	6.14	8.40

VC = variable cost; TC = total cost.

ANALYZING THE CASE

As noted earlier, this case reflects the new SCM thrust in managerial accounting, which involves something old and something new. The old is cost–volume–profit analysis and product profitability assessment. The new is a decision setting in which the financial analysis must be considered explicitly in the context of the strategy being followed. The analysis considers the appropriateness of that strategy from a financial perspective. This analysis is either financial from a strategic perspective or strategic from a financial perspective—take your choice. The specific decision setting is ostensibly pricing, but product-related development expenditures, capital investment, and performance evaluation and control also are at issue.

The case differs from conventional relevant cost analysis situations primarily in terms of the richness of the strategic context. The intent is to provide a case that allows the cost analysis to be imbedded in a strategic analysis that influences the cost analysis in a major way. The particular business (technologically innovative textile dyestuffs) is moving from high perceived product differentiation and low price sensitivity toward lower differentiation and higher price sensitivity.[1] Such drift is very common for products that are big winners when introduced but that begin to lose their luster over time. Even though the case looks at one product line, three distinct and different niches are present. In the case of the yellow dye, two competitors are manufacturing an identical product and competing aggressively on price. Thus, yellow dye easily can be deemed a commodity. The blue and red dyes are protected by patents and thus are still differentiated products to some extent. Blue has a close substitute that is priced much lower, but red does not (at least so far).

The roles of cost analysis and management control are very different for these three different situations.

Cost Analysis for Strategic Positioning

Profit contribution and full cost profit for the three Trubrite dyes can be calculated from the information in the first four exhibits. The results are summarized in exhibits 8–5 and 8–6.

Exhibits 8–1, 8–2, and 8–3 provide some evidence of how volume might move as price moves. There is strong indication that Trojan would meet any price cut for yellow dye, so that no major volume gain would result. Leading price back up would enhance profitability only if Trojan would follow, which seems unlikely given the history. Yellow dye seems to be priced to get high volume but with no net profit to show for the efforts. Because the factory is now operating at capacity, a good question is why any capacity is being allocated to a marginal profit pro-

EXHIBIT 8–5
Profit Contribution (per Unit) for Trubrite Dyes

	Current Sales Price	Variable Manufacturing Cost	Variable Sales Expense*	Profit Contribution
Yellow	$ 4.24	$3.30	$0.26	$ 0.68
Blue	16.40	7.22	0.26	8.92
Red	16.70	6.14	0.26	10.30

*In addition to variable manufacturing expenses, a total of $760,000 was incurred in sales commissions paid to a common sales force dealing with the Trubrite line (commissions based on the number of pounds sold).
Volume = 1285K + 573K + 1036K = 2894K
Cost per pound = $760,000/2,894,000 = $0.26

EXHIBIT 8–6
Full Cost Profit for Trubrite Dyes (Millions of Dollars)

	Sales	Variable Costs	Variable Sales Expense	Fixed Manufacturing Expense	Manufacturing Profit
Yellow	$ 5.4	$(4.2)	$(0.34)	$(2.1)	$ (1.24)
Blue	9.4	(4.1)	(0.15)	(1.6)	3.55
Red	17.3	(6.4)	(0.27)	(2.3)	8.33
Total	$32.1	$(14.7)	$(0.76)	$(6.0)	$10.64

ducer like yellow. Whether Monarch could drop yellow is a good question, regardless of whether they should do so. A three-color system perspective says you must carry all three colors, but Monarch is the only firm competing in all three colors. Yellow is a clear candidate for cost reduction if it is to stay as a profitable product, especially because the competitor, Trojan, has the newer plant. We come back to the cost management issue later.

Blue dye is an excellent example of cost–volume–profit dynamics. It makes a very high profit contribution (PC) per unit ($8.92) and has a sizable and modestly growing sales volume. The competing product is priced at about 50% of Monarch's price and has grown in volume from 458,000 pounds in 1981 to 2,013,000 in 1983. This increase is roughly 100% annual growth for two years! A very large share of the users who were buying non-light sensitive blue dye when the light sensitive price was $14 to $18 per pound are willing to buy light sensitive dye when the price is below $10 per pound. The competing product costs about $5.40 per pound to produce (variable cost only, based on 90% of Monarch's 1982 cost). If Monarch matched the competitor's price, it still would have a profit contribution of $1.52 per pound (9.00 – 7.48). Since Blue TB is superior, Monarch should get some of the competitor's volume. Monarch had about half the total volume as recently as 1981, just before the big price cuts on Blue 79. Why is Monarch allowing all this volume to go to the competitors?

The comparison in exhibit 8–7 is a good example of how higher volume is not always preferable in terms of profit contribution. Chasing the extra volume with deep price cuts would reduce profit substantially in the short run.

Monarch feels it isn't wise to try to compete on a price basis with a lower-quality product that is cheaper to make. Given this view, why did they cut prices in 1982 and 1983? A better idea now might be to raise the price back toward $18 to see if volume holds. The price-sensitive volume has already shifted to Blue 79. The remaining volume is the quality-conscious, price-inelastic segment. Why cut price here? Perhaps Mon-

EXHIBIT 8–7
Effects of Pricing on Monarch's Profit Contribution

Price	Contribution	Volume	Total PC
$16.40	$8.92	573K	$5,110K
$ 9.00	$1.52	1,293K (50% share?)	$1966K

arch could find some new innovation to add to the product that would justify returning the price to $18. Alternatively, perhaps the company could stay where it is on Blue TB but also introduce a Monarch Blue 79 to get some of the price-sensitive business as well as the quality-sensitive business. An evaluation of this option needs to consider the fact that this approach might involve too much obfuscation of Monarch's basic fabric dyes strategy—the Trubrite system.

Red dye also raises interesting cost–volume–profit (C-V-P) issues. Given the $10.30 contribution per pound, Monarch could certainly afford some price cutting if desired to hold volume. The real question is whether it is worth trying to buy the Red 66 volume at a discount price. This issue is similar to the blue situation where it is important to keep the strategic positioning of the product in mind. Is Monarch competing on a price basis (a commodity) or on the basis of a differentiated product with higher quality and better service? One could argue, based on a C-V-P analysis of the data in exhibit 8–3, the red dye is a technological leader (with an exclusive patent) where the key to maintaining market share is superior value, not a cheaper price.

Thus, Monarch is in a much different position regarding the tradeoffs across cost, price, penetration, and profitability for yellow, blue, and red dyes. The key conclusion is that an overall pricing strategy for yellow, blue, and red does not seem possible. Yellow is in a totally different strategic niche, and red and blue face somewhat different competitive situations. The point to emphasize is that product strategy drives the pricing question. Consistent pricing in only possible when strategies are the same.

In terms of the classic pricing triangle diagram shown in exhibit 8–8, pricing for all three colors was value-driven at the time of introduction of the new Trubrite system.

EXHIBIT 8–8
Which Leg Dominates in Setting Price?

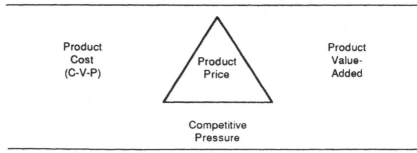

By 1983, red was still value driven, but blue was C-V-P driven and yellow was competition driven. Intelligent cost analysis in 1983 must take these differences into account.

Different Cost Management Systems for Different Strategies

At this point, we turn attention to the issue of differentiating cost management systems in accordance with the different strategic positions of the three Trubrite dyes.

Yellow Dye

Paraphrasing the classic maxim about real estate, there are three strategic keys here, given that Monarch does not and cannot have a differentiated product. The three are cost, cost, and cost. Monarch can continue to compete aggressively on a price basis only if they can reduce manufacturing costs. As shown in exhibit 8–9, cost savings are possible, depending on how aggressive one is about achievable cost targets.

In 1983, the company introduced a program of new management controls in which a major element was cost reporting that focused on theoretical ideal costs rather than on currently achievable standard costs. The manager in charge of the yellow dye was tightly held against continuous improvement targets related to ideal cost. By showing theoretical costs and emphasizing where actual costs fall short of the theoretical costs, the hope is that managers will have a strong incentive not to settle for the currently achievable standard. If the regular reporting system focuses month by month on opportunities (perhaps impractical in the short run) for cost improvement rather than on burying these challenges as part of so-called attainable standards, more progress can be made toward realizing those opportunities. Does it make sense, for example, to use high-priced diluents (which were part of the original high-value image) for yellow dye now that it is a cost-driven commodity product? The pros and cons of such a switch at least should be discussed. This behavioral argument is sound, and Monarch is trying to implement it. As an aside, we have also seen this same behavioral argument applied successfully in a major U.S. steel company. This idea has proved successful in real life for yellow Trubrite dye. By the end of 1983, the standard cost was down from $5.72 to $4.94. By 1984 it was down to $3.84 so that full cost profit could be shown at a $4.20 price. By 1985 the achievable cost was down to $2.98. The fixed cost savings were achieved largely through the

EXHIBIT 8–9
Yellow TB Dye: Standard Cost per Pound as of 1982

	Variable Cost	Share of Fixed Cost	Total Cost
Theoretical ideal	$2.18	$0.80	$2.98
Cost due to inefficient handling techniques	—	0.32	3.30
Yield losses from nonideal product formulation	0.54	—	3.84
Loss from inefficient drying techniques	—	0.56	4.40
Extra cost from use of higher priced diluents	0.54	—	4.94
Loss from inefficient product flow manufacturing	—	0.34	5.28
Cost premium from not using long-run supply contracts	0.44	—	5.72
	$3.70	$2.02	$5.72*

By focusing attention on the cost improvement opportunities through regular cost reporting of variances in the above format, the firm was able to achieve the following improvement in standard cost. Much of the improvement in fixed cost came from the factory modernization project.
1983—Standard cost = $4.94
1984—Standard cost = $3.84
1985—Standard cost = $2.98
*$5.72 is the attainable standard cost for 1982.

plant modernization project. But the variable cost savings from diluents and long-term supply contracts involve policy issues. This innovative and aggressive posture toward cost control in internal financial reporting helped Monarch achieve cost savings that permitted it to reduce price again by 10% (to $3.82) in 1985 and still show a 20% net margin on sales. As a result, Trojan exited the yellow dyes business altogether. Ideal cost reporting is a powerful strategic tool in those instances where cost leadership is critical. In terms of differentiated management controls, a key idea for yellow dye clearly was to focus on avenues for cost improvement via a reporting format such as shown in exhibit 8–9.

Red and Blue Dye

One could argue that the same cost reporting idea applies equally well to red or blue dye. We disagree, because cost leadership thinking is inappropriate for high value added and highly differentiated products. Under this view, the strategic thrust for red and blue dyes should be quality improvement, additional features, plenty of service, and aggressive promotion of product superiority—not cost cutting. For Red TB dye, the key issue is how to maintain product leadership. What investments can be made to prolong the leadership position of the product? Milestone reporting on the development project for hot spray dyeing is much more critical for Red TB dye than is cost cutting.

For blue dye the issue is niching versus penetration. A smaller share of the market may be better if margins can be maintained. A key strategic management control for Blue TB dye thus is reporting focusing on cost–volume–profit relationships via comparative profit contribution totals.

Is cost cutting applicable to all three? Whereas it might make sense to use lower-priced diluents in the yellow dye to save $0.54 per pound with no noticeable drop in quality, such thinking would be off base for red or blue. For Monarch, cost for red and blue rose during 1983–1985, while cost for yellow was dropping. This trend may not have been bad news, and it may not have been accidental. One does not seriously consider putting plastic upholstery in a Mercedes Benz. Peters and Pascarella echo a similar view when they say, "There is not an institution in the world that has the capability to walk and chew gum simultaneously. The managerial pie is only 360 degrees, and if 348 of those degrees are aimed at paper-clip counting, you are not going to be paying attention to quality, service, and the next generation of products." [2] Again, this assessment is behavioral. Whether or not one agrees with their conclusion or with the management control implications, it is imperative that management control thinking take explicit notice of the strategic positioning context in which it is being applied.

CHAPTER 9

NONFINANCIAL PERFORMANCE MEASURES

Another Key to Strategically Adapted Cost Management

Conventional reports of the financial performance of a business, both internal (budget or variance reports) and external (income statements or cash flow reports), are much like the scoreboard at a baseball game. The scoreboard tells a player whether he is winning or losing the game, but tells him little of what he is doing right or wrong in the mechanics of baseball. If he tries to play baseball by watching the scoreboard, he will not be successful in the game.

Traditionally, a scoreboard approach has been an acceptable role for financial reports, both internal and external. The role of accounting reports had been limited to providing periodic, ex post facto statements of financial performance without the expectation that they can provide insights into the factors causing that performance. Traditional accounting records have served the function of a scoreboard. Success, however, is a function of hitting, fielding, and pitching—not just watching the scoreboard.

As competition in industry has intensified, managers have looked for new sources of information on the key factors that contribute to success and how they can be measured. Many companies have looked to the financial statements and the standard cost systems for new insights, and to some extent these sources have yielded information. However, financial measures reflect the results of past decisions, not the actionable steps needed for surviving in today's competitive environment.

We see the rise of nonfinancial measures as an attempt to reassert the

---

This chapter was contributed by Joseph Fisher, assistant professor at the Amos Tuck School of Business Administration, Dartmouth College. A modified version of this chapter was published in the *Journal of Cost Management* (spring 1992). Reproduced with permission.

primacy of being operations driven. Nonfinancial measures try to capture progress on the actionable steps that lead to company success. Companies are trying to reemphasize that one must watch the ball in order to get a hit rather than study the scoreboard.

This chapter examines the use of nonfinancial measures based on a field study of five high-tech manufacturers (mostly makers of semiconductors). We synthesize the result from these field studies and describe the rise of nonfinancial measures as the primary tool of strategic control. We review why these firms felt that their prior accounting systems did not capture all the measures that were important for success. Finally, we examine the implementation and critical analysis of these new measures.

THE NONFINANCIAL PROCESS: AN OVERVIEW

In synthesizing the results of the analysis we documented that each company went through the six major steps shown in exhibit 9–1:

1. A shock to its operating environment.

2. The old control system was found inadequate.

3. Defining key success factors.

4. Finding objective, quantifiable performance measures.

5. Implementation.

6. Evaluating the new control system.

EXHIBIT 9–1
The Nonfinancial Implementation Process

Phase 1	Phase 2	Phase 3	Phase 4	Phase 5	Phase 6
Company perceives a shock to its operating environment	Company concludes its current control system is deficient	Company attempts to define key success factors that lead to competitive advantage	Company attempts to find quantifiable measures of success factors; many are nonfinancial	Implementation of new system	New Outcomes, both positive and negative

First, each company faced a perceived shock to its operating environment. This shock led management to conclude that their current practices did not lead to the desired results. The shock may have been as simple as a perception by management of an increasingly competitive environment or termination as a supplier to a major client. In another case, the shock consisted of moving the plant to a new location. Whatever the company's shock, it served as a catalyst motivating management to find new ways of managing, measuring, and controlling the manufacturing process.

In the second step, management concluded that the current control system, typically a variance system built on standard costs, was deficient. Therefore, rather than refining the current control system, a radically new method of control was needed.

In order to overcome the perceived shortcomings of the control process, the company had to determine what factors did or might give it competitive advantage. The third step consisted of defining these potential factors, called key success factors. This step required extensive senior management time in order to determine those factors and characteristics that would allow the firm to survive and thrive in its markets.

Once these key success factors were identified, the fourth steps involved attempting to find objective, quantifiable measures of these factors. The companies found that many of these measures were not financial. Many of the key success factors did not have an easy mapping to quantifiable measures. For example, assume a firm determines that innovation is a key success factor. A business strategy of innovation does not lead to easily quantifiable measures that indicate success on this strategy.

After identifying the key success factors and quantifiable measures, the fifth step was in implementing the new control system. Implementation was not a trivial task, and companies handled this step in very different ways. During this stage, the firms also attempted to find a benchmark for acceptable performance. This step can be considered analogous to setting the standard in a standard cost system; however, the firms used innovative methodologies in defining these benchmarks.

The last step the companies undertook was to evaluate the new measures along with the new control systems; this phase led to new outcomes, both positive and negative.

DEFICIENCIES OF TRADITIONAL ACCOUNTING SYSTEMS

Many complaints about traditional accounting systems led the companies to use nonfinancial measurements. Certain weaknesses are inherent in using a standard cost system to control an organization, while other deficiencies deal with the implementation of the standard cost system.

One of the major weaknesses of a standard cost system was the perception that a variance is not actionable at the operating level. The various departments of one plant had difficulty in interpreting a variance and tracing it to a specific problem. Because an unfavorable variance may have multiple causes, causality is very difficult to determine. Therefore, actions needed to bring the variance under control were not easily resolved.

Another weakness of the system was that production managers seldom saw a direct connection between actions they took on the factory floor and the numbers in the monthly standard cost report. One perceived cause of this problem was that the numbers were summarized on such an aggregate level that it became difficult to allocate individual responsibility for the variances. This problem led to frustration on the floor when the numbers were controlled using the variance methodology. As noted by one production foreman, "You have to be an accountant to understand cost variances, and if you're an accountant, you're probably not on the factory floor where you can do something about them." One senior manager stated, "In over forty years, I never learned to manage with standard costs."

Lack of actionability on a variance was a recurring theme in all the firms interviewed. One firm calculated machine hour variances on a monthly basis. However, this variance was made up of numerous activities that took place over the month. Thus, while the manager was told whether the machine was producing efficiently or inefficiently according to the standard cost system, the direct cause or solution was very difficult, if not impossible, to determine.

These problems were exacerbated when the cost accounting system relied exclusively on the typical volume-based allocation rules (i.e., labor or machine hours). Because the traditional accounting system sent faulty signals on cost causality, reliance on this information resulted in dysfunctional activities. For example, relying on a cost system that allocates cost based on direct labor may cause managers to make decisions as if overhead would decrease with decreasing direct labor. This causal link is faulty, of course; overhead does not decrease to the degree suggested by the cost accounting system.

Another danger is that the goal of maximizing an individual favorable variance may lead to dysfunctional activities at the firm level. The maximization of a single variance, in isolation from firm results, may be detrimental to overall firm profitability. An example of this potential dysfunctional variance optimization is the maximization of a positive price variance. In order to maximize a favorable price variance, a purchasing department may purchase cheap inputs. Low-grade materials, however, may result in increased manufacturing cost because of quality problems caused by the low-quality inputs. Another example is when standard costs include some elements of fixed costs. Standard cost systems show idle capacity as a negative variance. Therefore, managers may manufacture products in order to decrease the unfavorable volume variance even when the product is not needed.

Because the setting of standards is a very difficult and important step in a well-functioning standard cost system, this area also highlighted a weakness of the system. The firms in the sample competed in a very complex, swiftly changing environment. For example, several firms manufactured computer chips. These firms faced very steep learning curves in a relatively short period of time.

Given this very dynamic environment, the proper updating of standards was a difficult and costly process. Many managers argued that, given their own dynamic environments, the standards needed to be updated instantaneously. However, updating standards semiannually was the norm, and updating weekly was seen as being prohibitively expensive. Therefore, the standards were seen by the manufacturing floor as being constantly out of date.

In addition, managers argued that standards conflicted with the idea of continuous improvements. If the standards were not carefully set, the standards had the effect of setting norms rather than motivating improvement. Workers might be hesitant to perform to maximum ability if they realized that the standard for the future periods would be revised upward by current results. Observations from the factory floor led to the conclusion that the standard-setting process solidified the idea of norms and did not facilitate continuous improvement.

Finally, the standard cost systems in the firms we examined did not give timely signals. The typical standard cost system calculated variances on a monthly basis. After the close of a month, it would take at least two weeks for the accounting department to collect and calculate the results and return the results to the manufacturing floor. By the time it was disseminated, this information was considered by many on the factory floor out of date. Prompt reporting is especially important in a dynamic environment where the manufacturing process and operating environment are rapidly changing.

It should be noted that the firms we examined did not do away with their standard cost system. Most firms still needed the system for external reporting. However, the standard cost report was not disseminated throughout the firm and little managerial attention or control was placed on its results.

DETERMINATION OF KEY SUCCESS FACTORS

As mentioned previously, the firms studied were manufacturers of high-technology components. These firms found their market share under attack, mostly from Japanese firms. The firms were under pressure to implement more effective manufacturing methods and ways of controlling and measuring the effectiveness of these modern manufacturing methods.

The increased competition resulted in the firms reevaluating the important factors of success. Rather than relying on the signals from the current control system, the firms decided to reexamine their business strategy and determine the key success factors in order to compete successfully.

The business evaluation phase required large amounts of management time and attention. Typically, the firms determined imperatives that they considered essential to properly implementing their strategy. In fact, one firm concluded that these imperatives were essential for survival. Some of these imperatives were customer satisfaction, manufacturing excellence, market leadership, quality, reliability, responsiveness, and technological leadership.

Many of the key success factors were not based on cost considerations. Therefore, the standard cost system, with its heavy financial emphasis, was not seen as a good system for controlling the organization.

Determination of the Nonfinancial Measures

Once the key success factors were identified, the next step involved finding accurate, timely measures of these key success factors or imperatives. The following examples help to illustrate the process of linking key success factors with quantifiable measures.

Several firms determined that reliability with respect to promised delivery dates was an important aspect of competitive advantage. They found that charting on-time deliveries was a nonfinancial measure that addressed this company imperative. Therefore, the firms implemented control systems that tracked on-time delivery percentages. However, even a measure of on-time delivery needed to be fine tuned. One company initially used the metric of the percentage of shipments delivered on-time. Simple reliance on this measure motivated workers in the plant to fill an order that was on time before one that was already late because it was better to have one shipment very late and one on time than to have two moderately late shipments. Because the firm did not find this outcome desirable, they also added a chart that tracked the age of delinquent orders.

Responsiveness to the customer was another important aspect of competitive advantage identified by several firms. One firm determined that the proper quantification of this key success factor was the lead time required to fill an order. Previous to this choice they had tried using the number of new products introduced, but this measure proved to be a poor reflection of responsiveness. The number of new products did not strongly correlate with the time required to fill a customer's needs.

Another key success factor identified by all the companies was quality. With the advent of Just in Time manufacturing systems, the issue of product quality has increased in relevance. No longer is poor quality buffered by large inventories. Most firms measured this variable as a function of the outgoing quality rate. Other nonfinancial measures of quality included product yields and customer returns.

As noted by these examples, most of the nonfinancial measures were not directly based on cost considerations. These high-technology firms found that customers wanted a well-designed, well-functioning product delivered in a minimum amount of time. Cost considerations were perceived as secondary. A standard cost system, with its financial emphasis, at a minimum resulted in unnecessary dollarizing.

Finding effective nonfinancial measures of the key success factors is not a straightforward process. Many of these imperatives are multifaceted, so that several measures may comprise one key success factor; there is rarely a one-to-one mapping between a key success factor and a quantifiable measure. The quality key success factor, for example, may include outgoing quality rate, customer rejections, warranties, and other potential measures.

The use of nonfinancial control systems did not do away with the importance of financial results. However, the firms believed that positive financial outcomes would ensue from successfully implementing the key success factors through the nonfinancial controls. The firms felt that a byproduct of this control system would be superior financial results.

CONTROL THROUGH NONFINANCIAL MEASURES

After a firm determined the nonfinancial measures, the next issue it faced was how to run and control the organization using these measures. We noted two major issues facing the firms in this phase: (1) determining acceptable performance on the nonfinancial measures, and (2) placing responsibility within the firm for the individual nonfinancial measure.

Determining Acceptable Performance

The first issue facing the firm was how to determine effective performance. In a standard cost system, this step to analogous to determining the standard. However, the firms found the idea of setting a standard in the conventional sense unappealing for the reasons discussed previously. A couple of examples, meant to be illustrative rather than be exhaustive, show what processes the firms used to categorize performance.

Most firms stressed continuous improvement through the quantification of the learning curve. Once the learning curve was quantified, then actual results were compared with results predicted from the learning curve. It was believed that tying the standard to the learning curve motivated the firm to improve continuously.

One company found that there was a direct relationship between the learning curve and the complexity of the organizational setting in which the problem was being addressed. Problems addressable within one organizational subunit (department) tended to have short and steep learning curves. Problems that required coordination across organizational subunits boundaries but that were still addressable within one organization (multiple department within a division) tended to have longer learning curves. Finally, problems that required cooperation and coordination across independent organizations (a customer/supplier linkage) tended to have the longest and flattest learning curves.

One firm did not explicitly attempt to quantify the learning curve. This firm decided to base the standard on last period's actual outcome. Current period performance equal to the previous period's performance was unacceptable and the standard required improvement. Usually, progress was followed on a daily or weekly basis. The nonfinancial measures were plotted on graphs, with each graph showing continuous improvement as the goal.

Placing Responsibility

Once the nonfinancial measures were determined and performance could be measured and evaluated, the firms had to determine how to control the organization through these nonfinancial measures. The issue was how to place responsibility for these measures at the plant (or management) level.

At one company, committees were organized for each of the key success factors and charged with the responsibility of determining how to implement them. An important factor in the success of this process was the bringing together of people within the organization who were in a position to contribute to the identification of problems, underlying causes, and possible solutions.

These teams typically were staffed with several senior managers from the division as well as others who were familiar with the specific area. Frequently the teams would establish subteams to tackle a particular problem. After a team had been formed and its charter identified, the members began the process of problem solving.

The first step in this problem-solving process was the identification of the appropriate metric to use to measure performance. Once identified, team members collected data on that metric and analyzed the data to identify the sources of the failure. After the source was identified, possible corrective actions were listed and carefully considered. Several were tested before an acceptable action emerged. Once the best solution was determined, an implementation plan was developed and carried through. The process then began again. As already mentioned, these teams were held to a target learning curve. Actual results were compared periodically to the targets, and teams were required to explain both positive and negative deviations.

Another firm delegated responsibility for the nonfinancial measures to the various departments within the plant. The firm attempted to match departmental responsibility for a nonfinancial measure with the department that had the most influence on that particular measure. Each department then tracked and was responsible for its assigned nonfinancial measures. For example, the manufacturing department was controlled on manufacturing cycle times. The production planning department was controlled through on-time delivery percentages and inventory levels. The quality control department was controlled on the level of customer returns.

STRENGTHS AND WEAKNESSES OF THE NONFINANCIAL MEASURES

The firms noted many strengths of the new measures as compared to using the standard cost system for control purposes. First, the nonfinancial measures were more directly traceable to the strategy (key success factors) of the firm. Management felt that progress on these measures directly affected the success of firm strategy.

Another perceived benefit was that the measures were actionable. One of the major complaints about a standard cost system was that the cause and cure of a certain unfavorable variance were not always easily determined. In contrast, the nonfinancial measures were actionable at the plant level. For instance, a drop in quality was quickly determined under the system and remedial steps could be implemented to solve the problem. Or, if a firm had a poor response to customer orders, a typical standard cost system would not easily highlight this problem. However, nonfinancial measures of on-time performance (and possibly cycle times) would directly address this issue.

The nonfinancial system was also found to couple well with the new high-technology manufacturing systems. The close coupling of manufacturing systems within an organization through manufacturing technologies such as JIT resulted in increased importance for timely measures.

Role of Controllers

The role of the controller changed in these firms. As noted previously, they did not scrap their standard cost systems. Therefore, the controller's office still calculated standard costs for external financial reporting. The standard cost reports, however, typically were not disseminated beyond the controller's office.

In general, the controller's influence in the control process potentially could decrease because the controller's office was no longer the source of control reports. In these firms, the controller's (cost accounting) offices were not antagonistic toward attempts to implement a nonfinancial control system. In some of the firms, the controller's offices were actively involved in the design and implementation of the system and took a leading role.

In firms where the controller was actively involved in the process, the controller's role significantly altered. Rather than being the source of control information, the office's role was seen as facilitating and offering expertise on the control and measurement process. The controller's office helped in determining the new measures and implementation issues.

Problems with the Nonfinancial Measures

While the new measures were considered superior to the old methods of control, the nonfinancial system was not problem-free. One of the key difficulties of the nonfinancial system was the problem of how to assign dollar amounts to improvements in the nonfinancial measurements. The tie between improvements in the nonfinancial measures and profits was difficult to make. Managers were not sure that their efforts were being rewarded with improvements in the bottom line.

For example, a dollar quantification of decreasing cycle time was difficult, it not impossible. While dollar quantification is understandably a very difficult process, its absence detracts from the impact of the system. As another example, one of the benefits of an excellent on-time performance record may be repeat business from customers. However, a poor record on this measure may result in decreased sales or termination as a supplier. The typical financial accounting system may not explicitly pick up this opportunity cost of poor on-time performance. Therefore, in order to tie nonfinancial measures to the bottom line, the financial measurement system needs modification.

Going beyond the difficult tie between financial and nonfinancial measures, the measures may conflict in a short time horizon. For example, assume a firm decides to purchase new machinery in order to decrease manufacturing cycle times. The expenses of this purchase are easily traced to the income statement. On the other hand, the increased revenues are difficult to tie to the decreased cycle times, and therefore managers may perceive that this acquisition decreased net income. This tension is magnified when the division or plant is a profit center and upper management is controlled on divisional profit.

Another example of this phenomenon is shipping behavior at the end of a period. At the end of a period, a plant may ship high-margin goods ahead of schedule at the expense of on-time delivery of lower-margin goods. This practice results in improved short-run financial performance, but an unfavorable on-time delivery performance. The financial results mask the fact that the late delivery of the goods will invariably lower customer satisfaction, whereas recognizing the profit now or next quarter may have no lasting effect on corporate performance.

Need for an Overall Theoretical Framework

Another weakness of this implementation process is that without an overall theoretical framework, the nonfinancial measures may conflict with each other and make proper tradeoffs difficult to determine. As a simple example, assume that the manufacturing department is controlled on yields while the quality assurance department is responsible for customer returns. Rejections by quality assurance decrease customer returns but also decrease yields. Therefore a product that is borderline for rejection will probably be a source of contention between these departments if the departments are controlled on the respective measures. As a further example, decreasing manufacturing cycle times at the exclusion of all other factors may be detrimental. For instance, the wrong product or lot sizes may be produced in order to lower cycle times.

Gaming

As with all measurement systems, the problem of gaming of nonfinancial measures may arise. There are opportunities for managers to optimize their performance at the expense of optimal performance for the organization. The case of on-time delivery is a potential example of this motivation to game. If the nonfinancial measure is the percentage of shipments delivered on time, then there is an incentive for managers to sacrifice one late shipment for the sake of shipments that can be delivered on time. That is, on-time delivery performance looks better when nine shipments are shipped on time and one is ten days late than when ten shipments are delivered one day late. However, it may be better for the company to deliver several shipments a little late than one shipment very late.

CONCLUSION

The rise of nonfinancial control systems is the result of firms attempting to become operations driven. Many of the key success factors of firm strategy are not easily measured by the typical standard cost system. A nonfinancial control system attempts to address the actionable steps that lead to company success. However, as with all control systems, a nonfinancial system does not get rid of all dysfunctional behavior.

The implementation of nonfinancial systems is in its infancy. Firms are just beginning to design and implement these systems. Understanding the strengths, weaknesses, and tradeoffs in these systems is critical to the successful adoption of controls based on nonfinancial performance measures.

CHAPTER 10

WHAT DRIVES COST?

The Third Key to Strategic Cost Management

VOLUME AND COST

What variable best explains changes in cost per unit? For persons well trained in conventional financial analysis, the answer is easy—output volume. Examples of situations in which volume is the presumed cost driver are so widespread and so plausible that they have dominated thinking about cost for decades: fixed versus variable cost, break-even analysis, profit contribution analysis, marginal cost, flexible budgets, cost–volume–profit (CVP) analysis, and so on. There is no question that the notion is true. Average cost does decline in the short run as volume increases, other things being equal. Of course, other things are hardly ever equal for very long.

There is also no question that the notion that cost is driven by volume has strategic significance. If a firm somehow can double its throughput, it can achieve a major cost advantage that permits lower prices or more spending to achieve market differentiation or some combination of these two ideas. There is also much common-sense appeal in using the break-even point concept as a basic strategic variable.

But there is also no question that, upon careful reflection, this kind of cost driver analysis does not go very far. There are too many instances in which average cost is not lower for the firm with the most volume (Ford versus Mazda, for example). There are too many instances of firms in which average cost goes up, not down, as volume grows (Kodak in film from 1950 to 1980, for example). There are too many instances in which the distinction between fixed and variable cost is just not meaningful. Many now believe that variable cost is essentially use-less as a strategic concept. Think, for example, of how rich the discussion could be about labor as a fixed or variable cost in IBM, Digital

A modified version of this chapter will appear in *Advances in Management Accounting*, Vol. 2, 1993, JAI Press. Reproduced with permission.

Equipment Corporation, or Hallmark. Also, is it really easy to decide whether maintenance is fixed or variable? This choice is really strategic, just as for labor. Even raw materials cost is not necessarily variable when viewed from the perspective of long-term supplier–customer alliances. It is far more useful today to consider all costs as variable in a strategic sense. The trick is to be astute about the underlying bases of cost variability. What underlying strategic choices cause cost to vary over time and across firms?

Also, if volume were the necessary answer to cost leadership, Federal Express would never have gained success in competing with the Postal Service. If volume were the answer, NuCor Steel would never have succeeded in competing against U.S. Steel. If volume were the answer, Apple would never have gained a foothold against IBM, or Mercedes Benz against General Motors. Also, if bigger always means lower cost, why are the cement industry, the processed pasta business, and the milk processing industry dominated by small regional plants?

One of the primary themes in the emergence of the strategic consulting industry in the 1970s was that volume is an uninteresting answer to the question of what drives costs? Situations that lead to more volume as the best answer to better cost management are not encountered very often outside the pages of textbooks.

But if volume is not the answer, what is?

STRATEGY AND COST

The basic concept of strategic cost drivers is to get away from the notion that volume drives cost. As discussed in chapters 2 and 4, in the SCM framework (Shank, 1989) cost is caused, or driven, by many factors that are interrelated in complex ways. Understanding cost behavior means understanding the complex interplay of the set of cost drivers at work in any given situation. The basic outline of this strategic perspective on cost drivers is presented in chapter 2.

Restating the conclusions from chapter 2, whatever cost drivers are on the list, the key ideas are as follows:

- For strategic analysis, volume usually is not the most useful way to explain cost behavior.
- What is more useful in a strategic sense is to explain cost position in terms of the structural choices and executional skills that shape the firm's competitive position.

- Not all the strategic drivers are equally important all the time, but some (more than one) of them are very probably very important in every case.
- For each cost driver there is a particular cost analysis framework that is critical to understanding the positioning of a firm. Being a well-trained cost analyst requires knowledge of these various frameworks. Effective general management today requires awareness of these issues.

STRUCTURAL COST DRIVERS

Examples of the positive strategic impact of structural driver analysis are noteworthy in business history, if not widespread. Economies of scale were a major factor in the emergence of a small set of dominant players in automobiles and steel in the early twentieth century. Scale economies are also the major reason for allowing monopoly status for electric utilities. The economies of vertical integration were used to tremendous advantage by the original Atlantic & Pacific Tea Company in controlling the food distribution value chain all the way from farms, food processing plants, and truck fleets to supermarkets.

A more recent example of the role of an executional cost driver is the use of quality as a key strategic concept by Motorola in integrated circuits. The cost advantage it derives from its ability to achieve defect rates of only three units per million ("Six Sigma" quality) is a key aspect of its competitive strategy. Motorola has also recently announced their decision to enter the business of making billets for fluorescent lamps. They believe their quality skills can be the strategic lever for a successful entry into this business.

What do all these examples have in common? They all reflect a strategic perspective on achieving cost advantage. Can we quantify the strategic impact of cost drivers in more formal terms? The answer is a clear yes. Whether such quantification is strategically useful is a more difficult question. We illustrate here how the quantification typically works and then consider whether it is really useful.

Exhibit 10–1 shows the experience curve for dynamic RAMs (random-access memory chips) over the years from 1976 to 1984. The graph uses a log-log scale in which both the X and Y axes are converted to logarithms. It is a well known mathematical trick that graphs using log-log scales convert many curvilinear relationships into straight lines. Straight-line relationships seem more powerful to most people and give the appearance of a more definitive relationship. However, the relation-

EXHIBIT 10–1
The Experience Curve

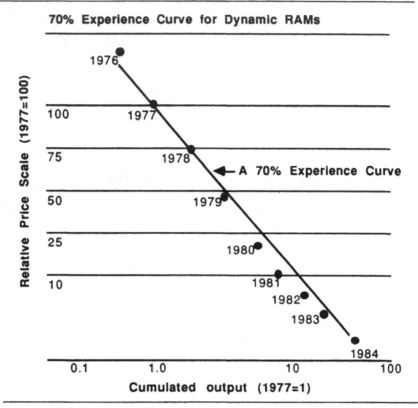

70% Experience Curve for Dynamic RAMs

The experience curve is based on a simple proposition: the more an industry performs an economic function, the better/cheaper it becomes at a predictable rate.

ship is not stronger just because we can find a way to make it look stronger. Consider, for example, exhibit 10–2. The basic data relationship is shown in panel 1 and graphed in panel 2. But most observers would think panel 3, using a log-log scale, suggests a stronger relationship than panel 2.

Exhibit 10–1 shows dynamic RAM prices falling in 1984 to less than 10% of their level in 1976 as cumulative output grew almost 100-fold. The presumption here is that the steep decline in prices reflects a corresponding decline in manufacturing cost.

The caption labels this line as a "70% experience curve." This relationship obviously shows a clear and direct drop in prices as output

EXHIBIT 10–2
Different Ways to Present the Same Data

CP = Cumulative Production   HTU = Hours This Unit

CP	HTU	CP	HTU	CP	HTU	CP	HTU
1	716	20	173	150	67	500	38
2	516	40	125	200	58	600	35
10	240	60	103	250	52	700	32
12	221	75	93	300	48	800	30
15	198	100	81	400	42	840	29

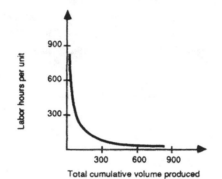

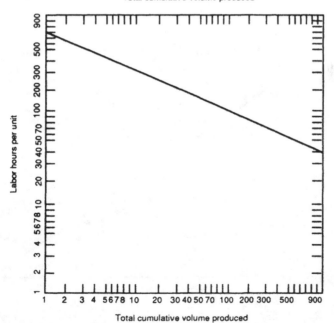

grows. But, what does 70% mean? The notion here is that price falls to 70% of its former level every time cumulative volume doubles. The line shows a 70% slope, where slope is interpreted as the reduction in the price level when volume doubles. Exhibit 10–3 shows a similar phenomenon, with passenger tire costs falling according to a 73% slope as cumulative passenger miles driven grew exponentially from 1921 to 1976.

The managerial notion here is that one can predict future cost behavior based on output growth. Bruce Henderson's Boston Consulting Group built a large consulting practice in the 1970s around the myriad implications of this simple notion about cost and cumulative experience. His strategic insights are summarized in the monograph, *Perspectives*

EXHIBIT 10–3
Tire Industry Experience Curve, 1921–1976

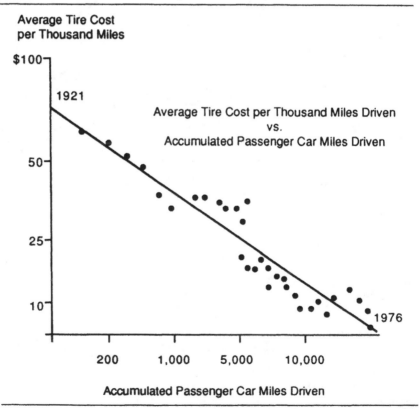

Accumulated Passenger Car Miles Driven

on Experience (Henderson, 1972). The appeal of searching for such a direct and strong relationship between cost and some single magic ingredient has not been limited to only the experience ingredient.

Exhibit 10–4 shows the same concept in the steel industry, with scale as the magic single ingredient that drives cost. Operating cost per ton is plotted against the size of the blast furnace, measured in thousands of tons. Again, graphed in log-log form, there is a strong linear relationship. The slope here is 75%, which means operating cost per ton drops 25% every time the capacity of the blast furnace doubles.

A third example, shown in exhibit 10–5, relates the unit cost of an automobile for General Motors and Ford to the volume of production per model. The proliferation of different models from 1965 to 1982 is a

EXHIBIT 10–4
Scale as the Cost Driver

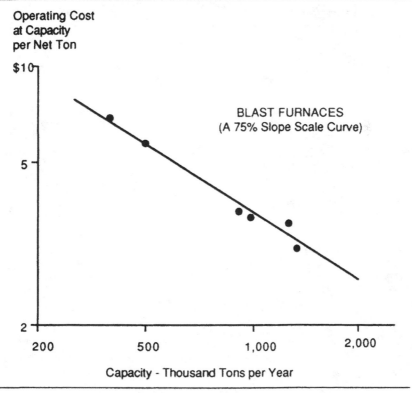

Capacity - Thousand Tons per Year

The scale curve is based on a simple premise: the larger a competitor's plant for a specific economic function, the cheaper the competitor is at performing the function.
Adapted from a Booz, Allen, Hamilton presentation.

EXHIBIT 10–5
Product Line Complexity as a Cost Driver

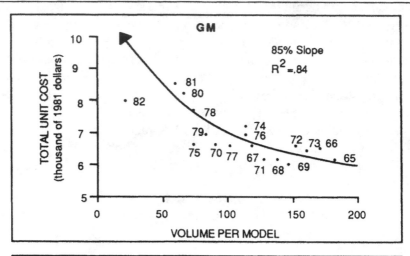

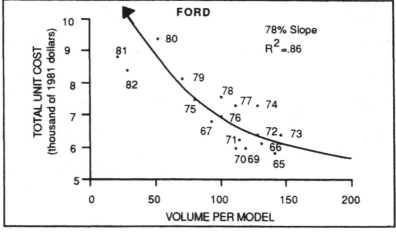

A striking example of complexity occurred in the automobile industry between 1965 and 1982, when the rise in real unit costs for U.S. auto makers was mostly driven by decreasing volumes per model (i.e., an increasing number of models per thousand sold).
Adapted from a Booz, Allen, Hamilton presentation.

proxy for product line complexity as a cost driver. This graph, which is not converted to logarithms, illustrates the strong diseconomies of product line complexity. When the number of models doubles (volume per model drops by half) unit cost rises 15% for General Motors and 22% for Ford.

These are all good examples from the strategic consulting literature of interesting business insights gleaned from formal cost analysis based on a single cost driver. But, if the concept can be applied to any one of several different cost drivers, which one should be picked? What if the graphs in exhibit 10–4 were drawn using experience instead of scale as the cost driver for steel cost? Or what if plant scale were used as the cost driver for tires instead of experience in exhibit 10–3? And who says there is always one critical cost driver? Don't larger scale and more experience often go together? What if one tried to measure the joint impact of experience, scale, and product line complexity in combination with each other? And what about considering more than just two or three cost drivers? Common sense suggests that many factors interact all the time in any real-world example. And yet, exhibits 10–1 to 10–5 are taken from the real world. Are these one-factor explanations anomalies, or are they typical?

STRATEGIC COST ARITHMETIC

Quantifying the financial impact of cost drivers, as in these exhibits, is fairly common practice among the strategy consulting firms. The underlying mathematical procedures are very straightforward. In fact, they probably are too straightforward. Because the procedures can be easily taught to staff consultants, it is risky to rely on them as truth without stringently challenging the underlying assumptions. As a basis for considering how managerially useful this type of quantification is, we present a summary of the underlying mathematical model upon which it is based. This awareness is necessary to build perspective on this form of cost analysis.

In the world of strategic cost arithmetic it is first necessary to assume that cost is a function of some set of cost drivers that interact in a multiplicative way:

$$\text{Cost} = \text{Factor } A \times \text{Factor } B \times \text{Factor } C \ldots$$

It is necessary to assume that all the factors are not equally important. The importance of each factor is reflected in an exponential weighting of that factor in the cost equation:

$$\text{Cost} = A^a \times B^b \times C^{\cdot} \ldots$$

The size of the exponent for each factor determines that factor's importance to total cost.

Why is it necessary to assume that cost factors interact multiplicatively, rather than, say, additively $(A \times B \times C)$ or in some other more complicated fashion? And why is it necessary to assume that each factor influences cost exponentially, as in A raised to the a power (A^a), rather than in some other fashion? The answer is simple. This formulation of the cost equation yields readily interpretable answers, whereas more complicated formulations are not mathematically tractable.

This formulation of the cost equation, when reduced to log-log form, can be estimated using the multiple regression technique, one of the most basic forms of analysis in the consultant's bag of tools. These assumptions are carefully chosen so that the analyst can use readily available and easily interpreted calculational techniques. This point is worth repeating. The assumptions shown here are chosen not because they are particularly plausible, but rather because they yield convenient mathematical answers.

Again, in equation form, if:

$$\text{Cost} = A^a \times B^b \times C^c \times D^d \text{ (assuming only four factors)},$$

then, it is also true that:

$$\log \text{Cost} = a \log A + b \log B + c \log C + d \log D.$$

This equation is now in a standard multiple regression equation format.

This format means that the cost equation can be estimated from a series of observations of each of the four explanatory factors and of actual cost over some time period. That is, if we have, for example, 36 monthly data points for the four cost factors and for overall cost, we can estimate the cost equation by using the logarithms of all the cost factor data points and the logarithms of the cost numbers for each of the 36 months as the inputs to a standard computer program to generate the regression equation and the estimates of the regression coefficients, a, b, c, and d.

Once we get this far, another mathematical trick lets us talk about how much overall unit cost will change if we were to double one of the cost factors. The trick is remembering that when a number doubles (from S to $2S$), the impact on the exponential form, S^s is given by $2^s \times S^s$.

This formula is just another way of saying $(2S)^s = 2^s \times S^s$. So if total cost (TC) can be represented as:

$$TC = A^a \times B^b \text{ (assuming only two factors)},$$

then, if we double the A factor to $2A$, we have:

$$\begin{aligned}
TC &= (2A)^a \times B^b \\
&= 2^a \times A^a \times B^b \\
&= 2^a \times (A^a \times B^b) \\
&= 2^a \times (TC \text{ before})
\end{aligned}$$

So,

$$TC \text{ after}/TC \text{ before} = 2^a$$

That is, the percent change in total cost when the A factor doubles is given by raising the number 2 to the a exponent, which is estimated as the a coefficient for the A factor from the regression equation. The slope is the quantity, $(1 - 2^a)$, expressed as a percentage.

For factors such as scale or experience where more of the factor leads to less cost, the quantity 2^a will lie between 0.5 and 0.99. The common-sense explanations for this result is that when doubling any one cost factor that reduces cost, average cost probably goes down, but not all the way down to half the earlier level. Thus, unit cost is reduced, but not as much as one half.

Summarizing the arithmetic of strategic cost drivers:

- Cost driver analysis can be quantified is a way that yields precise, neat mathematical answers to the question of how various structural or executional drivers affect total cost.
- Insights of the form "when cumulative experience doubles, unit cost falls 20%" are possible to generate.
- This analysis requires Herculean assumptions about how cost varies over time.
- The assumptions usually chosen are those that make the math easier, rather than those that are most plausible.
- Thus, the insights must always be considered with extreme caution. Are they real or just math tricks?

- On the other hand, the math techniques chosen often yield insights that have powerful strategic significance. For example, the learning curve idea was applied at Wright-Patterson Air Force Base in World II to demonstrate that the cost of manufacturing aircraft wings followed a clear declining progression as the number of wings produced grew. This finding was a clear indication that orders should be batched to allow a few producers to gain the learning curve benefits.

USING COST DRIVER ANALYSIS

Does anyone really use this sort of analysis? Yes. Many studies by such consulting firms as Bain, Booz Allen Hamilton, or McKinsey, as well as BCG mentioned earlier, explicitly use these techniques. These firms are mentioned because they are well known as leading strategy consulting firms.

Analysis like this is also widely used in public policy research. A major study reported in the *Bell Journal of Economics* (Friedlaender, Winston, & Wang, 1988) looked at the importance of manufacturing scale, among other factors, in explaining product cost in the automobile industry. The public policy implications are significant. If scale is important in reducing unit cost, concentration among auto firms has positive benefits. If scale is not important, legislation restricting concentration would not result in higher unit costs. The study found that scale was a significant cost driver, a result with appeal to the regulation-reluctant Reagan administration!

Obviously, this kind of cost analysis is fraught with major limitations. We must be able to identify and quantify all the factors that influence cost for some particular product or department. To guarantee easily interpretable results, we must further assume that the factors all fit together in an exponentially multiplicative form so that the equation can be estimated using readily available regression software after it has been converted to log-log form. And then we also have to assume that the calculated regression coefficients hold true over the strategically relevant ranges of all the important cost factors. How important are these limitations? Very. The limitations are so important that efforts to date to quantify cost drivers should be interpreted with a large dose of skepticism, no matter how appealing the conclusions may seem.

Then what is the future for efforts to describe in a quantitative way the impact on cost of various combinations of structural and executional cost drivers? Such efforts are extremely important in understanding what drives cost position. Strategic tradeoffs across cost drivers are made all the time by real businesses. Better understanding of the cost implications is an urgent need of strategic cost management.

For example, understanding the explicit impact of scale in a business is too important to be left undefined or simplistically defined. A major chemical firm entered the paint business and built a large plant to service a wide geographic area. This decision was based on an implicit belief in significant manufacturing scale economies, which certainly hold true for bulk chemicals. But, these economies are not true for paint. The minimum efficient scale for paint manufacturing is quite small. This firm did not gain any cost advantage in its large plant, but its freight disadvantage in shipping across a very wide area doomed the business. The absence of cost analysis of scale economies and diseconomies was a major strategic weakness in this situation.

Explicit knowledge of the minimum efficient scale (the smallest size that achieves full-scale economies) is a useful strategic variable that cries for more explicit attention. For example, as the minimum efficient scale in computers falls steadily from mainframes to minicomputers to superminis to personal computers to laptops, business advantage is won and lost based on understanding the impact on cost. Firms whose data processing strategy in 1993 is still based on the presumed economies of large-scale processing centers do not understand this phenomenon.

As another example, the tradeoff between scale and technology as cost drivers is revolutionizing the steel business today. Minimill technology using all of the scrap as the raw material and electric arc furnaces have eliminated the importance of scale that has dominated the industry for almost one hundred years. A minimum efficient scale plant is 3 to 4 million tons a year with conventional oxygen furnace technology but only 300,000 to 400,000 tons with electric furnace technology.

Recent reports in the business press suggest that in 1992 Bethlehem Steel still did not believe that a 300,000-ton-per-year mill could produce and deliver comparable quality steel at a lower cost than a 3-million-ton-per-year mill. But, NuCor Steel knew that Bethlehem was wrong. The decision announced by U.S. Steel in August 1992 to go forward with a minimill suggests that at least one of the major integrated firms had realized that scale economies, as a strategic weapon to build competitive advantage, are dead in the steel business.

It is interesting that as of 1993, the Japanese steel industry was also committed to megamills. It will be interesting to see how long it takes

Nippon Steel or NKK to understand the cost implications of the declining significance of one of their major strategic themes—bigger is better.

The authors also have participated in recent studies that suggest that, similar to the steel industry, minimill technology and recycled raw material technology can also dramatically reduce the importance of scale economies in the paper industry. We believe that by the year 2000, the lowest-cost producer is likely to be a 100-ton-per-day machine (with recycled fiber as raw material) located in the suburbs rather than a 1,000-ton-per-day megamachine located in a distant rural setting and using virgin fiber. Paper is also an industry currently dominated by large integrated firms operating through megamills and megamachines. Thus, the potential to benefit competitively from the change in underlying cost drivers is as significant here as it has become for steel. Cost driver analysis is the key to understanding this phenomenon.

As one final example of a firm using cost driver analysis effectively in strategic positioning, we cite the dramatic turnaround of Ford from 1982 to 1992. Based on its competitive position in 1981 via-à-vis General Motors, no one seriously would have predicted the reversal in fortunes of the two firms that became so obvious in 1993.

In 1981, it was clear that, whatever cost advantage had accrued from cumulative experience, General Motors (GM) was the big winner over Ford. GM had produced more than twice as many cars as Ford and was continuing this ratio every day. Also, whatever cost advantages had accrued from manufacturing or marketing scale and vertical integration, GM was the big winner over Ford. GM was large enough to achieve minimum efficient scale at every important stage of the manufacturing and distribution value chain. Ford could not hope to match GM on scale or vertical scope at every value chain stage.

Also, Ford could not hope to match GM on investment in new manufacturing technologies. Whatever cost advantages had accrued from new technological advances such as robotics or computer integrated manufacturing (CIM), GM was again the big winner over Ford. This overall scenario would be depressing if you were the senior management of Ford and were not content to be a weak number two forever! But Ford did not give up. They analyzed industry cost drivers very astutely and overtook GM in profitability in barely a decade.

What Ford came to understand, through strategic use of cost driver analysis, was that GM was not dominant in all cost drivers. Whatever advantages GM enjoyed in economies of scale, technology, experience, and vertical scope, they more than lost in the diseconomies of product line complexity. GM's product line, considering brand names, models, engines, body types, and options packages totaled more than 2×10^{17} combinations in 1986. That is 200 quintillion possibilities for the customer.

A minimum efficient scale auto assembly plant in 1986 produced 250,000 cars per year. This rate is roughly 1 car per minute for 16 hours a day, 250 days per year. An interesting statistic is to compare GM versus Honda in 1986 on the question, "how long would it take in this minimum efficient scale assembly plant to produce one each of every possible end unit combination for the auto company?" For Honda, the answer was 45 minutes (45 different end unit combinations were offered, including factory options). For comparison, the answer was 1 day for Toyota and 220,000 years for Chrysler. For GM, it was 7.8 quadrillion years (7.8×10^{15}).

Because GM made about 200 different models, the answer was still a staggering 36 trillion years for any one model, such as the Chevrolet Cavalier. Because Cavalier sold only about 250,000 cars in 1986, about nine quadrillion possibilities from the sales catalogues were never produced. The impact of this extreme degree of complexity in product choice on manufacturing cost is dramatic. Whatever value GM derived in the marketplace from this dizzying variety available (in theory) to its customers, it paid a tremendous price in the cost of the resulting manufacturing complexity.

Ford significantly reduced the number of models it offered, combined factory-installed options into fixed packages, and thereby gained significant unit cost advantage over GM. Ford also was fortunate that there were no significant cost advantages from the technological investments GM had made in robotics. The *Wall Street Journal* reported that in 1991 GM achieved its lowest assembly costs in old, labor-driven assembly plants with high worker morale and dedication to continuous improvement. Costs were higher in the new, technology-driven plants such as Hamtramck, Michigan, even after the company had spent about $45 billion on the transformation. This case is the largest single example of which we are aware of a diseconomy in the technology cost driver.

Finally, Ford also came to believe that GM was at a substantial disadvantage on a very significant executional cost driver—manufacturing quality. With its "Quality Is Job One" program, Ford achieved tremendous gains between 1985 and 1992 in unit cost and in market acceptance. GM is still trying to match this success.

Thus, Ford created a superior position in the quality and product line complexity cost drivers that more than offset GM's superiority in the scale, experience, and vertical integration cost drivers. The tremendous diseconomies that GM experienced on its major investment in the technology cost driver further eroded GM's once-dominant cost position.

Although this example is more intuitively than quantitatively analytic, it is an excellent demonstration of the potential strategic benefits of knowing what factors drive cost position and how to use cost driver analysis to gain competitive advantage.

THE FUTURE

We are convinced that much progress will be made over the next few years in further developing the techniques for quantifying the cost effects of particular structural and executional cost drivers, taken individually or in combinations. This area represents one in which cost analysis can be of tremendous benefit to strategic analysis in the future. We have tried in this chapter to highlight the potential significance of this topic area for the future, even though most of the examples we use are relatively simplistic or are more intuitive than analytic. The challenge is for cost management professionals to devote sufficient resources to this area to turn the potential benefits into realities and for general managers to push cost analysts to understand and explain cost position in strategic terms.

CHAPTER 11

PRODUCT LINE COMPLEXITY AS A COST DRIVER— ACTIVITY-BASED COSTING

Theory, Practice, and Limitations

Business history is filled with examples of firms that have bundled their product offerings with explicit realization that profitability differed markedly across the bundle:

Gillette—razors and razor blades

Kodak—cameras and film

IBM—computers and maintenance service

AT&T—telephones and telephone service

In these cases, the less profitable (or even loss leader) segment was consciously used as a market entree. Individual product costing was not as important as overall bundled profitability.

Business history and current practice are also filled with examples of firms that make and sell an extensive product line while hoping to earn a profit on each item. These firms recognize the value of variety in attracting customers, but they also expect individual product prices to recover all costs and an adequate return on invested capital. In other words, these firms do not explicitly (or even implicitly) acquiesce in cross-subsidization of profit across the line. For example, in the late 1980s, General Motors announced a dramatic reduction in the complexity of its product offering (fewer models, coupled with standard options packages). This reduction apparently was predicated on a realization

A modified version of this chapter appeared in *Accounting Horizons*, 2, 4 (December 1988), pp. 71–79. Reprinted with permission.

that the cost of complexity in their product line was not compensated by the value of variety.

For all of the companies that offer multiple products in a product line (or manufacture multiple product lines in common facilities) accurate product costing is critical to product pricing, product introduction, and product emphasis (Worthy, 1987). Explicitly managing the tradeoff between the value of variety in the marketplace and the cost of complexity in the factory or the distribution channel requires an accurate assessment of product cost.

This chapter demonstrates how traditional and even modern approaches to product costing can be dramatically deceiving about product profitability. The hero is a concept called activity-based costing (ABC) that we contrast with the villain—costing based on throughput or output volumes (volume-based costing, for short). We present a simple situation that illustrates the ABC methodology and, demonstrates its superiority. We also discuss the limitations of ABC when used as an ongoing cost accounting system and argue that the likelihood of achieving strategic benefits from ABC is inversely proportional to the extent that the concept is routinized as part of general ledger bookkeeping systems.

AJAX MANUFACTURING COMPANY

The case of Ajax Manufacturing Company consists of unit cost calculations for three different products under each of three different cost accounting systems—traditional volume-based, modern volume-based, and ABC. The company and situation described here have been highly simplified in order to keep the chapter to a reasonable length. The situation is not hypothetical, however. For much more extensive examples of essentially this same problem see Cooper (1986b, 1986c, 1987b) or Shank and Govindarajan (1987). We have named the company Ajax Manufacturing. Ajax manufactures three different products for an industrial market. This production constitutes a full line in the simplified context. The cost accounting system used by Ajax is a traditional one in the sense that is very much like the system literally thousands of firms have used for many years.

Sales prices and sales volume data for the three products are shown in exhibit 11–1 along with basic production and standard cost statistics. Target sales prices reflect the prices needed to achieve the planned 35% gross margin, given the product costs generated by the accounting sys-

EXHIBIT 11–1
Basic Product Information

Three Products

	A	B	C	Total
Production	10,000 units in 1 run	15,000 units in 3 runs	5,000 units in 10 runs	
Shipments	10,000 units in 1 shipment	15,000 units in 5 shipments	5,000 units in 20 shipments	
Selling Prices				
Target	$162.61	$134.09	$ 81.31	
Actual	162.61	125.96	105.70	

MANUFACTURING COST

	A	B	C	Total
Raw material	5 components @ $4 ea. = $20	6 components @ $5 ea. = $30	10 components @ $1 ea. = $10	
Labor usage				
Set-up Labor	10 hrs. per production run	10 hrs. per production run	11 hrs. per production run	150 hours
Run labor	1/2 hr. per part	1/3 hr. per part	1/4 hr. per part	11,250 hrs.
Machines usage	1/4 hr. per part	1/3 hr. per part	1/2 hr. per part 10,000 hrs.	

OTHER OVERHEAD*

Receiving department	$300,000
Engineering department	500,000
Packing department	200,000

Note: There is only one production department—machines—and it takes a little more than 1 labor hour for each machine hour (11,250/10,000) at the current product mix. (Labor = $20 hr. including fringe benefits; machine cost = $70 hr.)

*Again, the categories of manufacturing overhead have been greatly simplified for purposes of this case.

tem (product cost ÷ 0.65 = target price). The product costs are calculated as follows:

1. Charge each product for raw material cost (the sum of purchased components times the purchase price).

2. Charge each product for direct labor cost (labor hours per unit times the labor charge per hour).

3. Assign overhead costs to units based on a two-stage allocation for-
    mula. (Stage one) is to assign the costs of overhead departments to
    production departments based on some relevant measure of activ-
    ity (square feet of floor space for janitorial cost, machine value for
    insurance cost, employee head count for personnel cost, etc.).
    Then, after all costs have been assigned to production departments,
    stage two is to assign costs to units of product based on some mea-
    sure of throughput or output volume in the production depart-
    ments. The most frequently used measure of production volume in
    multiproduct plants traditionally has been labor dollars (of labor
    hours).

In our example, because there is only one production department
(machines), the first stage allocation is trivial. Because there is one production department, allocating all of the indirect overhead to it must be
correct. Yet even when the stage-one allocations are perfectly accurate,
meaningful product costing is not assured. The false belief that reason-
ableness of the allocations at stage one produces reasonable end unit
costs is part of the problem with volume-based costing.

Assuming set-up labor is included, the total overhead to be assigned
to the production in the machines department is shown in exhibit 11–2.
In a traditional costing system such as this, overhead is assigned to products based on direct labor dollars. Using this information, Ajax calculates the unit cost of products A, B, and C as shown in exhibit 11–3.
Product profitability data is summarized in exhibit 11–4.

As shown in exhibit 11–4, product A is achieving its planned margin.
Product B is achieving only 31% gross margin because this product has

EXHIBIT 11–2
Total Overhead Assigned to the Machines Department

Allocated overhead		
Setup	$ 3,000	
Receiving	300,000	
Engineering	500,000	
Packing	200,000	$1,003,000
Directly assignable overhead		
Machines cost (10,000 hours × $70/hr.)		700,000
Total Overhead		$1,703,000

EXHIBIT 11–3
The Traditional Approach to Calculating Unit Costs

		A	B	C
Raw material		$20.00	$30.00	$10.00
Direct labor		10.00	6.67	5.00
Overhead (Labor $ basis)		75.70	50.49	37.85
Set up	3,000			
Machines	700,000			
Receiving	300,000			
Engineering	500,000			
Packing	200,000			
	$1,703,000			
Total		$105.70	$87.16	$52.85

Overhead rate = $1,703,000/$225,000 = 757%

EXHIBIT 11–4
Data on Product Profitability

	A	B	C
Standard cost	$105.70	$87.16	$52.85
Target selling price	$162.61	$134.09	$81.31
Planned gross margin	35%	35%	35%
Actual selling price	$162.61	$125.96	$105.70
Actual gross margin	35%	31%	50%

come under heavy price pressure from foreign competitors. Ajax knows its factory is as modern and efficient as any in the world and thus is convinced that the foreign firms are dumping product B in the U.S. market. Ajax has dropped its price somewhat in response to the foreign firms, but it is very reluctant to cut further because of the low achieved gross margin. It sales volume for product B has fallen substantially, although B is still the highest-volume product.

Fortunately for Ajax, it has been able to offset the declining profits from B by significantly raising the price of C. Ajax was pleasantly surprised when customers readily accepted the price increases here. Also, even with the higher prices, competition has not challenged Ajax very much for this business. The result seems to be a very profitable low-volume niche that competitors don't invade. Management presumes that product C must have some unique characteristics that are very attractive to customers but that are not apparent to Ajax. Because of the market dominance it has achieved with C, Ajax still should be earning its target overall gross margin of 35%. But actual results consistently seem to lag the projected results. Management attributes the decline to "inexplicable" overhead creep—lack of management discipline.

Concern with costs and prices for its volume leader, product B, has led Ajax to experiment with some modern refinements to its cost accounting system. A new approach to product costing has been developed by the controller, even though top management has not yet seen his calculations. Still using only the information in exhibit 11–1, he has incorporated three refinements to the traditional system. His modern touches are:

1. Breaking out set-up labor from the overhead pool and charging it to each product based on set-up time per production run divided by the number of units in a production run. For example, for product A, one set up costs $200 (10 hours × $20/hour) and one run is 10,000 units. Set-up cost is thus 0.02 per unit ($200/10,000). This refinement goes beyond averaging set-up cost across the products to specifically identify it with the individual products. This refinement can be very important when products differ in set-up time, number of production set ups, or in length of production runs (or all three).

2. Breaking out the overhead that is more related to material cost (receiving or inbound inspection, for example) and charging it to products based on material cost rather than labor cost. Under this refinement a pool of material handling overhead is separate from the pool of production overhead. Material handling overhead is charged to products based on raw material dollars, rather than direct labor dollars. This refinement can be very important when products differ in raw material content.

3. Substituting machine hours for labor dollars (or labor hours) as the measure of production volume. As factories have become much less labor-paced and much more machine-paced, the notion of labor content as the best measure of throughput has lost its salience. When one worker tends several machines that perform different functions, run at different speeds, and differ markedly in cost and complexity, labor cost loses its meaning as a central element in product costing. The overhead rate of 757% (overhead ÷

direct labor) for Ajax is a clear signal that labor is no longer a dominant cost component.

In this case, direct labor cost is only 8% of total cost, a far cry from the factories of the past or of textbook lore. When direct labor cost dropped to 3% of total cost in Hewlett-Packard, management relegated it to another component of overhead in a two-component cost system—material cost and overhead.

For Ajax, where the machines are ostensibly identical and machine-specific cost is three times as high as direct labor cost, machine hours consumed can be viewed as a better measure of throughput and thus as a superior basis for assigning indirect overhead.

Using these three refinements, the controller has calculated product cost using raw material cost, direct labor cost, product-specific set-up cost, material handling overhead charged in proportion to material cost, and production overhead charged in proportion to machine hours consumed. Exhibit 11–5 shows the product costs of A, B, and C when calculated using these refinements.

The controller is almost ready to present his modern cost accounting system ideas to top management. He feels sure that this information will strengthen management's resolve not to cut prices on product B any fur-

EXHIBIT 11–5
The Modern Approach

		A	B	C
Raw material		$20.00	$30.00	$10.00
Material overhead				
(Material $ basis), (300K/700K = 43%)		8.60	12.90	4.30
Set-up labor		0.02	0.04	0.44
Direct labor		10.00	6.67	5.00
Other overhead				
(Machine hours basis)		35.00	46.67	70.00
Machines	$700,000			
Engineering	500,000			
Packing	200,000			
	$1,400,000			
Total		$73.62	$96.28	$89.74

Overhead rate = $1,400,000/10,000 = $140 hr.

ther. The new system shows that margins are even lower than management currently believes. The controller sees this as further evidence that foreign firms must be dumping product B to Ajax customers. Part of his hesitation in releasing the new cost data had been based on his concern about how management would view the news that C is not as profitable as they had thought, even though A is much more profitable. This concern had lessened recently when he heard the sales manager say that Ajax was experimenting with 15% price jumps for C in some regions. Amazingly, salespeople had found customers still willing to order normal quantities.

At this point, we turn to a description of a much different system for allocating indirect costs—activity-based costing. If Ajax were aware of this system, they would see how painfully inaccurate their cost system is, even with the refinements the controller wants to propose. The activity-based view of costs might lead to a dramatically different assessment of the options being considered.

ACTIVITY-BASED COSTING

In spite of the very good logic embodied in the controller's three refinements, the results still misallocate overhead to products. Fundamentally, each component of overhead is caused by some activity. Each product should be charged for a share of the component based on the proportion of that activity that it causes. Production scheduling cost, for example, is generated by the number of production runs to be scheduled and thus should be allocated based on the number of production runs each product generates. Products that generate a large number of relatively short production runs always bear a less-than-proportionate share of the cost under any volume-based allocation scheme. Scheduling cost is not volume dependent in the short run; it is not even dependent on production volume in the long run. In the long run, it is dependent on how many runs must be scheduled, not how many units are produced. Whether machine hours or labor hours is the better measure of output, using either measure of output volume misstates the extent to which the product with many short runs causes scheduling cost. The basic idea is that transaction volume (number of production runs) is a better proxy for long-run variable cost than is output volume.

This concept is not particularly subtle or counterintuitive—it is very much in line with common sense. But, in earlier days, factories tended to produce fewer different products, cost was labor dominated (high labor cost relative to overhead), and products tended to differ less in the amount of support services they consumed. Thus, the activity basis for overhead allocation was not likely to produce product cost results much different from a simple volume-driven basis tied to labor cost. Activity costing would involve much more work, so it was not worth the extra effort. Over time, the circumstances under which the more complicated activity approach would produce comparable results have eroded. But eroding along with them was our awareness that volume-based costing is useful only when the simplifications upon which it is based are reasonable.

Helping to reestablish that awareness is the purpose of this chapter. There is no question that an activity-based overhead allocation system adopts a long-run rather than a short-run focus on cost behavior. Activity costing does not imply that overhead can be saved in the short run if the transactions that cause it are stopped. There is almost always a lag between changes in the volume of activities and changes in the level of cost. Salaried production schedulers are not fired immediately if the number of production runs declines. Yet, over the longer run, scheduling cost is surely tied to one fundamental activity—the number of production runs to schedule. A similar logic applies to each component of production overhead, such as shipping orders for shipping cost or receiving orders for receiving cost.

The activity approach also disavows the notion that all overhead allocation is arbitrary and thus is not worth trying to do better. The approach presumes that meaningful allocation of fixed costs is possible and worth doing (Zimmerman, 1979). The gradual rise to prominence over the past thirty years of the two concepts that full cost is less useful than variable cost and that full costing is only an exercise in applied arbitrariness (Thomas, 1969) also helps to explain why activity-based allocation of fixed overhead has not received more serious attention.

Today, labor cost is not only dramatically less important, it is also viewed less and less as a cost to be varied when production volume varies. Labor is now part of the team in a large and growing number of companies. But business after business is choking on overhead. Indirect cost is now the dominant part of cost, and businesses are desperately seeking ways to understand why its growth so undermines their efforts to generate adequate profits. In the prototypical flexible factory, raw material is the only volume-dependent cost and the only cost that can be directly related to individual products. A meaningful assessment of full cost today must involve assigning overhead in proportion to the activities that generate it in the long-run.

For Ajax, exhibit 11–6 summarizes the distribution of cost-causing activities for each of the three indirect overhead departments: receiving orders for the receiving department, packing orders for the packing department, and work orders for the engineering department. This framework obviously simplifies a very complex phenomenon—determining what activities ultimately cause cost in any given department. Receiving cost, for example, is partly caused by bulk of receipts, partly by weight of receipts, and partly by fragility of receipts as well as by number of shipments received. For purposes of this example, however, the concept is demonstrated even though it is not fully amplified. The basic idea is that receiving cost is caused by receiving workload, rather than by production volume, and receiving workload for products may differ markedly from production volume.

Using activities volume to assign overhead to products is not difficult once one has the data in exhibit 11–6. Product A, for example, should

EXHIBIT 11–6
Overhead Activities Workload

	A	B	C
Receiving orders			
Receive each component once per run (a Just in Time inventory policy)	5 (4%)	18 (15%)	100 (81%)
Packing orders			
One packing order per shipment	1 (4%)	5 (19%)	20 (77%)
Engineering workload			
Distribution of workload in the engineering department is based on subjective assessment of long-run trends in number of engineering work orders for each product	25%	35%	40%
	The standard, smooth running product		The complex, special problems product

EXHIBIT 11–7
The ABC Approach

	A	B	C
Raw material	$20.00	$30.00	$10.00
Direct labor	10.00	6.67	5.00
Set-up labor	.02	.04	.44
Machine overhead ($70/hr.)	17.50	23.33	35.00
Receiving (12K/45K/243K)	1.20	3.00	48.60
Engineering (125K/175K/200K)	12.50	11.67	40.00
Packing (8K/38K/154K)	.80	2.53	30.80
Total	$62.02	$77.24	$169.84

absorb 4% of receiving cost ($12,000). Each unit of A thus should carry $1.20 of receiving cost ($12,000/10,000). In contrast, product C should absorb 81% of receiving cost because it causes 81% of the receiving workload. Both of the volume-based systems overallocate receiving cost to products A and B because these products generate more production volume as compared to product C. Unit C cost now includes:

Raw material cost

Direct labor cost

Product-specific set-up cost

Machines overhead charge per machine hour consumed

Indirect production overhead charged in proportion to the consumption of the activities that, in the longer run, cause the overhead

Following this activity-based approach, unit costs for products A, B, and C are as shown in exhibit 11–7.

MANAGERIAL IMPLICATIONS

Exhibit 11–8 is a summary of product costs and product profitability for A, B, and C under each of the three approaches. The essential message is that product C is dramatically undercosted under both volume-based systems, while products A and B are overcosted. The two volume-based systems give a different rank ordering of cost for A and B, but both products are overcosted by both systems.

EXHIBIT 11–8
Comparison of Costing Systems

	A	B	C
COST PER UNIT			
Conventional volume-based system	$105.70	$87.16	$ 52.85
Modern volume-based system	73.62	96.28	89.74
ABC	62.02	77.24	169.84
Selling price	162.61	125.96	121.55*
PROFITABILITY PER UNIT			
Conventional system			
Profit/unit	$56.91	$38.80	$ 68.70
Gross margin	35%	31%	57%
Modern system			
Profit/unit	$88.99	$29.68	$ 31.81
Gross margin	55%	24%	26%
ABC system			
Profit/unit	$100.59	$48.72	($48.29)
Gross margin	62%	39%	Negative!

*After the latest round of further price increases.

The general point is that the higher-volume products will be over-costed relative to the low-volume products to the extent that overhead cost is driven, in the long run, by activities that are not proportional to output volume. Much of the overhead in modern multiproduct factories is caused much more by the complexity of the product line and by the special handling of special low-volume items than by the volume of production as such. In these circumstances, the high-volume products are either overpriced or show low apparent margins. Conversely, the low-volume products are either underpriced or show high apparent margins. The high-volume products are subsidizing the low-volume ones, but the accounting system camouflages the subsidy.

The scenario opens the door for a firm pursuing a niche strategy to attack the high-volume segment with aggressively low pricing. This firm will not have low-volume products to subsidize. It is thus possible that foreign firms are not dumping product B at all; they just have a clearer knowledge of what B costs to make when it does not have to subsidize a low-volume special product like C. An all too common response by the full-line firm is to push even harder on the apparently profitable low-volume items. Their cost system indicates they cannot meet the competitor's low prices on the standard items, and the special items always look very attractive at the margin. A convenient rationale for this action is the all-too-popular adage, "make something that really meets the customer's needs; don't just try to sell the things that are easy to make."

Like most popular aphorisms, this one has enough truth behind it to appear compelling. However, when it is coupled with an accounting system that systematically misallocates costs, it can spell disaster for a firm, like Ajax, that is not even aware it is acting unwisely. The more the low-volume special items are emphasized, the more the indirect costs will grow in the long run. But this growth is charged largely to the higher-volume standard items, which become progressively more unattractive, and the downward spiral of profitability continues.

The symptoms of a seriously flawed cost accounting system have been enumerated by Cooper (1987a). Many of them are present in Ajax:

- Achieved gross margins are not easily explained. Ajax cannot explain its high margins on C or its low margins on B. In reality, costs are misallocated between C and B.
- Customers do not object strongly when prices are increased. Given what it really costs to make C, customers have been getting a tremendous bargain. Thus, what Ajax sees as major price increases the customers see as a reduction in the amount of windfall. Product C is not so great or so unique, it is just dramatically underpriced.
- What appear to be very high-margin products are not attacked by our competitors. If the margins are so good, why don't we have more competition? ABC reveals why competitors are not rushing to offer C. Even with the projected round of additional price hikes, product C will lose over $48 per unit! Ajax is much more likely to see competitors attack A than C.
- Even though the product mix is moving away from apparently lower-margin products toward apparently higher-margin products, overall profitability is declining. For Ajax, the reported margins are an illusion. The reality is that the high-volume standard products have much higher margins than reported and the low-volume special products have much lower margins than reported.

Ajax cannot really mount an effective strategic response to its competitive problems because it is using seriously flawed product profitability information. A classic example of this phenomenon is documented in the series of cases about the Schrader Bellows Division of Scovill Manufacturing Company (Cooper, 1986c). The dismal result for this firm was dismemberment following a hostile takeover made possible by poor stock market performance caused by declining profits. One Schrader Bellows factory produced 2,300 products that all showed up as profitable under their cost accounting system. Only 550 products were profitable once the ABC approach was applied. Virtually all the low-volume special items, which looked very profitable under their modern volume-based coating system, were big losers under activity costing.

Volume-based costing can seriously alter the way a firm looks at its strategic options and the way it assesses the profit impact of its pricing and product emphasis decisions. Activity-based costing can at least clarify the cost dimension of such decisions. Armed with accurate cost information, the firm has a much better chance to construct and implement a viable strategy.

Until preparers and users of management accounting reports come to grips with the problems of volume-based costing systems and begin to provide realistic activity-based cost data, we are aiding and abetting the charge that management accounting is part of the problem in U.S. industry today rather than part of the solution (Johnson, 1987; Kaplan, 1984).

ABC: STRATEGIC TOOL, NOT AN ACCOUNTING SYSTEM

There is very little doubt that volume-based approaches to product costing represent a very serious shortcoming of most management accounting systems today. Approaches that assign large portions of total cost (overhead) using direct labor or machine hour allocation rules are inaccurate and strategically useless in complex product line environments. There is also little doubt that the ABC approach is substantially more accurate in assigning total actual cost to the products that are causing the cost.

But, the superiority of ABC over volume-based costing in assigning current actual overhead to products does not imply that ABC is a strategic panacea or that formal cost accounting systems should be switched over en masse from volume-based rules to activity-based allocation rules.

When considering activity-based costing from the perspective of strategic cost management, ABC is seen as a very useful financial tool of strategic management. But ABC is not necessarily the primary financial tool, or even one of the most important. It is certainly not a management accounting panacea. Furthermore, our experience indicates that the benefits of ABC in product line assessment and activity management can best be achieved by avoiding its formalization as part of a general ledger bookkeeping system. The likelihood of achieving strategic benefits is inversely proportional to the extent the concept is routinized as part of general ledger bookkeeping systems. In the next chapter, we illustrate our arguments with a widely disseminated ABC case study that demonstrates the negative aspects of ABC as much as the positive aspects.

ABC: Three Basic Problems

At least three major problems with ABC as a formal cost accounting system deserve careful consideration before deciding where the ABC concept should fit into the broader context of strategically relevant cost management systems. We mention and briefly illustrate each of these three problems here and then expand more fully on them using a widely cited case study in the next chapter.

Problem 1: A Static Versus Dynamic View of Cost

ABC assigns all of the current manufacturing costs to products without any concern as to whether or not the cost is legitimate in a strategic sense. For example, receiving cost would be assigned to products in proportion to the share of receiving activity each generates. This evaluation is correct in a static sense, but it may be dangerous in a dynamic sense. Receiving, as a step in the value chain, does not add much value, if any, to the end product.

A dynamic view of strategically relevant product cost focuses on reducing or even eliminating all costs that are not value added, such as receiving. In a JIT environment, the receiving cost category is essentially eliminated as components are received directly at the relevant manufacturing work station only as needed; inbound storage and inspection and warehouse handling no longer exist.

Focusing on product costs that incorporate all current expenditure levels can be just as dangerous as using inaccurate cost assignment rules. In addition to assigning current activities to the products that currently consume them, a strategic product costing system must formally acknowledge the need to continually rethink which activities really add value to the customer and how to perform those activities in the most efficient manner. As indicated in exhibit 11–9, only activities in box A should be assigned to products. Activities in box D need to be examined for ways to improve their efficiency and, ultimately, those activities should be moved to box A. Activities in box C should be eliminated. One needs to examine whether the resources devoted to activities in box B can be redeployed in value-adding activities. The ideas contained in exhibit 11–9 give rise to the idea that firms need activity-based management (ABM) rather than activity-based costing systems (Turney, 1992).

Problem 2: Adherence to an Obsolete Distinction
Between Product and Period Costs

Like all general ledger-based accounting systems, ABC is caught up in the distinction between costs that will be inventoried and those that will

EXHIBIT 11–9
Value Engineering the Cost Structure

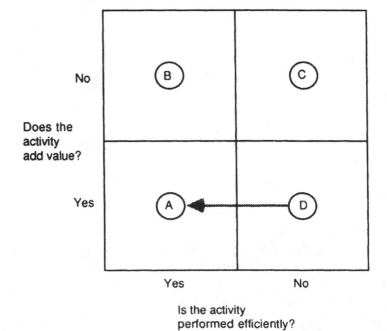

be expensed. From the standpoint of general ledger design it is, of course, absolutely necessary to worry about what is accumulated in the balance sheet in inventory accounts and what is expensed directly. But whatever relevance, if any, this distinction had for managerial purposes has long since gone. In most firms today, strategically relevant portions of product costs are incurred long before the product every reaches the manufacturing stage (e.g., research and development costs) and/or long after it leaves the factory (e.g., marketing and distribution costs). Whatever general ledger bookkeeping system is used, the costs incurred for design, development, selling, distribution, and customer service are very relevant components of product cost for strategic analysis.

In the illustration in this chapter, only conventional product costs are considered, even though cost management issues upstream and downstream from the factory probably have strategic relevance in evaluating individual products or product comparisons. Differences in selling and distribution costs, for example, can outweigh differences in manufacturing cost when considering products intensive in application engineering. Strategic cost management must consider full cost, in the broadest sense of that term, no matter how astutely costs in the manufacturing segment of the value chain are assessed.

Problem 3: Costing Products Through Today's Activity Chain Assumes Today's Strategy

Even when the focus is on full cost versus only manufacturing cost and when the emphasis is on only the value-adding activities versus all current activities, ABC still involves accounting for today's strategy. This assumption is dangerous when extended into tomorrow. This observation is not a criticism as much as it is a recognition of a limitation of any formal accounting system. Such systems necessarily account for today, not tomorrow. Much of strategic analysis and thus strategic cost management involves constantly reevaluating today's competitive positioning in favor of alternatives that would be better adapted to current perceptions of tomorrow's competitive environment.

Whenever a firm decides to change strategic direction, impediments always must be overcome. One important impediment to change is almost always the current accounting system. Accounting systems are typically perceived to be important in how success or failure is measured and thereby important as an indicator of how rewards will be distributed.

Because of the importance attached to accounting systems, major changes to them involve much resistance and anxiety. As a result, major changes occur infrequently. Firms must be very sure that such change is needed before investing the energy to bring it about and thereby using up part of a very scarce resource—the firm's tolerance for major revision to formal management systems.

In this context, a decision to replace one comprehensive general ledger-based product costing system with a different one deserves very careful consideration, even if the alternative seems demonstrably more accurate. Three points are relevant on this concern.

1. The insights from ABC about product profitability can be gleaned from special studies that are conducted outside the books of account. ABC does not necessarily require processing through the general ledger.

2. The insights that ABC can yield are not the kind that imply monthly monitoring. The implications are more long term. These insights thus do not require monthly updating through general ledger closing routines to enhance their significance. That is, an ABC study first done off the books can also be updated periodically in the same way. Annual or semiannual updating is usually a viable time frame for acting upon the new insights.

3. Investing the energy and tolerance for change that are necessary to convert a volume-based product costing system to ABC implies, at least indirectly, a continuing commitment to the current product line strategy. For example, in the illustration in this chapter, changing the general ledger accounting system for the current full product line suggests strongly that the full line strategy is being reaffirmed. But, one possible inference from the new insights revealed in the ABC study might be that the full line strategy is inappropriate. Perhaps concentrating on either the vanilla segment, with a cost leadership focus, or the special segment, with a value-added focus, might be smarter than trying to compete in both segments.

A strategic reassessment based on the insights from an ABC analysis typically will be much more difficult to bring about if the firm is also investing heavily in an accounting system redesign tied to the current product line. We have seen this problem in several major corporations in the past few years. A very useful reassessment of overall product attractiveness resulting from an analytic off-line ABC study does not lead to the implied improvements in strategic positioning. The investment of organizational energy in an accounting system redesign becomes a major barrier to seeing the need to invest organizational energy in the strategic repositioning that the new accounting insights should have fostered.

ABC and ABM are very useful tools for strategic analysis, but trying to lock them into the formal cost accounting system significantly reduces the probability that the insights they yield will be acted upon. The trick is to deemphasize the concept that general ledger systems are useful for strategic product cost analysis. Product costing for strategic product line management should be done off-line and only as frequently as product line decisions are reconsidered. Trying to use transactions bookkeeping systems tied to generally accepted accounting principles for such purposes is ill-conceived.

Directing attention and effort away from the currently prevalent volume-based general ledger product-costing systems that generate dangerously inaccurate monthly cost reports is clearly a step in the right direction. But, replacing them with alternative general ledger product-costing systems is a step in the wrong direction.

The next chapter presents an extended example taken from published case studies about the German electrical products and electronics firm, Siemens, that illustrates our perspective on what is useful about ABC and what is not.

CHAPTER 12

USING AND ABUSING
THE ABC CONCEPT

A Case Study

This chapter is based on our analysis and interpretation of two published case studies dealing with cost accounting and management control issues for the Electric Motor Works (EMW) plant of Siemens AG, one of the largest industrial products firms in Europe. One case appears in Kaplan and Cooper's *Cost Management Systems,* (1990), the other case appears in Anthony, Dearden, and Govindarajan's *Management Control Systems* (1992). We have no information about this situation other than what we have read in the two cases.

Our interpretation of the EMW situation is that, in spite of the very useful insights that emerge from the ABC analysis, it is an example of the negative role ABC can play in strategic cost management when it is seen as an issue in the design of formal cost accounting systems.

We are not aware of any other publicly available case history that illustrates so clearly how the benefits of ABC as a tool for strategic analysis dissipate when ABC is seen instead as an alternative cost accounting system. All three of the major pitfalls of ABC noted in chapter 11 are illustrated in the case.

To set the stage for our analysis, a highly condensed summary of the case studies is shown in exhibits 12–1 through 12–3 and 12–5.

ABC: THE USEFUL NEW INSIGHTS

As long as the product line was fairly simple (200 different products in the mid-1970s) and most products used about the same mix of factory resources, management believed that the conventional product costing system explained in exhibit 12–2 would produce a reasonably accurate assignment of overall factory cost to products. Once the strategy changed, however, between 1985 and 1987, neither of these two condi-

EXHIBIT 12-1
The EMW Situation

The cases are set in mid-1988 in Germany in Siemens' only facility for manufacturing small, low-wattage (0.06 to 18.5 kw) alternating current motors. The plant was originally built in 1937, aggressively expanded and modernized after World War II, and again in the mid-1970s. These motors are sold exclusively through 12 sales branches to a wide range of industrial products firms throughout Europe. These sales branches also sell a wide range of other products produced in other plants in Siemens' Manufacturing Industries Division, a part of the Energy/Automation Group. Siemens uses a complicated transfer pricing rule in the Manufacturing Industries Division between the manufacturing plants and the sales department in order to treat both of them as profit centers. The turnover shown for EMW is the transfer price to the sales branch. Profit for EMW equals transfer price minus factory cost and minus allocated overhead (division, group, and corporate). Profit for the sales department equals actual turnover minus transfer price minus sales and distribution cost and minus allocated overhead.

From the mid-1970s through the mid-1980s sales were cyclical, following the machine tool industry. The factory usually operated well below capacity, with 80% average utilization. The focus in EMW was on standard motors, produced in long runs and shipped from stock. In spite of this focus, about 20% of its production was custom motors. Because competition in standard motors was heavily price based, cost advantage was the key to profitable operations. Over this decade, EMW was never highly profitable on a sustained basis. By the mid-1980s management had concluded that its strategic emphasis on price-based competition for standard motors was never going to pay off because EMW's labor rates were always going to be substantially higher than those of its Eastern Bloc competitors.

EMW's success over the early 1980s in growing its penetration in the much higher-priced custom motors segment led to a formal study that concluded in 1985 that a primary strategic focus on low-volume, custom motors could be feasible. The key to success was perceived to be a "flexible manufacturing" environment designed explicitly for the batch size of one or a very few. Between 1985 and 1987 EMW invested DM 150 million to replace virtually every machine on the shop floor. By 1987 the conversion to flexible manufacturing was complete, with extensive use of numerically controlled machines, robotics, and flexible machining centers. As the factory was reconfigured, the strategic emphasis was changed to custom motors. Of the orders accepted in 1987, 74% were for fewer than 5 motors. But, standard motors still accounted for about 50% of production. From 1981 to 1987 annual

(continued)

EXHIBIT 12–1
The EMW Situation (Continued)

production of standard motors held fairly constant at a little over 300,000 units, while custom motors grew from about 100,000 units a year to more than 300,000. Of the three major European producers of small, low-wattage A/C motors, only Siemens produced both custom and standard motors in large quantities. One of the two major competitors focused primarily on standard motors and one primarily on custom motors.

In 1987, EMW received orders with a sales value close to DM 1 billion but could accept only DM 450 million dollar worth, even while running the factory at 115% of rated capacity. In contrast, the factory had accepted nearly every order it received in 1980 and still operated at far less than capacity. The deutsche mark value of incoming orders each year had virtually tripled over a ten-year period. By strategic intent, the growth in orders was primarily for small quantities of custom motors, each of which could sell for seven to ten times the price of a standard motor. Although orders were strong, 1987 was not a particularly profitable year for EMW. Results were even worse in 1988, with substantial losses reported at midyear in spite of continuing to operate at 115% of rated capacity.

Some production and turnover information is summarized in exhibit 12–5.

---

tions was met any longer. By 1987, the factory was producing more than 10,000 different products, and the mix of factory resources consumed by the standard motors was dramatically different from the mix consumed by custom motors. The resource mix also could vary dramatically across the set of different custom motors. Clearly, the old cost accounting system was inappropriate for the new strategy.

The accounting system was finally changed, as explained in exhibit 12–3, although the changes lagged the change in strategy by more than two years. The new system used the ABC concept and focused on two components within the support-related overhead category, order processing costs and special components processing costs. No other cost categories were deemed to require changes. Order processing costs included bidding, billing, order receiving, and shipping and handling and totaled DM 13.8 million in 1987.

Special components were the items EMW added to a base motor to create a custom motor. In 1987, the factory used 30,000 different special components, ranging from one to more than ten for any one custom motor. Special components processing costs included development, bidding, purchasing, receiving, handling, scheduling, production control, and inspec-

EXHIBIT 12–2
Product Costing at EMW Before 1987

Although the sales and manufacturing strategy had changed dramatically since 1980, the accounting system had not kept pace. Although it had frequently been expanded as the factory expanded, the basic structure of the product cost system was the same in 1987 as it had been when the factory was opened in 1937. Direct material and direct labor were charged directly to the products without significant problems; these two categories averaged 29% and 10% of factory cost, respectively.

Overhead was broken into three categories. Materials-related overhead (receiving and storage) averaged about 2% of factory cost and was assigned in proportion to direct material. Production-related overhead, which was about 33% of factory cost in 1987, included those costs traceable directly to one of the 600 production centers in the factory. Costs of each of these production centers were assigned to the products passing though based on either direct labor hours or machine hours, depending on the labor intensity of the center. The remaining overhead (engineering, tooling, and factory administration) was termed support-related and was allocated arbitrarily to products based on the sum of direct material, direct labor, materials-related overhead, and production-related overhead.

To illustrate the costing system, consider two products, one simple and one complex, for which costs cumulatively for the first four cost categories (materials, labor, materials overhead, and production overhead), are:

	Product A	Product E
The base motor	DM 240	DM 240
Special components:		
Number	1	10
Total cost	DM 24	DM 240

(For this example, the simplifying assumption is made that each of the 10 special components in motor E costs the same DM 24 (through the first four cost categories) as the one special component in motor A.)

For product A, cost for the first four of the cost categories is given as DM 264 (240 + 24). For product E, this subtotal is DM 480 (240 + 240). Under the before system, the fifth cost category, support-related overhead, is allocated at 35% of the sum of the first four categories. Derivation of the 35% number is straightforward: Because the first four categories total 74% of the factory cost (29 + 10 + 2 + 33), the fifth category must equal the remaining 26% (100 − 74).

(continued)

EXHIBIT 12–2
Product Costing at EMW Before 1987 (Continued)

Assigned in proportion to the sum of the first four categories, support-related overhead is thus 35% of that sum (26%/74%).

Product costs for products A and E under the before system thus are:

Product A DM 264 × 1.35 = DM 356 (1 special component)

Product E: DM 480 × 1.35 = DM 648 (10 special components)

For a comparable standard motor with no special components, the product cost under the old system would be DM 324 (DM 240 × 1.35).

---

tion and totaled DM 19.5 million in 1987. Each special component generated a work order each time it was used because the factory practiced Just in Time inventory management for these items. In 1987, the 30,000 different special components generated a total of 325,000 work orders, an average of more than ten production runs during the year for each item.

Clearly, there are major benefits of the ABC perspective in thinking about which orders to accept in situations in which EMW is simply a price taker or in setting prices for custom motors in situations in which EMW has some price flexibility. Exhibit 12–4 presents some direct comparisons of the old and new product costs for the three illustrative products for some of the relevant order sizes.

Exhibit 12–4 makes it clear that one E motor costs more than twice as much to make as the old system showed (DM 1400 versus DM 648). The price for one unit of E must increase dramatically if EMW is to earn the profit margin it was expecting on this product. It is also now clear that standard motors are significantly less expensive than the old system showed. EMW can be more aggressive on price, offering as much as 8% in cuts, and still be as well off as was indicated under the old system.

Obviously, the new product strategy cannot be successfully implemented without accurate product cost information. In this sense, these case studies represent a success story in that the manufacturing and sales managers in Siemens' low-wattage small A/C motors business used a new product-costing system to support their decision to change strategies. This result can be interpreted as a successful example of strategic cost management.

However, as noted earlier, we are not convinced of the success of this

EXHIBIT 12-3
EMW: The ABC System

Because the new ABC costing system involved changes to only two components in the fifth product cost category, support-related overhead, DM 61.2, of the total of DM 94.5 million in 1987, was still allocated in proportion to the sum of the first four categories. The remainder (33.3 million) is now shown in two new categories, order processing (13.8 million) and special components processing (19.5 million).

Order processing cost is assigned equally per customer order. Since 65,625 orders were processed in 1987, the charge is DM 210 per order (13.8 million/65,625). The logic is that each customer order consumes just about the same resources to process, regardless of the composition of the motor or the number of units ordered.

Special components processing is assigned equally for each special component work order processed. The logic is that each work order consumes just about the same resources to process, regardless of the number of items to be produced. The average cost per special component work order is DM 60 (19.5 million/325,000). Each customer order is assigned a cost of DM 60 for each special component in the motor, regardless of the number of motors ordered. Four steps are used to calculate the ABC cost:

1. Costs for the first four categories are the same as in the old system (direct materials, direct labor, materials overhead, production overhead).

2. Apply support-related overhead at 23% of the cost at step 1. This rate was 35% under the old system when the total to be applied was DM 94.5 million. Since the total to be applied now is only DM 61.2 million, the new rate is 23% (61.2/94.5 × 35%)

3. Apply order processing overhead at the rate of DM 210 for each order. As the number of units ordered increases, this cost will decline proportionately per unit. For example, for an order of 100 units, the per unit cost is only DM2; for an order of 1 unit it is DM 210.

4. Apply special components processing overhead at the rate of DM 60 for each special component in the motor being ordered. Thus, for a motor with one special component, the charge is DM 60, and for a motor with 5 special components the charge is DM 300 (DM 60 × 5). This cost will also decline proportionately on a per-unit basis as more than one unit is ordered.

Combining these four steps, the ABC cost for products A, E, and a comparable standard motor are as follows:

(continued)

EXHIBIT 12–3
EMW: The ABC System (Continued)

	Motor A	Motor E	Standard motor
Step 1	DM 264	DM 480	DM 240
Step 2	61	110	55
Step 3	210	210	210
Step 4	60	600	0
Total	DM 595	DM 1400	DM 505

EXHIBIT 12–4
Product Costs for Three Products

		Old Cost	New Cost	Percent Change
Motor A	1 unit	356	595	+ 67
	10 units	356	352	− 1
	100 units	356	328	−8
Motor E	1 unit	648	1,400	+116
	10 units	648	671	+ 4
	100 units	648	598	− 8
Standard motor	100 units	324	297	−8

ABC story, even though we agree that the new insights about product cost are definitely more accurate. As we show in the next section, the situation also can be viewed as illustrating each of the three major strategic pitfalls of ABC mentioned in the previous chapter.

PITFALLS OF THE ABC SYSTEM

Not Enough Attention to Activity Management Relative to Activity Costing

It is not uncommon today to see the statement that ABC can be a precursor to cost management. Measuring the cost of current activities is a start toward focusing on managing those activities more cost effectively or even eliminating those activities that do not add value to the end product. The authors of the Siemens cases suggest, without elaboration, that this situation represents a good example of the way activity costing could be a first step toward activity-based management. Mentioning the distinction between ABC and ABM is one thing, but it is much more difficult to avoid the pitfall of basing management decisions on ABC results that incorporate activity costs that have not been "value-engineered." Apparently, EMW has not avoided this pitfall.

One area in which the activity cost revealed in the ABC study seems inordinately high is the order processing cost of DM 210 per order. For perspective, DM 210 is fully 71% of the complete cost to manufacture a standard motor. It should not cost 71% as much to process the order as it costs to make the motor. In dollar terms, DM 210 was $140 at 1987 conversion rates. This cost is particularly troublesome for single-unit orders. Perhaps the fact that 80% of EMW's business before the mid-1980s was made to stock rather than made to order explains why they were not concerned about how expensive it was for them to process a low-volume order.

In a strategy that focuses on small orders in a factory that has been reconfigured to manufacture short runs cost effectively, it is ironic that the per-unit cost to process small orders is so high. This issue is mentioned in the teaching commentaries, although there is no indication that EMW was doing anything about it.

A second and even more troubling cost management issue in the case does not seem to have caught the attention of management. Specifically, there is no concern in the case about the cost effectiveness of the JIT policy for special components, even though the average special component is used more than ten times each year and processing each accompanying special component work order is very expensive. It seems noteworthy that an item costing DM 29.5 to make costs DM 60 for the work order to make it. Unless the cost of processing special component work orders can be reduced substantially, the tradeoff for these items between made to order and made to stock deserves very careful attention.

For example, for a typical special component that costs DM 29.5 to make and DM 60 to process, the total annual cost, assuming ten uses during the year, is DM 895 ($29.5 \times 10 + 60 \times 10 +$ zero carry cost). Suppose that some of the components are highly likely to be used frequently during the year and that inventory space is already available in the factory at no incremental cost. Space availability is likely because EMW recently switched away from a major make to stock strategy.

How would the cost change if this item were processed less frequently and stored for interim use?

Consider the case of two production runs of 5 units each (instead of 10 runs of 1 unit each). Average inventory would be 2½ units, and peak storage need would be 5 units. The total cost of this option would be:

Manufacturing cost:
Per run: $(29.5 \times 5) + 60 = $ DM 207.5
Per year: $207.5 \times 2 = $ DM 415

Carrying cost (assuming a 25% cost per year for cost of funds and cost of handling—space cost is assumed to be zero), calculated as average inventory times cost per unit times annual cost:
2½ units $\times$ 207.5/5 = 41.5 $\times$ 25%
Carry cost $= 2.5 \times 41.5 \times 0.25 = $ DM 26

Total cost, calculated as manufacturing cost plus carry cost:
DM 415 + DM 26 = DM 441

Compared to the current system, this option represents a saving of DM 454 or 51% (895 − 441). Assuming this system would be possible for one-third of the 30,000 special components used in a year, the saving would be DM 4.5 million, which is equal to the profit EMW earns in a good year.

We must conclude that the EMW situation presents unexploited activity management opportunities that effectively negate any attempt to use the activity-costing results for strategic planning purposes.

The Focus Is Too Narrow

A second problem with using ABC results for strategic planning purposes is that manufacturing cost is only part of the cost picture, yet this area is the sole focus of the EMW cases. In discussing the disappointing operating results in 1987 and 1988, the case notes that manufacturing contribution margins are acceptable at 40% on orders for 5–19 units, but are too low at only 20% on the orders for more than 100 units. Implicit here is the idea that EMW needs more small-volume custom orders and fewer big orders for standard motors.

The problem with this reasoning is that manufacturing is only part of the story in comparing commodity products with custom products. In a commodity-like industry with very little marketing or postpurchase customer service or sales engineering, gross margins of 20% may be acceptable. For example, major industrial paper companies average only 5% of sales for selling, marketing, and sales service costs. These firms also spend very little on research and development. On the other hand, a firm such as Hewlett-Packard in its instruments business can easily exceed 40% of sales in sales engineering, product marketing, distribution, and postpurchase customer service. In a business like theirs, 40% manufacturing margins would be very thin.

To the extent that the sales, marketing, distribution, and customer service needs are very different within EMW for standard motor customers and custom motor customers, no meaningful strategic inferences can be drawn about the two segments by focusing only on manufacturing cost and factory margin differences. We do not know how different the sales and sales support job is for the two segments, but we suspect the difference is substantial. We also suspect that there are substantial differences in costs upstream from the factory for product design and development.

In short, strategic planning for segment emphasis demands analysis of the firm's entire value chain, of which manufacturing in only one part. More astute analysis of the manufacturing costs using ABC is one important part of the story, but it does not provide a sufficient basis for drawing the conclusion that EMW's new strategy is a success. This example clearly illustrates the second major strategic pitfall with ABC—factory cost myopia.

More Concern with Generating Strategic Information Than Using It

The Siemens cases accept the efficacy of EMW's revised strategy, which is a primary focus on small orders for custom motors but with heavy (50%) continuing production of standard motors. In various passages, four reasons are noted for accepting the premise that the new strategy is working:

1. From a business that could do no better than 80% average capacity utilization, EMW achieved 115% of rated capacity for the second consecutive year and was turning away more than one deutsche mark in orders for every deutsche mark it accepted.

2. The order mix had moved substantially toward the new strategy, with 90% of orders for custom motors.

3. The new strategy was in its fourth year in 1988 and management
    was still staying with it.

4. Siemens' top management had given its approval through DM 150
    million of new capital spending in support of the strategy. Balanc-
    ing this observation is the fact that top management of Siemens cut
    off discretionary capital spending to EMW in 1988, partly because
    the flexible manufacturing program was complete and partly be-
    cause returns from the new strategy had not warranted further ca-
    pacity expansion, in spite of order requests running at more than
    200% of turnover.

Also, the basic premise of the case is that Siemens needs to address
management systems issues (transfer pricing) to facilitate implementation of the new strategy. This viewpoint presumes, implicitly, that the
strategy is appropriate. That is, lack of implementation success would
be attributable to faulty management systems only if one rejects the alternative view that the poor results indicate a poor strategy.

THE EMW STRATEGY: A COUNTER PERSPECTIVE

Although the new strategy could not have been successfully implemented without ABC, along with an appropriately designed set of rein-
forcing management systems, it probably could not have been successfully implemented anyway, even with the new cost accounting system
and regardless of the supporting management systems.

Our conclusion about the efficacy of the new strategy stems from the
following observations, all of which are taken directly from the cases or
commentaries. We emphasize that we are introducing no new information here. Rather, we are trying to apply a broad strategic analysis
framework to all the facts and judgments presented, without presuming
the new strategy to be appropriate. Exhibit 2–5 presents additional case
information related to these observations.

We find it hard to conclude the EMW's problem has much to do with
the transfer pricing system when we consider the following observations:

EMW was having its worst year, financially, in a long time (perhaps
    ever) in 1988, in spite of an excellent economy in Europe, a boom-
    ing order backlog, and an operating rate of 115% of rated capacity.

EXHIBIT 12–5
EMW: Turnover and Production Information

Turnover and production history

Fiscal year	Turnover (millions)	Production (1,000 units)	Average selling price
1982	DM 356	404 (80% standard motors)	DM 881
1983	334	351	DM 952
1984	417	473	DM 882
1985	468	519	DM 902
1986	499	550	DM 907
1987	450*	630 (50% standard motors)	DM 714

A breakdown of 1987 turnover

Number of motors in the order	Number of orders accepted	Number of motors	Turnover (millions)	Average selling price	Percent with selling price below cost
1	31,500	31,500	DM 64	DM 2032	1
2–4	17,062	44,100	74	1678	2
5–19	9,188	81,900	108	1319	2
20–99	5,906	195,300	135	691	56
> 100	1,969	277,200	69	249	87
Total	65,625	630,000	DM 450	DM 714	9

*0.9% of Siemens' total turnover

Siemens had withdrawn its support for more capital spending in spite of the huge backlog of potential orders. Top management questioned the return from the new EMW strategy.

Exhibit 12–5 shows that the average selling price for EMW fell more than 20% in 1987 (from DM 908 to DM 714), probably indicating an order mix moving back toward simpler motors and/or larger orders.

EMW is the only large player in Europe trying to maintain a significant presence in both standard and custom motors. We doubt that any small players straddle both segments either.

In spite of the change in product emphasis and the reconfiguration of the factory away from standard items and long runs, standard motors still account for 50% of production volume after four years.

After at least ten years of struggle, EMW still is not able to compete effectively in standard motors, even though they remain half of its volume. Exhibit 12–5 shows that almost 90% of the standard motor orders accepted in 1987 were priced below cost.

In very simplified form, the cases present an overall chronological scenario:

1. The company faces inadequate financial returns.

2. The company concludes its strategy is flawed.

3. The company changes the strategy.

4. Then the company changes the accounting system.

5. The new accounting system is much better adapted to the new strategy.

6. Management systems problems now limit the ability of the company to implement its new strategy effectively.

Although this chronology is not in dispute, as a scenario it fails to capture the strategic richness that can be gleaned from the cases. As a result, this scenario fails to focus management attention on the most appropriate next steps.

THE PLIGHT OF EMW:
AN ALTERNATIVE SCENARIO

We see a much different scenario in the cases. It is plausible that EMW enjoyed a reasonably good strategic position in standard motors in 1980 because of its modern factory, its rich combination of manual and automated technologies, and the market power of its huge parent company. But EMW was not able to keep its large factory busy with standard motors. The underutilization of capacity placed a heavy financial burden on operations. The cases tell us that product costs were set to absorb overhead when operating at the normal level of about 80% utilization. With overhead at 60% of manufacturing cost, the underutilization penalty could be as high as 12% of total cost (0.6 × 0.2). This penalty is a major cost disadvantage in a commodity-like business.

High-priced custom motors looked to management like a good way to earn incremental returns while utilizing the excess capacity. And EMW clearly had the engineering capability to design and build custom motors. But the accounting system was not sophisticated. The extra costs associated with custom motors were assigned across the full product line in proportion to total throughput, so that high-volume standard motors bore much of the brunt. As a result, standard motors showed unrealistically low returns and custom motors showed unrealistically high returns. This discrepancy is the classic cross-subsidization of low-volume special products by high-volume vanilla products in complex production situations that use volume-based product costing systems, as explained and illustrated in chapter 11.

Because of the apparent low margins of standard motors and apparent high margins of custom motors, management continued to gradually move the product mix toward the underpriced custom segment. And the cost impact was continually spread across the full line. When overall results did not show much improvement, management erroneously attributed the problem to the standard motors segment. We know, for example, that the accounting system understated the cost of one typical complex motor, the E motor, by more than 100%.

Management attention focused on EMW's high labor rates relative to Eastern Bloc competitors as a rationale for its inability to compete effectively in the commodity segment. It is possible to see this issue as much more an excuse than a reason. Direct labor was only 10% of factory cost for EMW. With such a low labor cost proportion, wage rate differentials cannot explain very much of product cost differences, particularly when productivity differentials and technology differentials would both favor EMW over the Eastern Bloc. An alternative explanation for the poor reported results for standard motors is the volume-based product costing system coupled with underutilization of capacity.

Once EMW decided to change its primary focus to custom motors, the plight of standard motors continued to deteriorate. Not only was the accounting problem of hidden cross-subsidization still there and growing, but now manufacturing was also a problem. The factory had been reconfigured to the detriment of standard motors. Manufacturing operations were now geared to very small batch sizes. This orientation gave EMW a tremendous advantage in supplying high-quality, complex motors very quickly and cost effectively, but it also meant the factory was no longer designed to be cost effective on long runs of standard motors.

But the story gets worse. EMW next revised the accounting system to eliminate the cross-subsidy problem. Custom motors then carried their full cost and standard motors were not penalized. But, of course, standard motors then had a much more serious problem: the factory was—by design and after great expense—no longer cost effective against the major competitors when running commodity products. And once custom motors began carrying their full cost, it became apparent how expensive they were. This problem was complicated further by the significant cost penalties to custom motors from order processing and special component work order processing that were noted earlier.

At the very high prices EMW had to charge for the one of a kind, complex motors the factory has been designed to produce, the demand was much more limited than when EMW had been substantially underpricing them. The level of incoming orders for complex motors was huge, but most of those orders would not support profitable prices, given the cost structure revealed in the ABC system. Herein lies a major irony in the factory redesign program just completed. At the subsidized prices EMW had been charging for custom motors before adopting the ABC costing system, there was a large and apparently growing market for them. The market seemed large enough to warrant converting EMW's large factory to supply it. After the factory was converted, however, EMW became aware that it was underpricing custom motors. After instituting new pricing levels more commensurate with the ABC costs, the demand apparently was not great enough to fully utilize the large, flexible manufacturing factory. EMW was left, again, with underutilized capacity.

But the story gets even worse. By 1988, it was too late to scale back the newly designed factory to a capacity level more consistent with the demand level that matched the very high prices required by the very high costs. So, in a tactic learned in the early 1980s, EMW began to accept orders that did not fit its strategy but that served to fill up otherwise idle capacity. In the early 1980s, they had accepted custom motors orders outside their standard motors strategy to utilize otherwise idle capacity; in 1988, they accepted standard motors orders that did not fit the custom motors strategy but did fill up idle capacity.

The tactics are identical in reverse, but the stakes were at least DM 150 million higher because of the capital spending program. The results were the same. The capacity level could not be utilized fully by selling only motors that fit the stated strategy. So EMW took on uneconomic orders to fill up the plant, but did not earn an overall return commensurate with the investment. The only difference is that ABC made them more aware of the pricing problem. In the early 1980s they took on custom motor orders at unrealistically low prices, unwittingly. Turnover grew, but not profits. In 1988 they took on standard motor orders at prices they knew were below their costs. Turnover was higher, but not profits.

This scenario just outlined is speculation on our part. But it is fully consistent with the facts presented in the published cases. Furthermore it accounts for the richness and subtlety of the situation in a way that suggests clearly that no amount of fine tuning of transfer pricing systems or organizational interfaces between factory management and sales management is likely to improve EMW's plight.

EMW: THE SCM PERSPECTIVE

The case starts with EMW in a reasonably good strategic position (in standard motors) but handicapped by heavy excess capacity. Management obfuscated the strategy in order to fill the capacity but could not achieve financial success. Seven years and DM 150 million later, the case ended with EMW in a reasonably good strategic position (in custom motors) but still handicapped by heavy excess capacity. As earlier, management again obfuscated the strategy in order to fill the capacity but still could not achieve financial success.

A major irony is that the investment in ABC for product costing did not help EMW's strategic positioning. Rather, it is possible to argue that the ABC accounting system hurt the firm more than it helped. ABC definitely helped in that it corrected for the cross-subsidization that was leading EMW to underprice custom motors. But ABC implicitly sanctioned the full line strategy by accounting for the full line as if custom motors and standard motors were both legitimate business for EMW. ABC accounting lagged the power curve of strategic assessment by sanctioning, implicitly, their current strategy, regardless of that strategy's efficacy.

How could cost analysis have played a more positive role, strategically, in this situation? Suppose EMW had undertaken an ABC analysis in 1985, with a strong ABM component, as a special study not tied to changes in general ledger systems. If the study had preceded the decision to invest DM 150 million to reconfigure the factory, it might have saved EMW that money. The strategic study would have shown that EMW had no real pricing problem with its standard motors business once the cross-subsidy penalty from custom motors and the underutilization penalty were eliminated. A careful assessment also would have shown that to be profitable in one-of-a-kind custom motors, the motors would have to be sold at such high prices that demand probably would not be high enough to keep the large factory any more busy than it already was. Then, if EMW really had felt committed to a factory as large as the current one, the trick would have been to create two focused businesses, one for custom motors and one for standard ones.

Value chain analysis and strategic cost driver analysis could be used to configure each of these businesses based on the differing underlying key success factors. Given that these two businesses are very different from each other, no real purpose would be served by trying to fit both of them into one product costing system. Thus ABC could be seen, in a much more constructive way, as a tool for strategic product line analysis rather than as an alternative cost accounting system. The organizational energy saved by not undertaking a major cost accounting system redesign could instead be invested in more careful strategic repositioning.

It is futile to expect a redesign of general ledger systems to facilitate strategic analysis. Furthermore, the effort expended and the scarce organizational energy consumed in the attempt build commitment to the current strategy—whether or not it deserves that commitment. Management needs to be extremely confident that the current strategy (the new custom motors focus in EMW's case) is sound, because once the effort is invested to better account for it, that strategy is locked in psychologically, for better or worse (for worse in EMW's case).

Whatever system of general ledger accounting EMW chooses, it should not be seen as a strategic management tool. The ongoing task of fine tuning the strategic position in whatever different segments remain should make use of the full range of strategic cost management tools that are appropriate, including ABC, as they are needed.

CHAPTER 13

MEASURING AND ANALYZING COSTS FOR ONE IMPORTANT EXECUTIONAL COST DRIVER—QUALITY

The SCM Perspective

As we argue in chapter 10, cost is caused, or driven, by many factors that are interrelated in complex ways. Understanding cost behavior means understanding the complex interplay of the set of cost drivers at work in any given situation. Each driver involves choices by the firm (e.g., whether to have a large-scale or a small-scale operation) that drive unit cost. In order to facilitate making the right choices, the cost calculus of each driver should be specified. In chapters 11 and 12, we described a methodology for understanding product complexity as a structural cost driver. In this chapter, we discuss cost analysis frameworks for one of the soft executional drivers—the management commitment to total quality. Many firms call this commitment total quality management (TQM). Many other firms believe the concept is best applied without creating yet another formal program with its own TLA (three-letter acronym).

A SURVEY OF TQM LITERATURE

Quality is now widely acknowledged as a key competitive weapon. Firms such as American Express, Ford, General Electric, and Xerox give quality a prominent place in their overall strategy. In this section we present an overview of the four main schools of quality management: Juran, Deming, Crosby, and the Japanese approach.[1] While there are similarities in these approaches, they also differ in several subtle, but

A modified version of this chapter will appear in *Journal of Cost Management*. Reproduced with permission important ways. Both Deming and Juran were mentioned briefly in chapter 2. A short description of all four of the approaches can help to focus our attention on the important cost analysis issues.

Joseph Juran

Juran (along with Armand Feigenbaum) was a pioneer of quality cost analysis in the 1950s. As noted in chapter 2, Juran divided quality costs into four categories: prevention costs, appraisal costs, internal failure costs, and external failure costs (Juran & Gryna, 1970). This method of classifying quality costs is still used widely today. According to Juran, control (i.e., prevention and appraisal) costs increase as quality increases, while failure (internal and external) costs decrease as quality increases. This relationship is shown graphically in chapter 2 with a U-shaped overall quality cost curve that suggests that the objective of a management program should be to find the appropriate level of quality (or number of defects) that minimizes the total cost of quality.

Conceptually and practically, there is no reason why the minimum total cost position in this model could not be 100% quality. That is, nothing in the concept requires optimum quality to be less than perfection. Where the optimum point falls is a function of the shape of the various curves. It always surprises us how many management groups we encounter in the 1990s who firmly believe in the U-shaped quality cost curve: "those last few defects are very expensive to eliminate."

W. Edwards Deming

Deming is perhaps the best-known scholar of quality management. Interestingly, Deming, who is an American, first achieved acceptance of his quality ideas in Japan, where there is now an annual Deming Prize for advancement in precision and dependability of product. It was not until much later that U.S. industry recognized the importance of his ideas, and it was not until 1987 that the Deming Prize was awarded to a U.S. firm (Texas Instruments).

Deming believes that the failure of many U.S. industries to compete in the international marketplace is caused by a lack of attention to quality (Deming, 1982). The fundamental tenet of Deming's view of quality is that the costs of nonconformance and the resulting loss of customer goodwill are so high that evaluation of the costs of quality is unnecessary. He sees attention to measuring quality costs and seeking optimum defect levels as evidence of failure to understand the problem. The proper objective in Deming's view is zero defects. His philosophy is summarized in his fourteen points, listed in exhibit 13–1.

Philip Crosby

Like Deming, Crosby believes that the cost of quality will be minimized by "making it right the first time" (Crosby, 1979). He believes that the objective for any operation should be zero defects.

But, like Juran, Crosby sees a need for measuring quality costs. Crosby divides quality costs into two components: the price of conformance (POC) and the price of nonconformance (PONC). The price of conformance includes all the costs incurred in doing things right the first time. The price of nonconformance includes all the costs of doing things wrong—or, more precisely, the cost of correcting things. According to Crosby, the price of conformance for a well-run company is typically 2–3% of sales, while the price of nonconformance of most firms is closer to 20–25% of sales (Crosby, 1984).

Crosby argues that there is no such thing as a quality problem; there are only engineering, manufacturing, labor, or other problems that cause poor quality. Crosby does not accept Juran's idea of quality cost analysis as a management control tool. As a tool for improving quality, Crosby proposes instead a "quality management maturity grid" (exhibit 13–2) that traces the development of quality thinking, from uncertainty through awakening, enlightenment, and wisdom, to certainty. Senior managers achieve certainty when they begin to consider quality management as an essential part of company operations.

While Crosby and Juran do not agree on quality costing as a management tool, their respective views on the elements of quality cost can be reconciled. Crosby's POC includes Juran's prevention and inspection costs, and his PONC includes Juran's internal and external failure costs. Also, although Crosby rejects the notion of ongoing cost of quality measurement systems, he does believe it is useful for a company to do a quality cost analysis once as it begins a formal quality management program to inform the company about how it stands on the maturity grid.

The Japanese Approach

Obviously, no one quality system is used by all Japanese firms. However, there are several common themes in the well-known Japanese

EXHIBIT 13–1
Fourteen Management Principles of Dr. W. Edwards Deming*
Requirements for a business whose management plans to remain competitive in providing goods and services that will have a market

1. Create constancy of purpose toward improving products and services, allocating resources to provide for long-range needs rather than short-term profitability.

2. Adopt the new philosophy for economic stability by refusing to allow commonly accepted levels of delays, mistakes, defective materials, and defective workmanship.

3. Cease dependence on mass inspection by requiring statistical evidence of built-in quality in both manufacturing and purchasing functions.

4. Reduce the number of suppliers for the same item by eliminating those that do not qualify with evidence of quality: end the practice of awarding business solely on the basis of price.

5. Search continually for problems in the system to constantly improve processes.

6. Institute training on the job.

7. Focus supervision on helping people do a better job: ensure that immediate action is taken on reports of defects, maintenance requirements, poor tools, inadequate operating definitions, or other conditions detrimental to quality.

8. Encourage effective, two-way communication and other means to drive out fear throughout the organization and help people to work together for the aim of the system.

9. Break down barriers between departments by encouraging teamwork, combining the efforts of people from different areas such as research, design, sales, and production.

10. Eliminate use of numerical goals, posters, and slogans for the work force that ask for new levels of productivity without providing methods.

11. Continually improve quality and productivity. Eliminate numerical quotas.

12. Remove barriers that inhibit the worker's right to pride of workmanship.

13. Institute a vigorous program of education and self-improvement.

14. Define top management's permanent commitment to quality and productivity and its obligation to implement all of these principles.

*As summarized by Process Management Institute, Inc.

EXHIBIT 13–2
Crosby's Quality Management Maturity Grid

Quality Management Maturity Grid

Rater		Unit		
Measurement Category	Stage I: Uncertainty	Stage II: Awakening	Stage III: Enlightenment	Stage IV: Wisdom	Stage V: Certainty
Management understanding and attitude	No comprehension of quality as a management tool. Tend to blame quality department for quality problems	Recognizing that quality management may be of value but not willing to provide money or time to make it all happen	While going through quality improvement program, learn more about quality management becoming supportive and helpful	Participating. Understand absolution of quality management. Recognize their personal role in continuing emphasis	Consider quality management an essential part of company system
Quality organization status	Quality is hidden in manufacturing or engineering departments. Inspection probably not part of organization. Emphasis on appraisal and sorting	A strong quality leader is appointed, but main emphasis is still on appraisal and moving the product. Still part of manufacturing or other department	Quality department reports to top management. All appraisal is incorporated and manager has a role in the management of the company	Quality manager is an officer of company. Effective status reporting and preventive action. Involved with consumer affairs and special assignments	Quality manager on board of directors. Prevention is main concern. Quality is a thought leader

(continued on next page)

Source: Philip Crosby, *Quality Is Free* (New York: McGraw-Hill, 1979), pp. 38–39. Reproduced with permission of McGraw-Hill.

EXHIBIT 13–2
Crosby's Quality Management Maturity Grid (Continued)

Quality Management Maturity Grid

Unit

Measurement Category	Stage I: Uncertainty	Stage II: Awakening	Stage III: Enlightenment	Stage IV: Wisdom	Stage V: Certainty
Problem handling	Problems are fought as they occur. No resolution. Inadequate definition, lots of yelling and accusations	Teams are set up to attack major problems. Long-range solutions are not solicited	Corrective action communication established. Problems are faced openly and resolved in an orderly way	Problems are identified early in their development. All functions are open to suggestion and improvement	Except in the most unusual cases, problems are prevented
Cost of quality as percent of sales	Reported unknown; actual 20%	Reported 3%; actual 18%	Reported 8%; actual 12%	Reported 6.5%; actual 8%	Reported 2.5%; actual 2.5%
Quality improvement actions	No organized activities. No understanding of such activities	Trying obvious motivational short-range efforts	Implementation of the fourteen-step program with thorough understanding and establishment of each step	Continuing the fourteen-step program and starting "make certain"	Quality improvement is a normal and continued activity
Summation of company quality posture	"We don't know why we have problems with quality"	"Is it absolutely necessary to always have problems with quality?"	"Through management commitment and quality improvement, we are identifying and resolving our problems"	"Defect prevention is a routine part of our operation"	"We know why we do not have problems with quality"

quality programs. Charles Fine describes the Japanese approach in the following way:

> Briefly described, the ultimate objective of Japanese quality management is to improve the quality of life for producers, consumers and investors. The Japanese define quality as uniformity around the target, and their goal is continual improvement toward perfection. The Japanese use cost of quality similarly to Crosby—for directing action, not as a goal in itself.
>
> The Japanese allocate responsibility for quality management among all employees. The workers are primarily responsible for maintaining the system although they have some responsibility for improving it. Higher up the ladder, managers do less maintaining and more improving. At the highest levels, the emphasis is on breakthrough.
>
> There are a number of now-familiar concepts associated with Japanese quality management. These include commitment to improvement and perfection, insistence on compliance, correcting one's own errors, and 100 percent quality checks. Various practices facilitate quality management in Japanese corporations—small lot sizes, minimal work-in-process inventory, housekeeping, daily machine checking, and quality circles. (Fine, 1985)

Continuing this metaphor, the basic notions of the Japanese approach are that quality is a journey rather than a destination and that quality enhancement is a fundamental way of life, not a business target.

Exhibit 13–3 summarizes the important features of each of the approaches described previously. While differences exist, the programs suggested by Juran, Deming, Crosby, and others have common themes that we collectively describe using the familiar catch-phrase total quality management.

TRADITIONAL VIEWS: PHASE I THINKING ABOUT QUALITY AND COST

The characteristics of TQM can be best understood by contrasting it with traditional views on quality as typified by General Motors cars in the 1970s, the airline industry in the 1980s, or the forest products industry in the 1990s. Exhibit 13–4 contains the key elements of TQM versus the traditional approaches to quality.

EXHIBIT 13-3
Summary of Approaches to Quality

	Deming	Juran	Crosby	Japanese
Definition of quality	Conformance to specs	Conformance to specs	Conformance to specs	Uniformity around target
Why worry about quality?	Competitive position	Profits/quality of life	Profits	Quality of life
Goal of program	Improve competitive position	Decrease cost of quality (COQ)	Decrease costs	Continual improvement
Quality of goal	Zero defects	Minimize COQ	Zero defects	Zero defects
How to select projects	Pareto analysis defects	Cost analysis	Cost analysis	Cost analysis
How to measure improvement	Direct measurement	COQ data	COQ data and direct measurement maturity grid	Direct measurement
Role of quality control department	Low	Extensive	Moderate	Low
Role of top management	Leadership, participation	Leadership, participation	Must stress zero defects	Breakthroughs and improvements
Role of workers	Maintenance and improvement	Moderate	Moderate	Maintenance and improvement
COQ emphasis	None	High	Moderate	Low
Statistical analysis	High use	For lower management	Mixed	High use
Cultural changes required	Great change required; participative management; need great threat	Little change required; fits traditional culture	New quality attitude; fits traditional culture	Great change required; participative management; need grave threat
Managing the transition state	No guidance, but much needed	No guidance, but little needed	Excellent treatment; classic example	No guidance, but much needed
Decision	Optimize direct measurement of quality (DMOQ) zero defects	Minimize COQ	COQ for management attention; DMOQ for implementation zero defects	Optimize DMOQ; zero defects

Adapted from Charles Fine (1985)

EXHIBIT 13-4
Contrasting Quality Paradigms:
Traditional Views on Quality Versus Total Quality Management

Traditional Paradigm	TQM Paradigm
RESPONSIBILITY FOR QUALITY	
Workers are responsible for poor quality	Everyone is responsible for poor quality
Quality problems start in operations	The majority of the quality problems start long before the operations stage
Inspect quality in	Build quality in
After-the-fact inspection	Quality at the source
Quality inspectors are the gatekeepers of quality reliability	Operators are responsible for quality
Quality control department has large staff	Quality control department has small staff
The focus of the quality control department is to reject poor quality output	The focus of quality control department is to monitor and facilitate the process
Managers and engineers have the expertise; workers serve their needs	Workers have the expertise; managers and engineers serve their needs
LINKAGES WITH SUPPLIERS	
Procure from multiple suppliers	Procure from a single supplier
Acceptance sampling of inputs at point of receipt	Certify suppliers who can deliver right quantity, right quality, and on time
	No incoming inspection
NEW PRODUCT /SERVICE DEVELOPMENT	
Separate designers from operations	Use teams with operations, marketing, and designers
Design for performance (with more parts, more features) not to facilitate operations	Design for performance and ease of processing
OVERALL QUALITY GOAL	
Zero defects is not practical	Zero defects is the goal
Mistakes are inevitable and have to be inspected out	Mistakes are opportunities to learn and become perfect
It costs too much money to make defect-free products	Quality is free
A reasonable tradeoff is the key	Perfection is the key; perfection is a journey, not a destination

Responsibility for Quality

According to the traditional paradigm, quality problems start in operations; workers primarily are responsible for poor quality. The best way to control quality, therefore, is to inspect it in. This approach requires a large quality control department whose job is to inspect the output and certify that it meets customer specifications. Here, an adversarial relationship typically develops between the operations personnel, whose objective is to maximize output, and the quality control staff, whose objective is to monitor output quality. Historically, many U.S. companies have placed a higher priority on the level of output than on quality, because customers did not demand defect-free products. The environment has drastically changed during the last decade. Customers now demand high quality, especially since many companies have been able to provide top quality at competitive prices.

According to TQM, responsibility for quality should be shared by everyone in the organization; most of the quality problems start long before the operations stage begins. Edwards Deming argues that a process can be separated into two parts—the system, which is under the control of management, and the workers, who are under their own control. Based on his experience, Deming has found that 85% of quality problems can be attributed to faulty systems and only 15% to workers. The system could be faulty for several reasons: designing a difficult-to-execute operation, procuring inferior inputs, providing inadequate equipment maintenance, having poor working conditions, and applying excessive pressure to maximize output, just to name a few. Because the system is designed by management, quality is primarily a management responsibility.

Under TQM, the overriding consideration is to build quality into the output rather than to inspect quality into the output. Errors should be detected and corrected at the source. Quality at the source implies that the worker should be held responsible for his or her work and should not pass defective work downstream. Instead of appointing quality inspectors to locate the defects that workers may have created, the workers in a TQM operation are their own inspectors. This philosophy also implies a fundamental change in the role of the quality control department—moving away from inspection and toward facilitation. Instead of inspecting quality at the output stage, the quality control staff should monitor the process and facilitate increasing the workers' ability to do things right the first time.

Linkages with Suppliers

The traditional view argues that obtaining inputs from several suppliers will give the firm bargaining leverage. Suppliers can be pitted against each other and the resulting competition among suppliers will lead to lower input prices.

The problem with the traditional view is that quality control becomes extremely difficult if there are numerous suppliers. If the firm starts with inferior quality inputs, it can prove to be very costly even if the process is in control. For instance, in 1984, the Ford Motor Company stopped production of the Tempo and Topaz models in four plants because of a faulty engine part purchased from an outside supplier. Ford thus lost the opportunity to produce about 2,000 cars each day once production was stopped.

Under TQM, supplier selection is far more influenced by quality and delivery dependability than by price alone. The firm certifies a few suppliers who can deliver defect-free inputs on time at a reasonable price. Typically, the firm will procure most of its requirements for each input item from a single supplier out of the list of certified suppliers. Developing long-term relationships with a single supplier pays off both in terms of higher quality and lower price over time. Between 1980 and 1985 Caterpillar reduced the number of drill bit suppliers from 24 to 3 and cut drill bits cost by 40%.

Sourcing from a single supplier results in higher quality for two reasons: (1) the company views the supplier as an integral part of its operations and has the time and the motivation to work with the supplier to improve supplier process quality; (2) the supplier, for whom the company's business is very significant, is motivated to produce and ship small lots with exact specifications and to work with the buyer to improve process quality.

In addition to higher quality, single sourcing can result in lower costs, for several reasons: (1) if the firm is confident of the supplier's process quality, the inputs can bypass incoming inspection and save inspection costs; (2) the firm can save the costs of poor quality downstream that are the direct result of processing inferior quality inputs; (3) given the significant purchasing volume from the company, the supplier can enjoy longer runs and the resulting benefits of scale and experience.

The single-sourcing concept suffers from the potential risk of a breakdown in supply for reasons such as strikes, machine breakdowns, or natural disasters. However, concerns regarding supplier risk typically are overstated. First, though the firm procures most inputs from the single supplier, one or two backup suppliers usually are qualified to supply and get an occasional order to keep the channel open. Second, the firm faces similar risks every day within its own operations because the downstream stages are completely dependent on the upstream stages.

The Development Stage

Companies operating under the traditional view separate designers from operations personnel. The charter for designers is to conceive new products and services that have high customer appeal. The designers are instructed not to be constrained by the current operations capabilities. The usual result of this approach too often is elegant designs that are very difficult to implement. Many quality experts insist that half of quality problems arise at the design stage. It is difficult to produce a product reliably if it has been designed for performance (more parts or more features) but is not designed with consideration of ease of manufacture.

According to TQM, the best way to assure quality is to get operations managers and designers closely involved in developing new products and services. If the designers thoroughly understand the operations process, they are more likely to create designs that not only have high customer acceptance but also fit the firm's operations capability.

Overall Quality Goal

The traditional paradigm argues that mistakes are inevitable and that it is too expensive to rectify all the defects. In contrast, TQM takes the position that zero defects should be the goal. The firm should analyze the causes of all errors and take actions to remedy them.

Exhibit 13–5 presents the conflicting viewpoints on the optimal number of defects. According to the traditional view, the lowest cost is attained at some nonzero level of defects. Proponents of this view argue that the cost of removing errors increases as more and more errors are detected and fewer errors remain. The last errors are the most expensive to detect and correct.

In sharp contrast, TQM maintains that the lowest cost is attained at zero defects. Supporters of this view reason that even though errors are numerous, it takes no more dollars to rectify the last error as compared to the first. Hence, the total cost keeps declining until the last error is removed. In this sense, TQM advocates argue that quality is free.

EXHIBIT 13–5
Contrasting Views on the Optimum Number of Defects

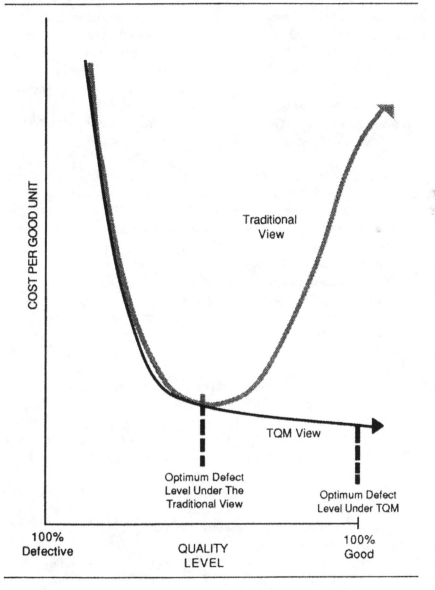

Contrasting Cost Management Paradigms

More and more companies are convinced that shifting from the tradi-tional quality philosophy to TQM is essential for success. Such a shift requires fundamental changes in management and worker attitudes to-ward quality. Far from facilitating this change, traditional cost account-ing systems can be a great hindrance to implementing TQM. The serious shortcomings of traditional cost accounting can be best understood by contrasting it with strategic cost management. Such a comparison is pre-sented in exhibit 13–6. Several points are noteworthy:

- Standard cost systems usually institutionalize waste such as scrap and rework by having normal allowances for them. The cost of the defective units are allocated to good units based on elaborate cost procedures. This practice of normal allowance for waste panders to the traditional views on quality that it is too expensive to rectify all the defects. In total quality management, on the other hand, there is no such thing as allowable waste.
- In a traditional system, overhead variances are used to evaluate performance. Overhead variance analysis encourages managers to maximize production volume—at the expense of quality—as a way to absorb overhead costs and avoid unfavorable vari-ances.
- Traditional systems highlight raw material price variances and pe-nalize managers for unfavorable price variances. This bias again reflects the traditional view on quality—source raw materials from a large number of suppliers; actively encourage competition among suppliers to lead to lower input prices. This view is detri-mental to firm profitability.
- Traditional systems do not directly reward nonfinancial measures of quality, such as parts-per-million defect rates, first-pass yields, on-time delivery, and shorter cycle time.
- Traditional systems emphasize meeting the standard costs. A reg-ularly exceeded standard is viewed as not tough enough. Under TQM, the emphasis is on continual improvement (*kaizen*).

In the next section, we describe in more detail the cost analysis framework that we believe is most helpful as companies work to shift from traditional views on quality to TQM.

EXHIBIT 13-6
Contrasting Cost Management Paradigms:
Traditional Cost Management Versus Strategic Cost Management

Traditional Cost Management	Strategic Cost Management
Standard cost system with normal allowance for scrap, waste, rework; zero defect standard is not practical	No allowance for scrap, waste, rework; zero defect is the concept
Overhead variance analysis; maximize production volume (not quality) to absorb overhead	Overhead absorption is not the key; standard costs and variance analysis are deemphasized, in general
Variance analysis on raw material price; procure from multiple suppliers to avoid unfavorable price variance; low price/low-quality raw materials	No control on raw material price; certify vendors who can deliver right quantity, right quality, and on time.
No emphasis on nonfinancial performance measures	Heavy use of nonfinancial measures (parts-per-million defects, percentage yields, scrap, unscheduled machine down times, first-pass yields, number of employee suggestions)
No tracking of customer acceptance	Systematic tracking of customer acceptance (customer complaints, order lead time, on-time delivery, incidence of failures in customers' locations)
No cost of quality analysis	Quality costing as a diagnostic and management control tool

CONTROL PHILOSOPHY

The goal is to be in the top tier of the reference group	The goal is *kaizen*
The annual target is to meet the standards	Industry norms set the floor
Standards are to be met, not exceeded	The annual target is to beat last year's performance
Standards are tough but attainable	Try to beat this year's target (continual improvements)
A regularly exceeded standard is not tough enough	Each achievement level sets a new floor for future achievement

QUALITY COSTING METHODOLOGY:
PHASE II THINKING

Cost of quality (COQ) analysis aggregates all the costs to the company of doing things wrong by not conforming to specifications. COQ is a comprehensive financial measure of conformance quality. COQ can be calculated for individual locations, individual business units, or for the entire firm. This framework attempts to put dollar figures on all the costs that are attributable to a nonconforming operation. As noted earlier, costs a company incurs to secure better quality can be grouped into four categories:

1. *Preventions costs:* The sum of all the costs associated with actions taken to plan the process to ensure that defects do not occur. For example, designing a defect-free manufacturing process, stable product design, employee training and development, quality circles, preventive maintenance, and the cost of managing supplier relations to increase the quality of raw inputs received.

2. *Appraisal costs:* Those costs associated with measuring the level of quality attained by the system, or, in other words, costs associated with inspecting to ensure that customer requirements are met. For example, prototype inspection and testing, receiving inspection and testing, in-process inspection, and quality audits of finished outputs.

3. *Internal failure costs:* Those costs incurred to rectify defective output before it reaches the customer. For example, scrap, rework, repair, redesign, reinspection of rework, downtime due to defects, and opportunity cost of lost sales caused by having fewer units of product to sell.

4. *External failure costs:* Those costs associated with delivering defective output to the customer. For example, warranty adjustments, investigation of defects, returns, recalls, liability suits, and loss of customer goodwill.

Exhibit 13–7 gives more extensive lists of the elements of each of the four categories.

Not all quality costs fit neatly into one or another of these categories. For example, the cost of inspecting raw material might be viewed as an appraisal cost (looking for defects) or as a prevention cost (preventing

EXHIBIT 13–7
Components of the Four Quality Cost Categories

PREVENTION COSTS	APPRAISAL COSTS
Receiving inspection	Quality engineering
In-process inspection	Quality planning
Laboratory inspection	Design and development of quality equipment
Outside laboratory endorsements	Design verification and review
Set up for testing	Quality training
Maintenance of test equipment	Quality improvement projects
Quality audits	Quality data gathering, analysis, and
Calibration of quality equipment	reporting
Maintenance of production equipment	Statistical process control
	Other process control activities used
	to prevent defects
	Cost accounting for production variances

EXTERNAL FAILURE COSTS	INTERNAL FAILURE COSTS
Warranty adjustments	Scrap
Repairs	Rework
Customer service	Reinspection of rework
Returned goods	Downgrading because of defects
Returned repaired goods	Losses caused by vendor scrap
Investigation of defects	Downtime caused by defects
Product recalls	Failure analysis
Product liability suits	
Lost revenue from customer "bad will" (an opportunity cost)	

defective raw materials from fouling the production process). In such cases, the allocation of costs to one category or another is somewhat arbitrary. As long as the company uses a consistent basis to classify the costs, trends over time in the categories can provide powerful insights.

Exhibit 13–8 presents the quality costs for a disguised manufacturing company, ABC Corporation, over an eight-year period. The example is adapted from an actual case history. Based on the experience of ABC Corporation and the quality cost studies completed by other companies, the following two general conclusions emerge:

1. *Cost of quality is a big opportunity.* When bad quality represents a significant cost item (25% of the total cost for ABC Corporation),

EXHIBIT 13–8
An Illustrative Example of Cost of Quality Analysis for ABC Corporation

Quality Cost Category	1982 (in thousands)	1984 (in thousands)	1986 (in thousands)	1988 (in thousands)
Prevention	$ 200	$ 400	$ 600	$ 800
Appraisal	400	800	800	400
Internal failure	200	2,400	1,600	600
External failure	4,000	800	400	200
Total	$ 4,800	$4,400	$3,400	$ 2,000
Total manufacturing cost	$20,000			$25,000
Total quality cost (TQC) as a percentage of total cost	25%			8%

quality management represents the most significant opportunity for improved profitability.

2. *Firms spend quality dollars in the wrong place.* Companies spend far more on internal and external failure costs than on prevention and appraisal costs, and more on appraisal than on prevention. This was true for ABC Corporation in 1982. In companies where TQC is in the range of 25% of sales, category 4 is usually the largest. When TQC is in the 5% range, category 1 is usually the largest.

Casting the Quality Net

One major issue in COQ analysis involves how broadly or narrowly to define quality costs. This decision, in many cases, is largely subjective. For example, no one would argue that the salary of a quality inspector is a quality cost. But what about the salary of an assembler who also inspects his own work before passing it on to the next stage of assembly? How much of his salary should be attributed to quality costs and how much to manufacturing costs? Since it is arguable that an assembler puts quality into the product while he is assembling (by doing it right the first time), perhaps his whole salary should be considered a quality cost. Or perhaps we should say that quality, in this case, is a free byproduct of the manufacturing process. There is no definitive answer to this dilemma. The subtlety and difficulty of obtaining meaningful COQ information must be considered, item by item, in doing cost-of-quality analysis.

The case of an automobile parts manufacturer is illustrative. To assemble a particular part, each unit passed through several departments (e.g., tooling, heating, grinding, assembly) before reaching the inspection department. The plant's accounting system recorded the inspection department as the only quality cost in the manufacturing process. But each department was doing some inspection and reworking before allowing parts to leave the department. In order to correctly measure the total quality cost for the plant it was necessary to determine how much time was spent in each department on inspection and repair. Workers within a department were reluctant to reveal how much time they spent on inspection and repair because they were supposed to be able to perform the task properly in the first place, without rework. As a result, it eventually became necessary to use a stopwatch to time workers on the amount of time spent on assembly versus repair. Needless to say, the total quality cost for the plant was much higher than the cost accounting system suggested.

This example illustrates another important point. After the quality costs for each department had been collected, it became clear that a few departments were incurring well-above-average quality costs (see exhibit 13–9). This gave plant management the opportunity to achieve substantial quality cost reductions quickly and simply by concentrating efforts on these departments.

Interaction Among the Four Categories

Spending money on prevention can result in more than off-setting cost savings on the other categories. It is possible to maintain or improve quality while, at the same time, dramatically lowering quality costs. For ABC Corporation in exhibit 13–8, as product quality increased over the eight years, total quality costs declined by 60%. The firm achieved this by consciously changing the mix of prevention, appraisal, and failure costs. Prevention and appraisal costs doubled, while internal and external failure costs declined by over 80%.

The implication is that improving quality by spending more on upstream activities (prevention costs) is a good investment for any organization. One rule of thumb in this area is that for every dollar the firm

EXHIBIT 13–9
Quality Cost Broken Down by the Departments Where It Is Incurred
(Isolating the High-Cost Departments)

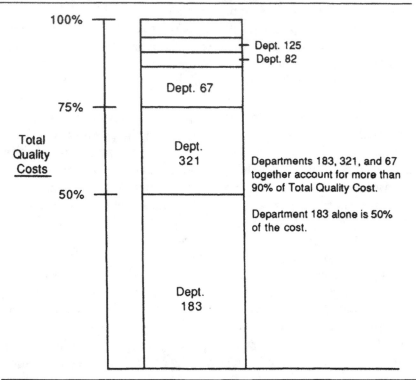

spends on prevention, it can eventually save ten dollars in appraisal and failure costs.

The impact of investing upstream can yield benefits over several years, but there is a time lag between expenditures on prevention and the resulting decrease in failure costs. When ABC Corporation doubled prevention costs in 1984, there was no immediate reduction in downstream costs. This lag suggests that when changing the mix, management must be prepared to see quality costs increase before they decrease.

Companies initiating TQM should anticipate interactions among the four categories of quality costs. As ABC Corporation doubled appraisal costs in 1984, the internal failure costs increased dramatically but the external failure costs decreased even more dramatically. This relationship makes sense. The improved inspection system caused more defects to be detected before reaching the customer. Management should not be surprised to see repair and rework departments exceeding their budgets as a result of increased appraisal spending. Similarly, warranty and customer returns costs should show a favorable trend. These trends could, of course, be anticipated in setting budgets during a period of changing the quality cost mix.

The Model Plant: Zero Defects, Near-Zero Quality Costs

A common theme among the four classes of quality costs is that they each have substantial fixed cost components. That is, the marginal cost of the last defective unit of output is extremely high. Consider the cost of quality of an operation that had zero defects. Because all the output from such a process would be defect-free, the internal and external failure costs would be near zero. No output would be returned by customers, none would need to be reworked, and none would be discarded as waste. It is also conceivable that appraisal costs would be zero. Because all output conforms to specifications, there is no point in inspecting for defects. The only quality costs of a zero-defect operation, therefore, would be the prevention costs incurred in designing the process to be defect-free in the first place and the cost of maintaining the defect-free performance. Fixed costs of appraisal and failure largely would be eliminated. It is the high fixed cost component to quality that leads Crosby and Deming to conclude that the only legitimate goal of quality management is zero defects. If an operation could achieve zero defects, and if, as a result, most of the fixed failure and appraisal costs could be avoided, then the total cost of quality would certainly be very low.

Conventional Reporting as a Barrier to TQM

Conventional reporting formats can be a barrier to TQM initiatives, whereas COQ reporting can help TQM. Conventional reports often discourage TQM efforts because any additional costs incurred in prevention appear immediately on a manager's performance report but the resulting benefits, such as a reduction in external failure, are not fully quantified and therefore are not recognized. For ABC Corporation, a manager's performance report in the conventional framework would report the total prevention, appraisal, and internal failure costs. These costs amounted to $800,000 in 1982 and they dramatically increased to $3,600,000 in 1984. This growth might imply an adverse performance, whereas COQ reporting tells us a very different story. The big gain is in external failure cost, most of which is an opportunity cost that does not show up in conventional reports.

One cautionary note should be offered about quality cost reduction. Quality costs, like many other costs, have the frustrating characteristic of being variable on the way up but fixed on the way down. That it, it is not as easy as one might think to reduce quality costs. We may be able to reduce the level of defective output by 25%, but that improvement may not enable us to reduce the rework department work force by 25%. Reducing that department requires a conscious management decision to scale back or even eliminate the function.

Just as quality costs will not disappear right away, quality revenues will not appear immediately. It is not always the case that customers are anxious to get better quality. Many successful firms have built up, over time, an infrastructure for dealing with the bad quality they receive from suppliers, such as raw material inspection systems or more sophisticated handling equipment. Because much of this infrastructure is a fixed cost, such a customer may find little immediate advantage in a supplier's higher conformance input. In addition, a customer who uses multiple sources of supply may find no advantage—indeed, there may be a disadvantage in the short term—in a higher-quality product offered by only one supplier. It may be that the industry leaders are those firms that have best learned how to neutralize the bad quality they are receiving. Thus, a supplier who begins to offer better quality may, strangely, be better able to sell to the less-successful firms that have not figured out how to offset bad incoming quality.

COQ Reporting

Because the impact of investments upstream yields benefits over several years, it is often sufficient to do quality reporting once a year. By preparing a COQ report once a year, the firm can keep the pressure on managers and workers to continually improve performance toward the ideal goal of zero defects.

COQ measurement cannot be the sole basis for facilitating TQM efforts. It needs to be supplemented with specific and timely feedback on nonfinancial measures of quality, as discussed in chapter 9. Some examples are:

Suppliers

- Number and frequency of defective units delivered, by each supplier.
- Number and frequency of late deliveries, by each supplier.

Product design

- Number of parts in a product.
- Percentage of common versus unique parts in a product.

Production process

- Percentage yields (good units to total units). This ratio is a measure of quality at the output stage and does not necessarily measure the firm's efforts at prevention.
- First-pass yields (percentage of units finished without any re-work). This measure reflects the results of the firm's efforts at prevention.
- Scrap.
- Rework.
- Unscheduled machine breakdowns.
- Number and duration of times the production and delivery schedules were not met.
- Number of employee suggestions. (General Motors averages 4 suggestions per employee per year, while Toyota averages 61.)

Marketing

- Number of customer complaints.
- Level of customer satisfaction by administering questionnaires to customers.
- Warranty claims.
- Field service expenses.
- Number and frequency of product returns.

There are two major advantages with these nonfinancial measures: most of them can be reported on an almost real-time basis, and corrective actions on these measures can be initiated almost immediately. Thus, reporting performance on nonfinancial measures is essential to provide continuous feedback to managers and workers in their pursuit of better quality. We view both COQ reporting and the related nonfinancial measures as providing useful information. COQ reporting provides the big picture, whereas the nonfinancial measures give the ongoing, actionable feedback on the implementation of TQM.

COST OF QUALITY ANALYSIS: PHASE III THINKING

There are several schools of thought on measuring quality costs that range from belief in regular cost of quality quantification and monitoring, at one end of the spectrum, to strict attention to zero defects but no attention to cost measurement at the other end. Among all these views, however, there are several common themes:

Poor quality costs far more than is typically realized by management.

Most firms spend on quality in the wrong places (fix it rather than do it right the first time).

Spending on prevention reduces the need for inspection and can potentially eliminate internal and external failure costs.

Large cost savings or revenue opportunities exist in creating customer goodwill by consistently providing conforming products.

Top management must be committed to and accept full responsibility for quality if quality programs are to be effective.

Conventional management accounting (standard costs, overhead variance analysis, analysis of raw material price variances, etc.) is a great barrier in implementing TQM.

There are three possible approaches to developing and using management accounting systems in support of TQM (exhibit 13–10). These approaches roughly correspond to the recommendations of Deming, Crosby, and Juran. A company adopting TQM for the first time might benefit by starting with Juran's approach, which calls for an explicit quantification of quality costs (the third approach in exhibit 13–10). The ultimate goal should be to make quality a part of the company's culture and way of life so that quality cost measurements become unnecessary (the Deming approach).

Some firms that have experimented with COQA (cost of quality analysis) reporting—such as Texas Instruments and Florida Power and Light—have decided that formalized reporting requirements are not an aid to enhanced quality. But for firms starting on TQM programs, we

EXHIBIT 13–10
Three Possible Management Accounting Approaches

Proponent	Approach	Role for Management Accountants
		Low
Deming	I. Don't do quality costing analysis. Just spend the money "upstream" to make the product "right"	↑
Crosby	II. Do a COQA as a "special" study (to assess the stage of quality management). Do not use this as a management tool on an ongoing basis by preparing periodic QC reports.	
Juran	III. Prepare quality costing reports on a periodic basis (say, once a year) as a management control tool.	↓
		High

believe the benefits of formal cost reporting are sufficiently important to warrant accepting some risk that the reporting engenders "game playing" that hinders the quality enhancement effort. We believe this risk can be managed.

As a firm's quality management program develops, the approach to COQ reporting can take several different forms. Four different approaches to the controllership role in TQM are:

1. COQA as a regular management reporting and control tool (per Juran's POC/PONC tradeoff).

2. Focus on PONC reduction, including opportunity losses.

3. Focus on nonfinancial, hard science production information to monitor TQM progress.

    a. Input measures—statistical process control.

    b. Output measures of conformance.

In the first approach, formal COQ reporting continues as a regular control tool. This strategy was applied by Ford throughout most of the 1980s and by Texas Instruments until about 1990. This approach also has been followed by Formosa Plastics, one of the largest Taiwanese manufacturing firms.

The second approach assumes that conformance costs (POC, in Crosby's terminology) will continue at a high level and will be managed via budgets and programmatic nonfinancial improvement indicators.

If POC spending remains consistently high, the reporting focus can switch to nonconformance costs (PONC, in Crosby's terminology), with specific inclusion of the opportunity cost of bad quality. The goal becomes a steady reduction in PONC toward a zero level. In 1992, many companies with a strong TQM commitment, such as Xerox, Westinghouse, and the Tennant Company, were following this approach.

Approach 3a deemphasizes formal COQ cost reporting systems in favor of formal nonfinancial reporting with a heavy emphasis on continuously improving quality in operations. One name for this approach is statistical process control (SPC). Notable examples of the success of this approach are Daishowa Paper Company and the Materials and Controls Group in Texas Instruments.

Finally, approach 3b also deemphasizes cost reporting in favor of nonfinancial measures, but the focus here is on output measures rather than input measures. Motorola's well-known Six Sigma program for customer-reported defects in its integrated circuits division is a good example. IBM has announced a similar program for eradicating customer-reported defects that it calls MDQ for market-determined quality. Analog Devices is another firm whose quality reporting emphasis is on defect-free deliveries rather than on cost reports.

Whichever approach a firm chooses, quality is such an undeniably important strategic variable that management accounting cannot ignore it. A strategically astute management reporting system must deal explicitly with the quality issue, one way or another.

CHAPTER 14

STRATEGIC ANALYSIS FOR ONE IMPORTANT STRUCTURAL COST DRIVER— TECHNOLOGY CHOICES

The charge has frequently been repeated in recent years that many firms fall behind in global markets because they are too slow in implementing new manufacturing technologies such as computer-integrated manufacturing, flexible manufacturing systems, advanced manufacturing technology, or the more familiar computer-aided design, engineering, and manufacturing (Jaikumar, 1986).

It has become popular to argue that a primary reason for this problem is that conventional methods of capital investment analysis do not capture the full richness of the technology change decision. A project-level net present value (NPV) framework, it is argued, places such a premium on short-term financial results and so little emphasis on difficult-to-quantify issues such as quality enhancement or manufacturing flexibility that major manufacturing breakthroughs do not pass the NPV test (Abernathy & Hayes, 1980).

Several approaches have been suggested in the literature to evaluate investments in technological change. One approach suggests that we discard all formal financial analysis (such as NPV analysis) and simply bet on new technologies. We can do better than this defeatist view. A second approach, proposed by Kaplan (1986b), calls for a refined NPV model; this framework does not give explicit attention to strategic issues and concerns. The approach, advocated by Porter (1985b), links technology decisions to strategic analysis but does not give explicit attention to financial analysis. An approach, suggested by Bromwich and Bhimani (1991), argues for an integrated "strategic–financial" analysis

A modified version of this chapter appeared as "Strategic Cost Analysis of Technological Investments" by John K. Shank and Vijay Govindarajan, *Sloan Management Review,* 34, 1 (fall 1992), pp. 39–51. Copyright 1992 by the Sloan Management Review Association. All rights reserved. Reprinted by permission of the publisher.

framework but is not pushed far enough to give meaningful guidance to managers in evaluating technology change investments.

In this chapter we offer our approach, which uses the strategic cost management theme presented in this book. Exhibit 14–1 presents a brief overview of the SCM theme as it applies to the technology choice problem. We illustrate the power of our framework by presenting a field study of a major technological innovation faced by a large forest products company. This case serves as a good summary of the major themes of SCM and shows how it can be applied to an important problem.

THE PROBLEM

Some writers argue that we should deemphasize, or even eliminate, formal investment analysis techniques when considering major manufacturing technology issues. Evidence has been cited of studies in which as many as 40% of firms used no formal evaluation for advanced manufacturing technology projects (Woods, Polorny, Lintner, & Blinkhorn, 1984). This approach is conceptually troubling in that it reduces some of the most important choices a firm faces to technology roulette—place your bet, spin the wheel, and hope. This process is not without its own risks. There have been many well-known failures from poorly conceived technology experiments:

- General Motors pushed the concept of robotics in their factories very hard in the early 1980s. Westinghouse made a major investment in robotics manufacturing in 1983. Their investment in this alternative manufacturing technology was in excess of 1 billion dollars. Yet the projected improvements proved difficult to achieve. Many of the robots purchased were never used at all. Westinghouse closed down its robotics subsidiary in 1989.
- General Electric's spectacularly abortive venture in new condenser technology for refrigerators cost the firm hundreds of millions of dollars and irreplaceable momentum in product leadership.
- The widely heralded $2 billion experiment in satellite distribution of TV signals (wireless cable), Sky Channel, by RCA, News Corporation, and CableVision was disbanded in the face of mounting costs and implementation problems.

The point of these examples certainly is not that technological experimentation always is a mistake. Nor is it that conventional NPV analysis

---

EXHIBIT 14–1

A Strategic Cost Management Approach to Technological Investment Analysis

---

Investments in technological change must be guided by undertaking all three of the following analyses:

1. *Value chain analysis:* The value chain in any business is the linked set of value-creating activities all the way from basic raw materials through component suppliers to the ultimate end-use product delivered into the final consumers' hands. Even though a firm may participate in only a part of the value chain, the firm should analyze its technological investments from the standpoint of their impact throughout the chain—the impact on its suppliers, the impact on the firm itself, and the impact on its customers. Value chain analysis can be contrasted with value-added analysis, which is typically used in the conventional NPV framework. Value-added analysis starts with payments to suppliers (purchases) and stops with charges to customers (sales) while focusing on maximizing the difference, the value added (sales minus purchases) for the firm. Value-added analysis is far too narrow a view because it misses the importance of linkages upstream and downstream in the value chain.

2. *Strategic positioning:* Technological choices cannot be justified by just understanding the value chain. Another key component involves analyzing whether technological change enhances the way the firm has chosen to compete—either on the basis of cost or on the basis of differentiation.

3. *Cost driver analysis:* Value chain and strategic positioning analysis alone are not a sufficient test of the desirability of changing technology. A third necessary component is that technology choice must be an important cost driver. Costs are a function of structural drivers (such as scale, product line complexity, scope of operations, experience, and technology) and executional drivers (such as total quality management, capacity utilization, and work force participation). In short, there are multiple drivers of cost. Technology must be an important driver of cost at critical steps in the chain.

Blending these three themes represents the most powerful way to focus cost analysis for technological change—strategic cost management. Each of the three is a necessary component of the SCM analysis, but a sufficient analysis must involve all three.

techniques must be used in spite of their limitations. We also do not mean to imply that firms cited here made some simplistic mistake that they readily could have avoided. Deciding when and how to implement change in product or process technologies is a very difficult, and at the same time critically important, task that demands the best thinking senior managers can muster. But to argue that no formal analysis is a plausible alternative to overly restrictive financial analysis seems just as misguided. The idea is to find an appropriate analytic framework.

TECHNOLOGY AND COMPETITIVE ADVANTAGE: THE CONTEXT

As background for our approach to analyzing technology investments, we summarize Porter's (1985b) perspective on the relationship between technological change and competition. Technological change is often viewed as valuable for its own sake. Any technological modification a firm can pioneer is believed to be good because it represents progress. But, from a business perspective, technological progress is not always a good thing. For example, the windsurfing and snowskiing industries are suffering from continuing technological evolution that does not translate into profits. The products are overengineered for the average customer. From a business perspective, technological change is only important to the extent that it affects competitive advantage and/or industry structure.

Technology, however, does pervade a firm's value chain. It extends far beyond those technologies associated directly with the product. There is no such thing as a low-technology industry if one takes a broader view. Viewing any industry as technologically mature can lead to strategic disaster. For example, magazine publishing today is in turmoil because of the emergence of desktop publishing in an industry deemed technologically mature just ten years ago. The belief that the old technology for page layout, color separations, or typesetting is still the way to go is preventing many large firms from competing effectively in the new arena. Moreover, many important innovations for competitive advantage are mundane and involve no scientific breakthroughs. The emergence of overnight delivery by Federal Express is a good example of a dramatic innovation that involved no new technology. Of course, the erosion of overnight delivery market share by the fax technology is a counter example. But, innovation can have important implications for low-tech as well as high-tech companies.

Technology and Competition

Everything a firm does involves technology of some sort, even though one or more technologies may appear to dominate the product or production process. For example, imaging technology may dominate the copier business, but paper feed technology is also an issue. Any particular technology is important for competition if it significantly affects a firm's competitive advantage or industry structure.

Technology and the Value Chain

The basic tool for understanding the role of technology in competitive advantage is the value chain. A firm, as a collection of activities, is a collection of technologies. Technology is embodied in every value activity of the firm, and technological change can affect competition through its impact on virtually any activity. Every value activity uses some technology to combine materials and machinery with human resources to produce some output. This technology may involve several scientific disciplines or *subtechnologies*. The existing technology of a value activity represents one combination of these subtechnologies.

The technologies in different value activities can be related. This linkage is a major source of competitive advantage within the value chain. For example, product technology can be linked to the technology for servicing a product (self-diagnosing computer systems that relay maintenance information directly to the manufacturer). Or, component technologies can be linked to end-product technology. Desktop layout of advertising pages, for example, makes possible a lower-cost magazine. Thus a technology choice in one part of the value chain can have implications for other parts of the chain. In extreme cases, changing technology in one activity can require a major reconfiguration of the value chain. For example, when the basic oxygen furnace replaced the open hearth furnace in steel making, scale became much less important. This development opened the door for the emergence of the minimill, which has fundamentally changed the structure of the steel industry.

A firm's technologies are also clearly interdependent with it's buyers technologies. The points of contact between a firm's value chain and its customers' or suppliers' chain define another area of potential interdependence of technologies. For example, Union Camp put PCs linked to its warehouses into paper distributors' offices and increased sales by offering immediate product availability and order status information. A firm's product technology influences the product and process technology of the customer, and vice versa.

Technology and Competitive Advantage

Technology affects competitive advantage if it has a significant role in determining relative cost or differentiation position. Because technology is embodied in every value activity and is involved in achieving linkages among activities, it can have a powerful effect on both cost and differentiation. The rise of computer reservations systems in the airline business represents an excellent example of technology affecting differentiation (American Airlines and the Saber system, for example). Technology affecting relative cost is illustrated by the rise of continuous casting in steel making. Continuous casters significantly reduce manufacturing cost for firms that use them.

In addition to affecting cost or differentiation in its own right, technology affects competitive advantage through changing or influencing the other drivers of cost or uniqueness. For example, the development of the interstate highway system dramatically changed the basis of competition between trucking and railroads in many basic ways. The successful railroads today (Burlington Northern, for example) are the ones that have adapted to those changes.

Tests of a Desirable Technological Change

The link between technological change and competitive advantage suggests a number of tests for a desirable direction of technological change. According to Porter (1985b), technological change by a firm will lead to sustainable competitive advantage under any of four circumstances.

1. The technological change lowers cost or enhances differentiation, and the firm's technological lead is sustainable. For example, Procter & Gamble's patented dry fluffing technology for tissue papers provides softer paper at no increase in drying cost.
2. The technological change shifts cost or uniqueness drivers in favor of a firm. For example, a new assembly process that is more scale sensitive than the previous one will benefit a large-share firm that pioneers it, even if competitors eventually adopt the process.
3. Pioneering the technological change translates into first-mover

advantages besides those inherent in the technology itself. A firm that moves first may establish a reputation as the pioneer or leader, a reputation that emulators will have difficulty overcoming. Kodak in film or Coca-Cola in beverages have gained this advantage. A first mover also may be first to serve buyers and thus to establish relationships where there may be loyalty.

It is interesting how many firms that were first movers have remained leaders for decades. In consumer goods, for example, such current leading brands as Crisco, Ivory soap, Life Savers, Coca-Cola, Campbell's soup, Wrigley gum, Kodak film, and Lipton tea were already leaders by the 1920s. Of course, early leaders do not always persist, as is evidenced by Singer sewing machines, Bowmar calculators, Bulova watches, and RCA television sets.

A first mover may be at a disadvantage if early investments are specific to the current technology and cannot be modified easily for later generations. In semiconductors, for example, Philco moved early for leadership with a large automated plant. It enjoyed a period of success, but the later development of a different manufacturing process for semiconductor chips made its earlier investment obsolete. Similarly, the early movers will be disadvantaged if its product or process reflects factor costs or factor quality levels that have changed.

Technological discontinuities can also work against the first mover by making its investments in the established technology obsolete. Technological discontinuities are major shifts in technology to which a first mover may be ill prepared to respond given its investment in the old technology. Weyerhaeuser, for example, pioneered the introduction of the technology for oriented strand board (a plywood substitute). But later innovations cut the cost of a new plant in half, leaving Weyco at a competitive disadvantage in its early plants. Discontinuity favors the fast follower who does not bear the high cost of pioneering.

4. The technological change improves overall industry structure. For example, the jet engine improved the competitive position of all airlines versus other substitute forms of transportation.

Although Porter's approach to understanding technological change investments is clearly very insightful at a conceptual level, it does not explicitly link the strategic framework to financial analysis. Without such a linkage, it is difficult to decide on specific technological investments. Thus, we have found no examples in the literature using Porter's framework to resolve technological choices in the eight years since it was introduced. This is in strong contrast to the extensive literature applying and testing other aspects of Porter's model.

THE SCM FRAMEWORK

Our framework builds explicitly on Porter's approach but also explicitly considers the financial issues. The SCM perspective, as emphasized in this book, involves three key themes that are taken from the strategic management literature:

1. Value chain analysis

2. Strategic positioning analysis

3. Cost driver analysis

Each of the three represents a stream of research and analysis about strategy in which cost information is cast in a much different light from that in which it is viewed in conventional management accounting. Blending the three themes represents the most powerful way to focus cost analysis for strategic choices. Each of the three is a necessary component of the SCM analysis, but a sufficient analysis must involve all three.

We illustrate the application of the SCM framework to analyzing technology investments by presenting a field study about a major technological innovation faced by a large forest product company.

The SCM Perspective on Technology Costing: A Field Study

The field study deals with the choice of equipment for logging operations in the Virginia timberlands owned by Yakima-Olympia Corporation (disguised), a multibillion dollar, highly vertically integrated, forest products company. The prevailing technology for logging is clear cutting using feller-bunchers, which are similar to large farm tractors and have heavy-duty scissors attached at the front to shear off standing trees at ground level. These tractors also are equipped with large clamps that can hold several tree trunks at a time in an upright position so that the tractor can shear off a bunch before stopping to dump the load on the ground. The machine literally fells trees in bunches. After felling, the bunches of trees are dragged (skidded) to a roadside staging area (the deck) by another variety of tractor called a skidder. The feller bunchers and skidders leave no trees standing as they move through a wood lot. At the deck, workers use hand-held chain saws to delimb the trees as best they can, usually leaving many short stub limbs on the log. Cranes then load the logs onto flatbed trucks for transport to woodyards. In the woodyards, logs are sorted and cut into segments for saw mills, plywood mills, or pulp mills, depending on the quality and species of the trees.

The tempo and pace of this process best can be described as helter skelter pandemonium. There is no sophistication involved, only brute force applied in an environment that is hot, insect ridden, snake infested, and alternately thick with dust or deep in mud. This process represents the latest technological state in the evolution of a process geared to cutting down and moving as many trees as possible in as short a time as possible. Those methods achieve high volume throughout but also result in serious damage to the trees and the land and in great discomfort and danger for the workers involved.

The alternative technology, widely used in northern Europe but still virtually unknown in the United States, involves sophisticated computerized machines that resemble Star Wars robots. A harvester is a closed-cab tractor that uses computer programs as it moves carefully through the woods, selecting individual trees for cutting based on current needs in the processing mills. The machine fells each tree with a smooth saw cut (as opposed to a scissors cut), removes the limbs from each log precisely flush to the stem, cuts the stem into sections of predetermined lengths, and gently drops the sections in neat piles. A forwarder then picks up the logs according to computer programmed sequences and carries them to the roadside. Later the forwarder will load the cut logs onto trucks destined for specific processing mills, bypassing the woodyard step altogether. In this system, the wood lot is not clear cut. Only the fully mature trees whose size and specie meet current processing mills' needs are harvested.

In terms of tempo and pace, this system resembles ballet dancers performing an elegant pas de deux in the words. The harvester/forwarder system represents the latest technological stage in the evolution of a process in which the logger sees each individual tree as a precious object and takes full responsibility to deliver clean, undamaged, sorted, and cut logs to specific processing mills, based on their current needs, while doing minimal damage to the land. The work is performed safely and cleanly from air conditioned cabs.

Speculation about how these two approaches to logging developed in such dramatically opposed ways in northern Europe and the United States is beyond the scope of this chapter. The issue for Virginia loggers in 1990 was whether to stay with feller-buncher/skidder technology or switch to harvester/forwarder (H/F) technology for Yakima Olympia's 450,000 timberland acres in the tidewater region.

Yakima-Olympia (Y-O), like many major forest products companies, was vertically integrated from research-intensive farms that developed and planted genetically improved seedlings through to wholesale and retail distribution of paper and solid wood products. The only step in this chain in which Y-O did not participate was logging. Primarily for cost reasons (nonunion wages and work practices), most of the forest products firms had long ago exited the business of cutting their own trees. Private logging contractors were hired to cut the mature trees from Y-O's lands and transport them to Y-O's processing mills.

How to evaluate the proposal to switch logging technologies is the subject of the field study.

Technology Costing: The Three Components of the SCM Perspective

This section considers in turn each of the three components of the SCM perspective as it applies to the choice of logging technology. We start with the value chain component.

The Value Chain Theme

In the SCM framework, managing costs effectively requires a broad focus, external to the firm. Porter has termed this perspective the value chain (Porter, 1980). To recapitulate the ideas from chapter 4, the value chain for any firm in any business is the linked set of value-creating activities all the way from basic raw materials (starting ultimately with the periodic table of the elements) through to component suppliers, to the ultimate end-use product delivered into the final consumers' hands, and, in today's world, perhaps through recycling to the beginning of a new value chain cycle. The focus is external to the firm, seeing each firm in the context of the overall chain of value-creating activities of which it is only a part. We are aware of no firms that span the entire value chain in which they participate. Value chain analysis is contrasted with value-added analysis, which starts with payments to suppliers (purchases) and stops with charges to customers (sales) while focusing on maximizing the difference, the value added (sales minus purchases) for the firm.

Value-added analysis is far too narrow a view because it misses the importance of linkages upstream and downstream in the value chain. In the context of computer-integrated manufacturing, the principal benefits of new investment may fall elsewhere in the value chain than where the investment takes place, as the logging example illustrates.

The power of the value chain perspective for this situation is highlighted by its contrast with a conventional project-level, value-added analysis. Exhibit 14–2 shows the conventional analysis for a logging contractor comparing the two alternative logging systems. From the logger's perspective, the return is virtually identical for the two options. Given the comparable economic returns, the logger currently using feller buncher technology is not inclined to switch. The new technology involves a significantly larger investment for a small businessman, a much heavier reliance on skilled labor (versus low-wage, day-rate laborers for conventional logging), much more complex maintenance issues, and a much more complex job task (cut selectively and treat each stem with great care versus cut them all down as fast as you can, and don't worry).

Y-O had experimented with the new technology in test sites. Senior management in Y-O knew that there were tremendous potential benefits, but the logger does not really stand to gain directly from any of them. From this perspective, there is really no way to bring about technological innovation on the part of the logger. Exhibit 14–3 summarizes the anticipated financial returns from adopting the new technology, broken down by where in the value chain they are realized. As shown in exhibit 14–3, although the switch to harvester/forwarder logging technology can save Y-O an estimated $33.6 million per year in just one of its several timberland regions, none of the gains are realized at the stage of the value chain where the investment must be made. Applying a value-added perspective in a project evaluation mode at the logging stage will never lead to the change. Applying a value chain perspective in a business unit evaluation mode reveals the tremendous potential benefits from the change.

Even if logging is potentially an important step in the value chain, a sufficient test for investing in the new logging technology requires that the benefits achievable are consistent with the strategic positioning adopted by the firm. This requirement leads to a consideration of the

EXHIBIT 14–2
A Net Present Value Comparison of Feller-Buncher/Skidder Technology
Versus Harvester/Forwarder Technology for Virginia Logging

CAPITAL COST
A. One harvester/forwarder pair = $608,000
B. One feller-buncher with two skidders and one crane = $370,000

A. Can work two shift with lights on the equipment
B. Can only work one shift
Running two shifts, A processes 17,600 cunits of wood in one year which is equal to what B can process working one shift

FINANCIAL SUMMARY

	A	B
Capital cost	$608,000	$370,000
Cash operating costs		
Labor	94,000	105,000
Fuel	15,000	75,000
Supplies, repair, and maintenance	91,000	91,000
Insurance and taxes	3,000	3,000
Supervision	50,000	35,000
Total	$253,000	$309,000
Depreciation (5 years)	122,000	74,000
Salvage value (after year 5)	60,000	18,000

ASSUME 36% COMBINED TAX RATE

	A	B
Processing revenue (for 17,600 cunits)	407,000	407,000
5-year NPV (at 12%)	(70,000)	(42,000)
5-year internal rate of return	7.4%	7.3%

For purposes of this example, the comparison is framed in Internal Rate of Return (IRR) terms rather than NPV to avoid the issue of risk-class comparability between the two options. The well-known caveats about ranking projects in IRR terms are acknowledged, but are not a concern in this context.

second component from the SCM framework for technology costing— strategic positioning analysis, as discussed in chapter 6.

The Strategic Positioning Theme

In the SCM perspective, understanding the implications of how the firm chooses to compete is fully as important for cost analysis as understand-

EXHIBIT 14–3
Comparing Annual Returns from Switching to Harvester/Forwarders for Y-O's 450,000 Acres (About 15,000 Acres Harvested Each Year)

A Value Chain Perspective

Returns to the landowner	
Improved product mix selection	$2.6 million
Saved stem damage waste (saw cut is better than shear cut)	0.3 million
Saved cost for site repair (H/F does much less damage to the residual land	0.2 million
	$3.1 million
Returns to the logger	
Virtually none	$ 0.0
Returns to the processing mills	
For pulp mill wood supply:	
Saved processing cost from precise sorting classification	$26.0 million
For solid wood supply (saw mills and plywood mills):	
At the woodyard:	
Saved cost of sawing trees to logs in the woodyard	$ .5 million
Saved trim loss in the woodyards	1.6 million
Saved cost from logs misapplied by the saw operators in the woodyard	0.5 million
Saved wood loss from woodyard saw spacing	0.3 million
	$2.9 million
At the processing mills:	
Kiln drying savings from more precise sorting	$0.2 million
Savings by using lighter-duty debarkers	0.1 million
Savings from double handling of off-grade logs in the plymills and sawmills	1.3 million
	$1.6 million

ing the value chain and understanding the key strategic cost drivers at critical steps in the chain. As articulated by Porter (1980) and discussed widely in the strategy literature, the basic choice on how to compete is between cost leadership and differentiation. How these different strategies affect technology choices is illustrated by the logging industry field study.

Y-O, as a corporation, has pursued a differentiation strategy in its solid wood operations for more than twenty years. The strategy is built around plantation forestry to plant and grow genetically improved trees that will yield a wood mix with a much higher-than-average value at maturity. With an approximately 35-year growing cycle in the Virginia tidewater region, the strategy still has about 15 years to go before it can be fully implemented.

By the year 2000, if conventional logging is used, Y-O timberlands will be yielding each year about 80 percent of the high-grade logs that its expanded set of saw mills and plymills will require. This figure is up from the 67% supplied internally in 1985, but still well below total requirements. The remaining twenty percent will have to be met by outside purchases, as shown in exhibit 14–4.

If the H/F technology were to be used, the net supply of high-grade logs from the same acreage would increase by 50,000 units each year. This increase would save the saw and ply mills more than $5,000,000 each year in purchased logs. Thus, adopting the new logging technology moves Y-O substantially closer to self-sufficiency in supplying the high-grade log needs of the expanded set of ply and saw mills it has built as part of its high-value extraction strategy. These savings are in addition to the quality savings shown in exhibit 14–3 from stem damage, sorting losses, kiln drying losses, and double handling.

The relevance of the strategic positioning choice to the technology choice in this situation is highlighted by noting the situation for one of Y-O's major competitors, Marathon Paper Company (disguised), which also owns substantial timberlands in the coastal southeast. Whereas Y-O's strategy emphasizes grade extraction (saw and ply mills logs) and distribution in global markets, Marathon's strategy emphasizes fiber extraction (pulp mill logs) and concentrates primarily on domestic markets. Because Marathon sees its timberlands primarily as a source of low-value pulp logs to supply its pulp mills, it has a much smaller commitment in saw and ply mills and is not nearly as concerned about the problems of conventional logging. Marathon uses a much shorter grow-

EXHIBIT 14–4
Estimated Wood Supply and Demand

Year		Pulp Mills	Saw/Ply Mills
1985	Demand	1,500,000 units	300,000 units
	Supply from Y-O timberlands	600,000 (40%)	200,000 (67%)
2000	Demand	1,500,000 units	500,000 units
	Supply from Y-O timberlands:		
	Using conventional technology	500,000 (33%)	400,000 (80%)
	Using H/F technology	500,000 (33%)	450,000 (90%)

ing cycle (22 years), and does not spend the money each year in its forests (fertilizing, burning, pruning, and thinning) to achieve a high-value wood mix.

It is not necessarily obvious, but growing better trees is only justifiable if there is a strategy in place to subsequently extract that extra value in end-product markets. Furthermore, whether or not a high-value timber strategy is superior to a low-value strategy depends on a complex set of assumptions that play out over a 25–35-year growth cycle. Different forest products firms make different choices on this issue. In 1992, Procter & Gamble sold its pulp mills and timberlands because it no longer saw a need to be vertically integrated into raw material for its paper products plants.

Conventional logging technology with its emphasis on high-volume (but lower-value) throughput is fully consistent with Marathon's strategy of lower value and low cost. At exactly the same time, Y-O is moving ahead aggressively to find gain-sharing mechanisms to induce its logging contractors to switch to the H/F technology, which represents a much better fit with its strategy of a longer growth cycle with higher cost, but higher value.

Even if logging is a key step in the value chain and the technology investment is consistent with the firm's strategic positioning, a sufficient test for investing in the new equipment is that technology choice is an important cost driver. Thus we must consider the third SCM component, strategic cost driver analysis, as it relates to this field study. Although each of the three themes is a necessary element in the analysis, a sufficient test must consider all three together.

The Cost Driver Theme

As discussed in chapter 10, in conventional management accounting, cost behavior is seen largely as a function of volume. In SCM, output volume as such is seen to capture very little of the richness of cost behavior. In this regard, SCM draws much less upon the simple models of basic microeconomics and much more upon the richer models of the economics of industrial organization.

Structural cost drivers relate to explicit strategic choices by the firm regarding economic structure, such as scale, product line complexity, scope of operations (vertical integration), or experience (Riley, 1987). Technology investments also represent structural choices about how to compete. There are also executional cost drivers that are major determinants of a firm's cost position and hinge on its ability to execute successfully within the economic structure it chooses (Riley, 1987). What structural and executional factors are driving success or failure at the logging stage, and how important is the technology factor compared to other cost drivers?

Of the structural drivers, scale does not prove to be very important in this context. Minimum efficient scale for logging is quite small. One or two sets of equipment is adequate to spread the supervision cost element, which is the only cost element with any scale effects. Vertical scope also yields no economies in this context. Because of union wage rates and work practices in the large forest products firm that are avoided by the private logger, there are actually diseconomies of vertical scope. Learning is also not a major cost driver with conventional equipment. The job is learned quickly and high labor turnover does not generate a significant cost disadvantage. Learning is a more important issue with H/F equipment, for which high labor turnover could destroy many of the benefits. However, learning is still not, in itself, a dramatic cost driver—the job can be learned in about twelve months and requires only average intelligence and diligence.

Product line complexity is not an important cost driver, either, because the mix of tree species and sizes is very narrow in this region. The area was logged once near the turn of the century and again in the 1950s. The fact that all the land already has been harvested once or twice in the past seventy-five years greatly enhances the homogeneity of the forest.

As summarized in exhibit 14–3, technology choice is a critical cost driver in this field study. The brief overview here indicates that, of all the structural cost drivers, technology choice is the single most important factor is this situation. The next step is to consider the executional drivers to see if they offset or reinforce the structural impact of the technology factor.

Layout of the production process is a neutral factor here. It is important in the sense that proximity of the mills to the trees is critical, but it is not a variable in the current context. Similarly, product formulation is also neutral. Developing genetically improved seedlings is an important issue, but it is also not a variable in the current context. Nor is capacity utilization a factor, because the small scale of operations for any one logger means they all tend to stay busy all the time. Chronic oversupply is not nearly as big an issue here as it is for the pulp and paper operations of Y-O.

Participative management, continuous improvement philosophy

(*kaizen*), and total quality management are all important here, as they almost always are, and they all reinforce the technology factor. The H/F technology is much more amenable to a high-quality and high commitment work force management program than is the clear-cutting technology, which seems almost to assume and guarantee an alienated work force.

These considerations bring us to the linkages issue, which in this case is of equal importance to the technology issue. Unless the contract loggers can be induced to see and value the overall benefits across the value chain from the high-tech logging option, there is little hope of achieving the benefits. The linkage between the loggers and the landowners and the linkage between the loggers and the processing mills are dramatically underexploited. Unless Y-O were to decide to do the logging itself, thus eliminating the need to deal with loggers as independent businesses, some form of gain sharing to induce a tighter linkage along the value chain must be developed. The diseconomies of vertical integration make Y-O very reluctant to participate in the logging business. In order to make the technology change investment attractive to loggers, they thus must address the linkage problem by sharing the potential benefits that are likely to accrue ahead of and behind the logger.

An interesting dilemma is how much sharing of potential gains will be necessary to get loggers to make the switch. Overcoming risk avoidance attitudes and inertia may require more profit sharing than might seem rational in purely financial terms. If Y-O cannot induce the technology change without giving away what they see as a disproportionate share of the benefits, they may come to see the diseconomies of vertical scope as less significant and reenter the logging business. How overall returns are shared along a value chain is a very complex issue. How enhancements to the overall value created by one player reach an equilibrium distribution across all the players is an equally complex issue.

Technology Choices: A SCM View

In this field study, Yakima-Olympia, faced a significant problem in the logging operation stage of the value chain. The prevailing technology for logging was cost effective for firms pursuing a strategy of high volume and low value-added wood products, but not for firms pursuing a strategy of differentiation and high value-added wood products. Because logging was done by independent contractors, there was no direct way for Y-O to control the choice of technology by the loggers.

Conventional project-level financial analysis does not suggest to the logger that a change of technology is a good business decision. The benefits from the new technology fall ahead of and behind the logger in the value chain, but the logger must incur the cost and assume the risks. A strategic perspective perspective is required that blends the conceptual framework proposed by Porter with explicit financial analysis.

Y-O had tried to convince the contract loggers it hired to move from feller/buncher technology to harvester/forwarder technology using conventional project-level financial analysis. It failed to persuade any loggers to change. Even careful attention to intangible factors, coupled with hurdle rate subsidies (investment guarantees) and appeals to long-run declines under current logging methods could not induce the contractors to switch. Subsequent attempts to couch the decision in strategic terms, for the loggers, gained somewhat more receptivity to change, but still nowhere near the groundswell Y-O felt it needed.

No real progress was made until Y-O was persuaded to adopt an SCM framework in thinking about the problem. First, viewing the problem from a value chain perspective clearly revealed the paradox that, although the change would involve major financial benefits, the stage in the chain where the investment must be made would earn none of the resulting benefits under current pricing regimes. Second, the strategic positioning perspective revealed that, although this technology change was not compelling under all conceivable strategic postures, it was compelling under the positioning strategy to which Y-O had committed, virtually irrevocably, for the next ten to fifteen years. Third, the cost driver perspective revealed that technology choice was a key structural cost factor that was further reinforced by executional cost factors. Each of these three components of the SCM analysis was necessary to establish the rationale for the new investment.

Whether Y-O could affect a voluntary changeover to H/F logging among its contractors is still not clear. It would certainly be necessary to explicitly consider gain-sharing mechanisms across the supplier-customer linkages to encourage the logging system Y-O believed to be optimal. If the loggers decided that the incentives Y-O was willing to offer were inadequate to motivate the change, Y-O might be forced to reconsider its decision to exclude the logging step from its vertical integration chain. In SCM terms, this would be a realization that, given Y-O's strategic position, the potential economies from technological change would be great enough to offset the diseconomies from vertically integrating at this value chain step if gain-sharing mechanisms to induce more explicit customer-supplier linkages were not successful.

CONCLUSION

This field study is an excellent example of how the strategic cost management framework provides a more useful way to apply the power of cost analysis concepts to technology investment opportunities within a fully articulated strategic analysis context.

One essential step in effective management of technology change clearly is effective analysis of the investment opportunities. We believe that strategic cost management is a useful way to structure the analysis of such opportunities and thus represents an important component of technology management.

EPILOGUE

To get the bad customs of a country changed and new ones, though better, introduced, it is necessary first to remove the prejudices of the people, enlighten their ignorance, and convince them that their interests will be promoted by the proposed changes, and this is not the work of a day.

—Benjamin Franklin (1781)

There is nothing more difficult to plan, more doubtful of success, nor more dangerous to manage than the creation of a new order of things . . . Whenever his enemies have occasion to attack the innovator they do so with the passion of partisans, while the others defend him sluggishly so that the innovator and his party alike are vulnerable.

—Niccolo Machiavelli (1513)

The most innovative member of a [group] is very often perceived as a deviant from the social system.

—Everett Rogers (1983)

Without the adoption of strategic management accounting, the control and monitoring of strategic objectives may have to take place outside the financial management system using disaggregated measures thereby losing the ability to easily consider the overall impact of the enterprise's achievements in these areas.

—Colin Drury (1992)

NOTES

CHAPTER 1   AN INTRODUCTION TO STRATEGIC COST MANAGEMENT

1. See, for example, Andrews (1971), Chandler (1962), Henderson (1979), and Porter (1980, 1985a).
2. See, for example, Mintzberg (1978), Hambrick (1981), Gupta and Govindarajan (1986b), or Govindarajan (1986a).
3. See, for example, the newest edition of Horngren and Sundem (1987) or Horngren and Foster (1987).

CHAPTER 2   STRATEGIC COST MANAGEMENT

1. The Japanese firms achieve a much higher schedule stability because of dramatically lower levels of complexity in their product lines.
2. See, for example, Dess and Davis (1984), Gilbert and Strebel (1987), Hall (1980), Hambrick (1983), or Karnani (1984).
3. See Gupta and Govindarajan (1984b), Wright (1987), or Shank and Govindarajan (1986).
4. See, for example, chapter 1 in Horngren and Foster (1987), Garrison (1988), or Anthony and Reece (1989).
5. For a recent comprehensive reference, see (Liao (1988).
6. See, for example, Deakin and Maher (1984) or Kaplan (1982).
7. See, for example, Ghemawat (1986) or the Titanium Dioxide Case series (Porter, 1986a).
8. Juran and Gryna (1970); Crosby (1979), Garvin (1987), Simpson and Muthler (1987).

CHAPTER 3   DEMONSTRATING STRATEGIC VERSUS CONVENTIONAL ANALYSIS

1. During the past twenty years, several books (e.g., Andrews, 1971; Henderson, 1979; Porter, 1980 as well as articles (e.g., Buzzell et al., 1975; Hambrick, 1981; Snow & Hrebiniak, 1975 have been published in the

field of strategic management. In addition, two new journals (*Strategic Management Journal* and *Journal of Business Strategy*) have been introduced in the strategy area. Also, traditional management journals such as *Administrative Science Quarterly, Academy of Management Journal,* and *Academy of Management Review* have started to regularly publish articles on strategic analysis.

2. The U.S. bicycle industry had become very volatile in recent years. From 1967 through 1970 sales averaged about 7 million units a year. By 1973 the total was up to a record 15 million units. By 1975 volume was back down to 7.5 million units. By 1982 volume was back up to 10 million units, still well below the peak years.

CHAPTER 6 EXPLICIT ATTENTION TO STRATEGIC POSITIONING

1. This section draws from an extensive body of research focused on strategy implementation issues at the business unit level. Some of the key references are: Govindarajan (1988, 1989), Govindarajan and Fisher (1989, 1990, 1991), Govindarajan and Gupta (1985), Gupta and Govindarajan, (1984a, 1984b), Hall (1987), Sata and Maidique (1980), Shank and Govindarajan (1989), Simons (1987).

2. "Executive Compensation: Looking to the Long-Term Again," *Business Week* (May 9, 1983), p. 81.

3. L. Reibstein, "Firms Trim Annual Pay Increase and Focus on Long Term: More Employers Link Incentives to Unit Results," *The Wall Street Journal* (April 10, 1987), p. 25.

4. B. Uttal, "The Gentlemen and the Upstarts Meet in a Great Mini-Battle," *Fortune* (April 23, 1979), pp. 98–108.

5. K. Ohmae, "The Long and Short of Japanese Planning," *The Wall Street Journal* (Jan. 18, 1982), p. 28.

6. B. G. James, "Strategic Planning Under Fire," *Sloan Management Review* 24, 3, (summer 1984), pp. 57–61.

7. J. Salamon, "Challenges Lie Ahead for Dynamic Citicorp After the Wriston Era," *The Wall Street Journal* (Dec. 18, 1981), p. 1.

8. Richard F. Vancil, "Corning Glass Works: Tom MacAvoy," in *Implementing Strategy,* R. F. Vancil, ed. (Boston: Division of Research, Harvard Business School, 1982), pp. 21–36.

CHAPTER 8 DIFFERENTIATING COST MANAGEMENT SYSTEMS BASED ON STRATEGIC POSITIONING

1. W. Kiechel, "The Decline of the Experience Curve," *Fortune* (Oct. 5, 1981), pp. 67–76.

2. T. Peters and P. Pascarella, "Searching for Excellence: The Winners Deliver on Value," *Industry Week* (April 16, 1984), pp. 61–62.

CHAPTER 13 MEASURING AND ANALYZING COSTS FOR ONE IMPORTANT EXECUTIONAL COST DRIVER—QUALITY

1. As explained later, there is no such thing as a monolithic Japanese approach. The term is the creation of quality researchers and writers who have tried to find common themes in the approaches to quality ex-explified by many Japanese firms.

BIBLIOGRAPHY

Abel, Derick F., and John S. Hammond. 1979 *Strategic Market Planning*. Englewood Cliffs, NJ: Prentice Hall.

Abernathy, W. and R. Hayes. 1980. "Managing our way to economic decline," *Harvard Business Review*, 58, 4, pp. 67–77.

Abernathy, W. J., and J. M. Utterback. 1979. "Patterns of Industrial Innovation," *Technology Review*, 80, 7 (June–July), pp. 40–47.

Alchian, Armen. 1959. "Costs and Outputs," in *The Allocation of Economic Resources*, M. Abromowitz, ed. Palo Alto, CA: Stanford University Press.

Allen, Bruce T. 1971. "Vertical Integration and Market Foreclosure: The Case of Cement and Concrete," *The Journal of Law & Economics*, 14, 1 (April), p. 251.

Andrews, Kenneth R. 1980. *The Concept of Corporate Strategy*. Homewood, IL: Richard D. Irwin.

Ansoff, H. I. 1965. *Corporate Strategy*. (New York: McGraw-Hill.

Anthony, R. N., J. Dearden, and V. Govindarajan. 1992. *Management Control Systems*. Homewood, IL: Richard D. Irwin.

Anthony, Robert. 1956. *Accounting*. Homewood, IL: Richard D. Irwin.

Anthony, Robert, and James Reece. 1989. *Accounting: Text and Cases*. 8th ed. Homewood, IL: Richard D. Irwin.

Baba, Y. 1989. "The Dynamics of Continuous Innovation in Scale-Sensitive Industries," *Strategic Management Journal*, 10, pp. 89–100.

Baiman, Stanley. 1990. "Agency Research in Managerial Accounting: A Second Look," *Accounting, Organizations and Society*, 15, 4, pp. 341–71.

Berliner, Callie, James Brimson, ed. 1988. *Cost Management for Today's Advanced Manufacturing*. Cambridge, MA: Harvard Business School Press.

Bessant, J., and B. Haywood. 1986. "Experiences with FMS in the UK," *International Journal of Operations and Production Management*, pp. 44–56.

Blank, Leland, 1990. "Planning and Evaluating CIM Systems," in *Emerging Practices in Cost Management*, Barry J. Brinker, ed. New York, NY: Warren, Gorham and Lamont.

Booz, Allen, and Hamilton. 1987. *Manufacturing Issues*. New York, Booz, Allen, and Hamilton.

Bower, Joseph L., Christopher A. Bartlett, Roland C. Christensen, Andrall E. Pearson, and Kenneth R. Andrews. 1990. *Business Policy: Text and Cases,* Homewood, IL: Richard D. Irwin.

Briers, Michael, and Mark Hirst. 1990. "The Role of Budgetary Information in Performance Evaluation," *Accounting, Organizations and Society,* pp. 373–98.

Bromwich, Michael, and Al Bhimani. 1991. "Strategic Investment Appraisal," *Management Accounting* (March), LXXII, 9, pp. 45–48.

Bruns, William, and Robert Kaplan. 1987. *Field Studies in Management Accounting and Control.* Cambridge, MA: Harvard Business School Press.

Bulow, Jeremy I., John D. Geanakoplos, and Paul D. Klemperer. 1985. "Multimarket Oligopoly: Strategic Substitutes and Complements," *Journal of Political Economy,* 93, 3, pp. 488–511.

Burrell, G., and G. Morgan. 1979. *Sociological Paradigms and Organizational Analysis.* Portsmouth, NH: Heinemann.

Butler, John E. 1988. "Theories of Technological Innovation as Useful Tools for Corporate Strategy," *Strategic Management Journal,* 9, pp. 15–29.

Buzzell, R. D., and F. D. Wiersema. 1981. "Modelling Changes in Market Share: A Cross-Sectional Analysis," *Strategic Management Journal* 2, 1, pp. 27–42.

Buzzell, R. D., G. Bradley, and R. G. M. Sultan. 1975. "Market Share—A Key to Profitability," *Harvard Business Review,* 53 (Jan–Feb.), pp. 97–106.

Camillus, John C. 1986. *Strategic Planning and Management Control.* Lexington, MA: Lexington Books.

Carlton, Dennis W., and Jeffrey M. Perloff. 1990. *Modern Industrial Organization.* Glenview, IL: Scott, Foresman/Little, Brown Higher Education.

Carr, Lawrence. 1992. "Applying Costs of Quality to a Service Business," *Sloan Management Review,* 33, 4 (Summer), pp. 72–78.

Chandler, Alfred A. 1962. *Strategy and Structure: Chapters in the History of American Industrial Enterprise.* Cambridge, MA: The MIT Press.

Clark, John 1985. "Costing for Quality at Celanese," *Management Accounting,* LXVI, 9 (March), pp. 42–47.

Conley, Patrick. 1970. "Experience Curves as a Planning Tool," a special commentary published by *The Boston Consulting Group,* reprinted from *IEEE Spectrum* (June).

Cooper, Robin. 1986a. *Cases in Product Costing—An Overview,* Cambridge, MA: Harvard Business School.

Cooper, Robin. 1986b. *Mueller Lemkuhl Case.* Cambridge, MA: Harvard Business School.

Cooper, Robin, 1986c. *Schrader Bellows Cases.* Cambridge, MA: Harvard Business School.

Cooper, Robin, 1987a. "Does Your Company Need a New Cost System?" *Journal of Cost Management,* 1, 1 (Spring), Cambridge, MA: 45–49.

Cooper, Robin, 1987b. *John Deere Company Cases.* Forthcoming. Harvard Business School.

Cooper, Robin, 1989. "You Need a New Cost System When. . . . ," *Harvard Business Review,* 67, 1 (Jan.–Feb.), pp. 77–82.

Cooper, Robin, and Robert Kaplan. 1988. "Measure Costs Right: Make the Right Decisions," *Harvard Business Review,* 66, 5 (Sept.–Oct.), pp. 96–105.

Cooper, Robin, and Robert Kaplan. 1991. "The Design of Cost Management Systems: Text, Cases, and Readings," Englewood Cliffs, NJ: Prentice-Hall.

Crosby, Phillip B. 1979. *Quality Is Free.* New York: McGraw-Hill.

Crosby, Phillip B. 1984. *Quality Without Tears.* New York: McGraw-Hill.

D'Aveni, Richard. 1991. "Sources of Competitive Advantage Associated with Business and Corporate Level Strategies," Hanover, NH: The Amos Tuck School of Business Administration, Dartmough College, Working Paper, 1991.

Davidson, Sidney. 1963. "Old Wine into New Bottles," *Accounting Review,* XXXVIII, 2 (April), pp. 278–84.

Davidson, Sidney, et al. 1985. *Managerial Accounting.* 2nd ed. New York, NY: The Dryden Press.

Deakin, E. B., and M. W. Maher. 1984. *Cost Accounting.* Homewood, IL: Richard D. Irwin.

Deming, W. Edwards. 1982. *Quality, Productivity and Competitive Position.* Cambridge, MA: MIT Center for Advanced Engineering Study.

Dess, G. G., and P. S. Davis. 1984. "Porter's (1980) Generic Strategies as Determinants of Strategic Group Membership and Organizational Performance," *Academy of Management Journal,* 27, pp. 467–88.

Donaldson, Gordon. 1984. *Managing Corporate Wealth.* New York: Praeger.

Drucker, Peter F. 1985. The Discipline of Innovation," *Harvard Business Review,* 63 (May–June), pp. 67–72.

Feigenbaum, A. V. 1983. *Total Quality Control: Engineering and Management.* New York: McGraw-Hill.

Fine, Charles. 1985. "Managing Quality: A Comparative Assessment." *Booz Allen Manufacturing Issues.*

Forbis, John, and Nitin Mehta. 1981. "Value-Based Strategies for Industrial Products," *Business Horizons,* 24, 3 (May), pp. 44–52.

Foster, George, and Charles T. Horngren. 1988. "Cost Accounting and Cost Management in a JIT Environment," *Journal of Cost Management,* 1, 4 (winter), pp. 4–14.

Foster, George, and Charles T. Horngren. 1990. "Flexible Manufacturing Systems: Cost Management and Cost Accounting Implications," in *Emerging Practices in Cost Management,* Barry J. Brinker, ed. New York, NY: Warren, Gorham and Lamont.

Freeman, C. 1974. *The Economics of Industrial Innovation.* Harmondsworth, Eng.: Penguin.

Friedlaender, Ann F., Clifford Winston, and Kung Wang. 1988. "Costs, Technology, and Productivity in the U.S. Automobile Industry," *The Bell Journal of Economics*, 20, 1, pp. 1–20.

Frohman, A. L. 1985. "Putting Technology into Strategic Planning," *California Management Review*, 27 (winter), pp. 48–59.

Galbraith, J., and R. Kazanjian. 1986. *Strategy Implementation: The Role of Structure, Systems and Process*. St. Paul, MN: West.

Garrison, Ray. 1988. *Managerial Accounting*. 5th ed. Homewood, IL: BPI.

Garvin, David. 1987. "Competing on the Eight Dimensions of Quality," *Harvard Business Review*, 65, 6 (Nov.–Dec.), pp. 101–111.

Garvin, David A. 1988. *Managing Quality: The Strategic and Competitive Edge*. New York: The Free Press.

Ghemawat, Pankaj. 1985. "Building Strategy on the Experience Curve," *Harvard Business Review*, 63, 2, (March–April), pp. 143–49.

Ghemawat, Pankaj. 1986. *The Arithmetic of Strategic Cost Analysis*. Cambridge, MA: Harvard Business School.

Ghemawat, Pankaj. 1989–1990. "Industry and Competitive Analysis," a Note for Instructors. Cambridge, MA: Harvard University, Graduate School of Business Administration.

Gilbert, Xavier, and Paul Strebel. 1987. "Strategies to Outpace Competition," *Journal of Business Strategy*, 8, 1 (summer), pp. 28–37.

Gold, Bela. 1988. "Charting a Course to Superior Technology Evaluation," *Sloan Management Review*, 30, 1 (fall), pp. 19–27.

Gold, Bela, et al. 1970. "Diffusion of Major Technological Innovation in U.S. Iron and Steel Manufacturing," *Journal of Industrial Economics*, (July).

Govindarajan, V. 1984. "Appropriateness of Accounting Data in Performance Evaluation: An Empirical Evaluation of Environmental Uncertainty as an Intervening Variable," *Accounting Organizations and Society*, 9, 2, pp. 125–35.

Govindarajan, V. 1986a. "Decentralization, Strategy and Effectiveness of Strategic Business Units in Multibusiness Organizations," *Academy of Management Review*, 11, 4 (Oct.), pp. 844–56.

Govindarajan, V. 1986b. "Impact of Participation in the Budgetary Process on Managerial Attitudes and Performance: Universalistic and Contingency Perspectives," *Decision Sciences*, 17, 4, pp. 496–516.

Govindarajan, V. 1988. "A Contingency Approach to Strategy Implementation at the Business Unit Level: Integrating Management Systems with Strategy," *Academy of Management Journal*, 31, 4 (Sept.), pp. 828–53.

Govindarajan, V. 1989. "Implementing Competitive Strategies at the Business Unit Level: Implications of Matching Managers to Strategies," *Strategic Management Journal*, 10, pp. 251–69.

Govindarajan, Vijay, and Joseph Fisher. 1989. "The Interaction Between Strategy and Controls: Implications for Managerial Job Satisfaction." Working paper. Hanover, NH: The Amos Tuck School of Business Administration, Dartmouth College.

Govindarajan, Vijay, and Joseph Fisher. 1990. "Impact of Output Versus Behavior Controls and Resource Sharing on Performance: Strategy as a Mediating Variable," *Academy of Management Journal* 33, 2, (June), pp. 259–85.

Govindarajan, Vijay, and Joseph Fisher. 1991. "Incentive Compensation, Strategic Business Unit Mission, and Competitive Strategy." Working paper. Hanover, NH: The Amos Tuck School of Business Administration, Dartmouth College.

Govindarajan, V., and A. K. Gupta. 1985. "Linking Control Systems to Business Unit Strategy: Impact on Performance," *Accounting, Organizations and Society,* 4, 1, pp. 51–66.

Govindarajan, V., and J. K. Shank. 1986. "Cash Sufficiency: The Missing Link in Strategic Planning," *The Journal of Business Strategy,* 7, 1, pp. 88–95.

Govindarajan, Vijay, and John Shank. 1989a. "Concepts in Strategic Cost Analysis: The 'Famous' Crown, Cork and Seal Case," *Journal of Cost Management,* 2, 4 (winter), pp. 5–16.

Govindarajan, Vijay, and John Shank. 1989b. "Profit Vairance Analysis: A Strategic Focus," *Issues in Accounting Education,* 4, 2 (fall), 396–410.

Govindarajan, V., and J. K. Shank. 1992. "Strategic Cost Management: Tailoring Controls to Strategies," *Journal of Cost Management,* 6, 3, pp. 14–25.

Gupta, A. K., and V. Govindarajan. 1984a. "Build, Hold, Harvest: Converting Strategic Intentions into Reality," *Journal of Business Strategy,* 4, 3, pp. 34–47.

Gupta, A. K., and V. Govindarajan. 1984b. "Business Unit Strategy, Managerial Characteristics, and Business Unit Effectiveness at Strategy Implementation," *Academy of Management Journal,* 27, 1, pp. 25–41.

Gupta, A. K., and V. Govindarajan. 1986b. "Resource Sharing Among SBUs: Strategic Antecedents and Administrative Implications," *Academy of Management Journal,* 29, 4, pp. 695–714.

Hall, G. E. 1987. "Reflections on Running a Diversified Company," *Harvard Business Review* (Jan.–Feb.), 65, 1, pp. 84–92.

Hall, Robert. 1983. *Zero Inventories.* Homewood, IL: Dow-Jones Irwin.

Hall, Robert W. 1987. *Attaining Manufacturing Excellence: Just-In-Time, Total Quality Control, Total People Involvement.* Homewood, IL: Dow-Jones Irwin.

Hall, William. 1980. "Survival Strategies in a Hostile Environment," *Harvard Business Review,* 58, 5 (Jan.–Feb.), pp. 75–85.

Hambrick, Donald. 1981. "Environment, Strategy and Power Within the Top Management Team," *Administrative Science Quarterly,* 26, pp. 253–76.

Hambrick, Donald. 1983. "High Profit Strategies in Mature Capital Goods Industries: A Contingency Approach," *Academy of Management Journal,* 26, 687–707.

Hamermesh, R. G. 1986. *Making Strategy Work.* New York: John Wiley.

Hax, A. C., and N. S. Majluf. 1991. *The Strategy Concept and Process.* Englewood Cliffs, NJ: Prentice-Hall.

Hax, Arnoldo C., and Nicolas S. Majluf. 1984. *Strategic Management: An Integrative Perspective.* Englewood Cliffs, NJ: Prentice-Hall.

Hayes, Robert, and William Abernathy. 1980. "Managing Our Way to Economic Decline," *Harvard Business Review,* 58, 4 (July/Aug.), pp. 67–77.

Hayes, Robert H., and Steven C. Wheelwright. 1989. *Restoring Our Competitive Edge: Competing Through Manufacturing.* New York: John Wiley.

Henderson, Bruce. 1972. *Perspective Experience.* Boston: Boston Consulting Group.

Henderson, B. D. 1979. *Henderson on Corporate Strategy.* Cambridge, MA: Abt Books.

Hergert, M., and D. Morris. 1989. "Accounting Data for Value Chain Analysis," *Strategic Management Journal,* 10, pp. 175–88.

Hofer, C. W., and M J. Davoust. 1977. *Successful Strategic Management.* Chicago: A. T. Kearney.

Hofer, C. W., and D. E. Schendel. 1978. *Strategy Formulation: Analytical Concepts.* St. Paul, MN: West.

Horngren, Charles. 1962. *Cost Accounting: A Managerial Emphasis.* Englewood Cliffs, NJ: Prentice-Hall.

Horngren, Charles, and George Foster. 1987. *Cost Accounting—A Managerial Emphasis.* 6th ed. Englewood Cliffs, NJ: Prentice-Hall.

Houlihan, John. 1987. "Exploiting the Industrial Supply Chain," in *Manufacturing Issues.* New York: Booz, Allen, and Hamilton.

Howell, Robert, John K. Shank, Stephen R. Soucy, and Joseph Fisher. 1992. *Cost Management for Tomorrow: Seeking the Competitive Edge.* New York, NY: Financial Executives Research Foundation series on Innovative Management.

Howell, Robert, and Stephen Soucy. 1987. "Operating Controls in the New Manufacturing Environment," *Management Accounting,* LXIX, 4 (Oct.), pp. 25–31.

Huettner, David. 1974. *Plant size, Technological Change, and Investment Requirements: A Dynamic Framework for the Long-Run Average Cost Curve.* New York: Praeger.

Jaikumar, Ramchandran. 1986. "Postindustrial Manufacturing," *Harvard Business Review,* 64, 6 (Nov.–Dec.), pp. 69–76.

Johnson, H. Thomas. 1987. "The Decline of Cost Management: A Reinterpretation of the 20th-Century Cost Accounting History," *Journal of Cost Management,* 1, 1 (spring), pp. 5–12.

Johnson, H. Thomas, and Robert S. Kaplan. 1987. *Relevance Lost: The Rise and Fall of Management Accounting.* Boston: MA: Harvard Business School.

Jones, Thomas, and Franklin Udvare. 1986. "Just in Time Challenges for U.S. Auto Suppliers' Industry," *Manufacturing Issues.* New York: Booz, Allen, and Hamilton.

Juran, Joseph. 1985. "The Quality Edge: A Management Tool," *PIMA* (May).

Juran, Joseph, and Frank Gryna. 1970. *Quality Planning and Analysis.* New York: McGraw-Hill.

Kackar, R. N. 1986. "Taguchi's Quality Philosophy: Analysis and Commentary," *Quality Progress* (Dec.).

Kantrow, A. M. 1980. "The Strategy-Technology Connection," *Harvard Business Review,* 58 (July–Aug.), pp. 6–21.

Kaplan, Robert, 1982. *Advanced Management Accounting.* Englewood Cliffs, NJ: Prentice-Hall.

Kaplan, Robert S. 1984a. "The Evolution of Management Accounting," *Accounting Review* LIX, 3 (July), pp. 390–418.

Kaplan, Robert. 1983. "Measuring Manufacturing Performance, A New Challenge for Management Accounting Research," *Accounting Review,* LVIII, 4, pp. 686–705.

Kaplan, Robert. 1986a. "Accounting Lag: The Obsolescence of Cost Accounting Systems," *California Management Review,* XXVIII, 2 (winter), pp. 174–99.

Kaplan, Robert. 1966. "Must CIM Be Justified on Faith Alone?" *Harvard Business Review,* 64, 2 (March/April), pp. 87–95.

Kaplan, Robert. 1987. *John Deere Cases.* Cambridge, MA: Harvard Business School.

Kaplan, Robert S., and Anthony A. Atkinson. 1989. *Advanced Management Accounting.* Englewood Cliffs, NJ: Prentice-Hall.

Kaplan, Robert S., and Robin Cooper. 1988. Get Your Costs Right," *Harvard Business Review,* 66, 5, 96–105.

Kaplan, Robert R., and R. Cooper. 1990. *Cost Management Systems.* Englewood Cliffs, NJ: Prentice-Hall.

Kaplan, Robert, and Thomas Johnston. 1987. *Relevance Lost! The Rise and Fall of Management Accounting.* Cambridge, MA: Harvard Business School Press.

Kerin, Roger A., Vijay Mahajan, and P. Rajan Varadarajan. 1990. *Contemporary Perspectives on Strategic Market Planning.* Boston: Allyn and Bacon.

Kotha, S., and Orne, D. 1989. "Generic Manufacturing Strategies: A Conceptual Synthesis," *Strategic Management Journal,* 10, pp. 211–31.

Kuhn, Thomas. 1970. *The Structure of Scientific Revolutions.* 2nd ed. Chicago: University of Chicago Press.

Lee, John. 1987. *Managerial Accounting Changes for the 1990s.* New York, NY: McKay Business Systems.

Lee, John Y. 1991. "Investing in New Technology to Stay Competitive," *Management Accounting,* LXXII, 12 (June), pp. 45–48.

Lieberman, Marvin B. 1984. "The Learning Curve and Pricing in the Chemical Processing Industries," *Rand Journal of Economics,* 15, 2 (summer), pp. 213–28.

Lieberman, Marvin B. 1987. "The Learning Curve, Diffusion, and Competitive Strategy," *Strategic Management Journal,* 8 (Sept.), pp. 441–52.

Maidique, M. A., and P. Patch. 1988. "Corporate Strategy and Technological Policy," in *Readings in the Management of Innovation.* 2nd ed. M. L. Tushman, and W. L. Moore, eds. Cambridge, MA: Ballinger.

Manes, R. P., K. C. Chen, and R. Greenberg. 1985. "Economics of Scope and Cost-Volume-Profit Analysis for the Multiproduct Firm," *Journal of Accounting Literature,* 1, 1, pp. 77–111.

Mansfield, E. 1981. "How Economists See R&D," *Harvard Business Review,* 59 (Nov.–Dec.), pp. 98–106.

McBride, Mark E. 1981. "The Nature and Source of Economies of Scale in Cement Production," *Southern Economic Journal,* 48, 1 (July), pp. 105–15.

Meredith, Jack, 1987. "The Strategic Advantages of New Manufacturing Technologies for Small Firms," *Strategic Management Journal,* 9, pp. 249–58.

Miles, R. E., and C. C. Snow. 1978. *Organizational Strategy, Structure and Process.* New York: McGraw-Hill.

Milgrom, Paul, and John Roberts. 1990. "The Economics of Modern Manufacturing: Technology, Strategy, and Organization," *The American Economic Review,* 80, 3 (June), pp. 511–28.

Miller, A. 1988. "A Taxonomy of Technological Settings, with Related Strategies and Performance Levels," *Strategic Management Journal,* 9 (May–June), pp. 239–54.

Mintzberg, Henry. 1978. "Patterns in Strategy Formulation," *Management Science,* 24, 9, pp. 934–48.

Monden, Y. 1983. *Toyota Production System: Practical Approach to Production Management.* Atlanta, GA: Industrial Engineering and Management Press.

Monteverde, K., and D. J. Teece. 1982. "Supplier Switching Costs and Vertical Integration in the Automobile Industry," *The Bell Journal of Economics,* 13, 1 (spring), p. 206.

Morone, Joseph. 1989. "Strategic Use of Technology," *California Management Review,* 31, 4 (summer), pp. 91–109.

Morse, W., and H. P. Roth. 1987. *Quality Costs.* Montvale, NJ: National Association of Accountants.

Noble, Jean L. 1990. "A New Approach for Justifying Computer-Integrated Manufacturing," in *Emerging Practices in Cost Management,* Barry J. Brinker, ed. New York, NY: Warren Gorham and Lamont.

Norman, G. 1979. "Economics of Scale in the Cement Industry," *The Journal of Industrial Economics,* 27, 4 (June), pp. 317–37.

Oster Sharon. 1982. "The Diffusion of Innovation Among Steel Firms. The Basic Oxygen Furnace," *The Bell Journal of Economics* (spring).

Oster, Sharon M. 1990. *Modern Competitive Analysis.* Oxford, England: Oxford University Press.

Parker, J. E. S. 1978. *The Economics of Innovation.* 2nd ed. New York: Longman.

Patell, James. 1987. "Cost Accounting, Process Control and Product Design: A Case Study of the Hewlett Packard Personal Office Computer Division," *Accounting Review,* LXII, 4 (Oct.), pp. 808–39.

Porter, Michael. 1979. "How Competitive Forces Shape Strategy," *Harvard Business Review,* 57, 2 (March–April), pp. 137–45.

Porter, Michael, E. 1980. *Competitive Strategy.* New York: The Free Press.

Porter, Michael. 1983. "The Technological Dimension of Competitive Strategy," in *Research on Technological Innovation, Management and Policy, 1,* R. S. Rosenbloom, ed.

Porter, M. E. 1985a. *Competitive Advantage.* New York: The Free Press.

Porter, Michael. 1985b. "Technology and Competitive Advantage," *Journal of Business Strategy,* 5, 3 (winter), pp. 60–78.

Porter, M. E. 1986a. *DuPont in Titanium Dioxide.* Cambridge, MA: Harvard Business School.

Porter, M. E. 1986. *GE vs. Westinghouse in Large Turbine Generators.* Cambridge, MA: Harvard Business School.

Prahalad, C. K., and R. A. Bettis. 1986. "The Dominant Logic: A New Linkage Between Diversity and Performance," *Strategic Management Journal,* 7, 6, pp. 485–502.

Primrose, P. L., and R. Leonard. 1987. "Performing Investment Appraisals for Advanced Manufacturing Technology," *Journal of Cost Management,* 1, 2 (summer), pp. 34–42.

Pryor, Thomas E. 1988. "That Old Time Accounting Isn't Good Enough Any More," *Business Week* (June 6), p. 112.

Quinn, James B. 1980. *Strategies for Change: Logical Incrementalism.* Homewood, IL: Richard D. Irwin.

Quinn, J. B. 1985. "Managing Innovation: Controlled Chaos," *Harvard Business Review,* 63 (May–June), pp. 73–84.

Quinn, J. B., and H. Mintzberg. 1991. *Strategy Process.* Englewood Cliffs, NJ: Prentice-Hall.

Ramanujam, Vasu. 1990. "Thinking Strategically About Costs." Cleveland, OH: Seminary presented at the Center for Management Development, the Weatherhead School of Management, Case Western Reserve University.

Rappaport, Alfred. 1987. "Linking Competitive Strategy and Shareholder Value Analysis," *The Journal of Business Strategy,* 7, 4 (spring), pp. 42–48.

Riley, Daniel. 1987. "Competitive Cost Based Investment Strategies for Industrial Companies," in *Manufacturing Issues.* New York: Booz, Allen, and Hamilton.

Robinson, Michael, and M. Edgar Barrett. 1988. "The Content of Managerial Accounting Curricula," *The Accounting Educators Journal* (spring).

Rosenberg, N. 1982. *Inside the Black Box: Technology and Economics.* Cambridge, England: Cambridge University Press.

Ross, Gerald H. 1990. "Revolution in Management Control," *Management Accounting,* LXXII, 5 (Nov.), pp. 23–27.

Roth, Harold P., and Wayne J. Morse. 1983. "Let's Help Measure and Report Quality Costs," *Management Accounting* (Aug.), LXV, 2, pp. 50–53.

Rothschild, W. E. 1976. *Putting It All Together: A Guide to Strategic Thinking.* New York: AMACOM.

Salter, M. S. 1973. "Tailor Incentive Compensation to Strategy," *Harvard Business Review,* 51, 2 (March–April), pp. 94–102.

Sata, R., and M. A. Maidique. 1980. "Bonus System for a Balanced Strategy," *Harvard Business Review,* 58, 6 (Nov.–Dec.), pp. 156–63.

Scherer, F. M. 1980. *Industrial Market Structure and Economic Performance.* 2nd ed. New York, NY: Rand McNally.

Scherer, F. M., Alan Beckenstein, Erich Kaufer, R. Dennis Murphy, with assistance from Francine Bougeon-Maassen. 1975. *The Economics of Multi-Plant Operation.* Cambridge, MA: Harvard University Press.

Schonberger, R. J. 1986. *World Class Manufacturing: The Lessons of Simplicity Applied.* New York: The Free Press.

Schroeder, Dean M. 1990. "A Dynamic Perspective on the Impact of Process Innovation upon Competitive Strategies," *Strategic Management Journal,* 11, pp. 25–41.

Shank, J. K. 1982. *Contemporary Management Accounting: A Casebook.* 5, 4 Englewood Cliffs, NJ: Prentice-Hall.

Shank, J. K. 1982 "Midwest Ice Cream Company," *Contemporary Management Accounting: A Casebook,* pp. 157–73. Englewood Cliffs, NJ: Prentice-Hall.

Shank, J. K. 1991. "Strategic Cost Management: New Wine or Just New Bottles?" *Journal of Management Accounting Research,* 1, 1 (fall), pp. 47–65.

Shank, J. K., and N. C. Churchill. 1977. "Variance Analysis: A Management-Oriented Approach," *The Accounting Review,* 5, 4 (Oct.), pp. 950–57.

Shank, John, and Vijay Govindarajan. 1987. "Transaction-Based Costing for the Complex Product Line: A Field Study." Working paper. Hanover, NH: Amos Tuck School of Business Administration, Dartmouth College.

Shank, John K., and V. Govindarajan. 1988a. "Making Strategy Explicit in Cost Analysis: A Case Study," *Sloan Management Review,* 29, 3 (spring), pp. 19–29.

Shank, John K., and V. Govindarajan. 1988b. The Perils of Product Costing Based on Output Volumes," *Accounting Horizons,* 2, 4 (Dec.), pp. 71–79.

Shank, J. K., and Vijay Govindarajan. 1988c. "The Perils of Volume-Based Costing," *Accounting Horizons,* 2, 4 (Sept.), pp. 71–79.

Shank, John K., and V. Govindarajan. 1988d. "Transaction-based Costing for the Complex Product Line: A Field Study," *Journal of Cost Management,* 2, 2 (summer), pp. 31–38.

Shank, J. K., and V. Govindarajan. 1989. *Strategic Cost Analysis.* Homewood, IL: Richard D. Irwin.

Shank, John K., and Vijay Govindarajan. 1991. "Strategic Cost Management: The Value Chain Concept," in *Handbook of Cost Management,* Barry J. Brinker, editor. New York, NY: Warren, Gorham, and Lamont.

Shank, John, and Vijay Govindarajan. 1992. "Strategic Cost Analysis of Technological Investments," *Sloan Management Review,* 34, 1 (fall), pp. 39–52.

Shank, J. K., and V. Govindarajan. 1992a. "Strategic Cost Management: The Value Chain Perspective," *Journal of Management Accounting Research,* 4, pp. 179–97.

Shank, J. K., and V. Govindarajan. 1992b. "Strategic Cost Management and the Value Chain," *Journal of Cost Management,* 5, 4, pp. 5–21.

Shank, John K., Vijay Govindarajan, and Eric Speigel. 1988. "Strategic Cost Analysis: A Case Study," *Journal of Cost Management,* 2, 3 (fall), pp. 25–32.

Shillinglaw, Gordon. 1961. *Cost Accounting: Analysis and Control.* Homewood, IL: Richard D. Irwin.

Simmonds, Kenneth. 1981. "Strategic Management Accounting," *Management Accounting (U.K.),* LXIII, 10 (April), pp. 54–63.

Simon, Herbert, et al. 1954. *Centralization Versus Decentralization in Organizing the Controller's Department.* New York, NY: the Controllship Foundation.

Simons, Robert. 1987. "The Relationship Between Business Strategy and Accounting Control Systems: An Empirical Analysis," *Accounting, Organizations and Society,* 5, 4 (July), pp. 357–74.

Simpson, James, and David Muthler. 1987. "Quality Costs: Facilitating the Quality Initiative," *Journal of Cost Management,* 1, 1 (spring), pp. 25–34.

Snow, C. C., and L. G. Hrebiniak. 1975. "Strategy, Distinctive Competence, and Organization Performance," *Administrative Science Quarterly,* 20, pp. 546–58.

Spence, Michael. 1983. "Contestable Markets and the Theory of Industry Structure: A Review Article," *Journal of Economic Literature,* 21 (Sept.), pp. 981–90.

Storm, David J., and Steven J. Sullivan. 1990. "CIM Investment Justification: The 'Fresh Start' Approach," in *Emerging Practices in Cost Management,* Barry J. Brinker, editor. New York, NY: Warren, Gorham and Lamont.

Stuart, A. 1981. "Meatpackers in Stampede," *Fortune,* 104, 1 (July 29), pp. 67–73.

Sullivan, L. P. 1986. "The Seven Stages in Company-Wide Quality Control," *Quality Progress* (May).

Thomas, Arthur. 1969. *The Allocation Problem in Financial Accounting Theory.* Sarasota, FL: Studies in Accounting Research No. 3. American Accounting Association.

Torantzky, L. G., J. D. Eveland, M. G. Boyland, W. A. Hetzner, E. C. Johnson, E. Roitman, and J. Schneider. 1983. *The Process of Technological Innovation: Reviewing the Literature.* Washington, DC: National Science Foundation.

Troxler, Joel W. 1990. "Estimating the Cost Impact of Flexible Manufacturing," in *Emerging Practices in Cost Management,* Barry J. Brinker, ed. New York, NY: Warren, Gorham and Lamont.

Turney, Peter, and Bruce Anderson. 1989. "Accounting for Continuous Improvement," *Sloan Management Review,* 30, 2 (winter), pp. 37–48.

Turney, Peter. 1992. *Common Cents: The ABC Performance Breakthrough.* Hillsboro, OR: Cost Technology.

Walleigh, Richard C. 1986. "What's Your Excuse for Not Using JIT?" *Harvard Business Review,* 64, 2 (March–April), pp. 38–54.

Weick, Karl. 1979. *The Social Psychology of Organizing.* 2nd ed. Addison-Wesley.

Wells, John R. 1984. "In Search of Synergy: Strategies for Related Diversification." Doctoral Dissertation, Harvard Business School.

Wood, M., M. Polorny, V. Lintner, and M. Blinkhorn. 1984. "Investment Appraisal in the Mechanical Engineering Industry," *Management Accounting* (UK) LXVI, 4 (Oct.), pp. 32–37.

Worthy, Ford S. 1987. "Accounting Bores You? Wake Up," *Fortune,* 116, 2 (Oct. 12), pp. 43–56.

Wright, Peter. 1987. "A Refinement of Porter's Strategies," *Strategic Management Journal,* 8, 1, pp. 93–101.

Wright, R. V. L. 1975. *A System for Managing Diversity.* Cambridge, MA: Arthur D. Little.

Zimmerman, Jerald L. 1979. "The Costs and Benefits of Cost Allocation," *The Accounting Review,* LIV, 3 (July), pp. 504–21.

INDEX

265

ABOUT THE AUTHORS

JOHN SHANK is Noble Professor of Management Accounting at the Amos Tuck School of Business Administration at Dartmouth College. He has published twelve books and is an active consultant.

VIJAY GOVINDARAJAN is Professor of Strategy and Control also at the Amos Tuck School of Business Administration at Dartmouth College. He has published two books and has received several honors, including "outstanding teacher of the year."